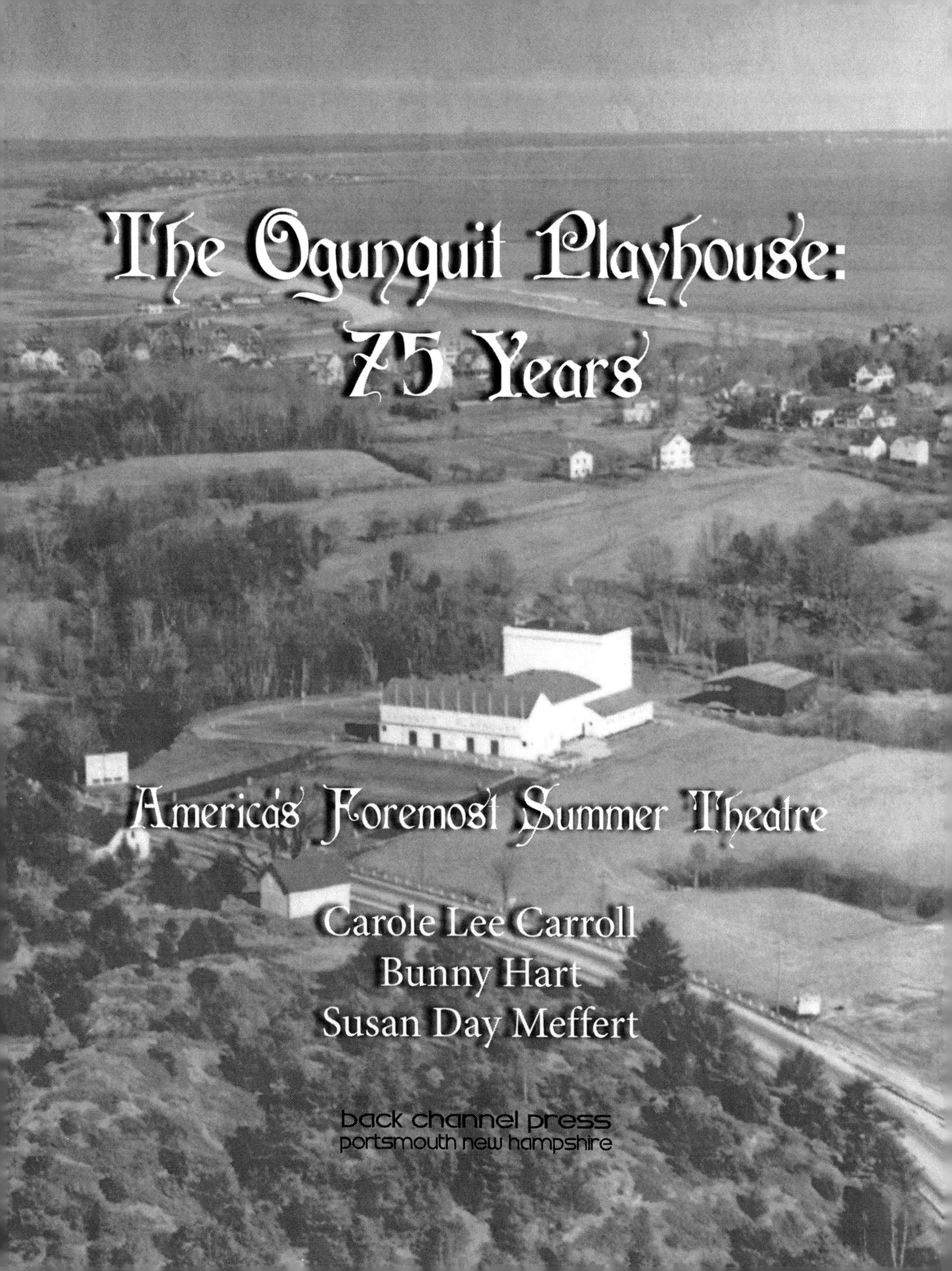

The Ogunquit Playhouse: 75 Years

America's Foremost Summer Theatre

Carole Lee Carroll
Bunny Hart
Susan Day Meffert

back channel press
portsmouth new hampshire

OGUNQUIT PLAYHOUSE: 75 YEARS
Copyright © 2007 by the Ogunquit Playhouse Foundation
ISBN: 978-1-934582-00-8

All rights reserved. No part of this book may be reproduced or utilized in any form or by any means, electronic or mechanical, including photocopying, scanning, recording or by any information storage and retrieval system now known or hereafter invented, without permission in writing from the Ogunquit Playhouse Foundation, except by a reviewer who may quote brief passages in review. Inquiries should be addressed to:

Ogunquit Playhouse Foundation
P.O. Box 915
Ogunquit, Maine 03907

BACK CHANNEL PRESS
170 Mechanic Street
Portsmouth, NH 03801
www.backchannelpress.com
Printed in the United States of America

Design and layout by Nancy Grossman
Library of Congress PCN 2007930882

Dedications

Bunny Hart

To John Lane, for having the courage to hire me in 1963 as publicity director of his very fine and famous summer theatre, and for introducing me to Ogunquit which he said I would love and never want to leave. He was right. And I am still here almost 45 years later.

Carole Lee Carroll

To Daniel Frohman, who supported Walter Hartwig in his great adventure and in addition built the most beautiful theatre in New York. To Maude Hartwig, who allowed her Playhouse to become my playground, and to Francis Dixon who worked there so his family could have the benefit of many splendid Ogunquit summers.

Susan Meffert

To my mother and father, Harriet and George Smith, who afforded me the most elegant and exciting teenage years a person could have. For their 35-year vision for Dunelawn, that made George's summer home such a wonderful retreat for John and his actors, and for being constant supports in my growing up. To my classy Aunt Barbara and her Lobster Bar. And to Henry Weller, who really was the glue.

To Debbie -
Happy remembering!
Susan Jaffer

Contents

viii   Table of Color Plates

ix   Acknowledgements

x   From the Foundation

xi   Foreword by Bradford Kenney

xiii   Prologue

1   The Hartwig Years

67   The John Lane Years

143   The Manhattan Theatre Colony

165   The Foundation

179   The Seasons

207   The Staff

Color Plates

I. "Bride of Ogunquit." Oil on paper/board by Charles Woodbury.
II. John Lane's hands. Oil painting by Helen Lane.
III. Mort Mather and Karen Maxwell in front of the challenge board with $500,000 raised, 1996.
IV. Cast of the *Thank You, John Lane* Gala, 1996.
V. *Grease,* 2000.
VI. Liz Sheridan and John Sloman in *Something's Afoot,* a mystery musical based on *Ten Little Indians,* 1998.
VII. Felicia Finley and David Brummel in *Evita,* 2003.
VIII. *The Tale of the Allergist's Wife,* 2003.
IX. *Annie,* 2003.
X. *Beehive,* 2006.
XI. *42nd Street,* 2001.
XII. *Cinderella,* 2006.
XIII. Leslie Uggams in *Cinderella,* 2006.
XIV. *Ain't Misbehavin',* 2003.
XV. *Joseph and the Amazing Technicolor Dreamcoat,* 2001.
XVI. Sally Struthers in *Hello, Dolly!,* 2006.
XVII. Set design by Don Jenson, for *Captain Brassbound's Conversion,* 1961.
XVIII. Darold Perkins's set design and notes for *The Little Foxes,* 1968.
XIX. Crew list painted on scene shop wall, 1988.
XX. Ogunquit Playhouse birdhouse.

Acknowledgements

We would like to thank the following people for sharing with us their memories and photographs of the Ogunquit Playhouse, and for helping us in the development of this book.

Adrian and Ellie Asherman	Sydney Henderson	Madeline Nowell
Dwight Bardwell	Tammy Heon	Stuart Nudelman
Jean Benda	Joseph C. Hill	Ogunquit Heritage Museum
Benita Braggiotti Carey	Barbara Hilty	Roy Rogosin
Carole Lee Carroll	Historical Society of Wells & Ogunquit	Sylvia Rubin
Tom Clarie	Mike and Helen Horn	James B. Russell
Ann C. Clark	Jaclynn Jones	Harold Shaw
Monty Compton	Bradford T. Kenney	Carol Collery Shuttleworth
Graham Cookson	Rich Latta	Mary-Leigh Smart
Paula Cummings	Mary and Richard Littlefield	Virginia Spiller
Kristine Cuzzi	Ian MacKenzie	Richard Therrian
Betty Dixon	Maine Historic Preservation Commission	Sada Thompson
Richard Ellis	Maine State Library	Robert Townsend
Linda Frye	Paul Mason	Louise Tragard
Beverly Hallam	Barbara Mather	Steve Twombly
Bunny Hart	Mort Mather	Henry Weller
Ron Hayes	Susan Meffert	Barbara and Peter Woodbury

The Billy Rose Theatre Divison of the New York Public Library for the Performing Arts, Astor, Lenox and Tilden Foundations. And the Ogunquit Playhouse Archives.

On October 28, 2006, the Ogunquit Heritage Museum held an oral history, *"Do You Remember," Part V, The Ogunquit Playhouse.* It was hosted by Henry Weller, General Manager of the Playhouse for almost fifty years, and current member of the board of the Ogunquit Playhouse Foundation. Many recollections in the text come from that oral history. Thank you to the Ogunquit Heritage Museum, to Jordan Freedman who video-taped it, and to the many townspeople and others who came.

Some of those people were Brad Sterl, Gary and Grace Littlefield, Ellie and Adrian Asherman, Carol Shuttleworth, Monty Compton, Ian MacKenzie, Donna Lewis, Susan Levinson, Joe Hill, Bobby Treen, Peter and Barbara Woodbury, Mike and Helen Horn, Richard Littlefield, Betty Dixon, Carole Lee Carroll, Barbara Hilty, Bradford Kenney, Jaclynn Jones, Tammy Heon, Henry Weller, and Jordan and Muriel Freedman.

From the Foundation

When John Lane passed the stewardship of the Ogunquit Playhouse to the Foundation Board created in 1996, he entrusted the Board with so much more than the beautiful white building we see today at Ten Main Street. The Foundation Board has endeavored to provide the resources to protect and promote the history that is so lovingly put forth in these pages.

From our first Board President and founder, Mort Mather, we have all taken the baton and continue to offer the leadership and seek the funding necessary to preserve and improve the capital aspects of what has now grown to be a 26-acre campus inclusive of the Playhouse, the Lodge, and the Chloë Checkoway Pavilion at the Colony.

As the curtain goes up on our 75th season, we gratefully acknowledge the commitment of all of Foundation Board members, past and present who have given generously of their time, talent and treasure behind the scenes to ensure a long and continued history yet to be written, or rather—performed.

The Ogunquit Playhouse Guild, formed in 1997, is a wonderful addition to the Playhouse family and the source of hundreds of hours of volunteer time and thousands of dollars used to fund improvements. To them, we give a hearty, standing ovation!

We cannot fully express our thanks to the entire staff for their commitment to this wonderful theatre. It is not always easy, but when that curtain goes up, it is always amazing.

Karen M. Maxwell
President
Ogunquit Playhouse Foundation
Board of Directors

Foreword

On behalf of the staff and Board of Directors of the Ogunquit Playhouse, we hope you enjoy learning about and reliving the glorious history of our wonderful Playhouse as we continue our stewardship during this 75th anniversary season.

Not only does this book preserve and annotate some of the most important years and events since Walter and Maude Hartwig first brought their Manhattan Repertory Company to Ogunquit in 1933, but it will help us, who are more recently arrived on the scene, to understand the way in which this marvelous national treasure has come about, grown and evolved over those 75 years.

We are truly blessed by the rich heritage of this nationally significant Playhouse and by the support we have received from our community here on the New England Seacoast and throughout the entertainment field. We work to honor and learn from our past every day, and see that the future of the Ogunquit Playhouse matches and outshines its remarkable past.

Enjoy this marvelous book and we'll see you at the Playhouse!

Bradford T. Kenney
Executive Artistic Director

Prologue

2007 is the 75th anniversary of the opening of the Ogunquit Playhouse. Actually, if you count Mrs. Merry Delle Hoyt's annual pageants and productions, this has been a theatre town for even longer. The Playhouse has survived where many others have succumbed to rising costs and, generally, the American love affair with television and movies.

It began as the dream of a very determined showman named Walter Hartwig. Hartwig believed that good theatre was possible outside of New York and that if you put on good material with highly professional people, audiences would come. He brought with him to Ogunquit a very accomplished resident company – one that he had started building in Peterborough, NH in 1927, and in Bristol, CT, during 1930 and 1931. Critics and journalists from Portland, Boston and New York called Hartwig an indefatigable entrepreneur, an old fashioned gentleman, and a visionary. Certainly, he brought early fame to Ogunquit with appearances by theatrical luminaries like Ethel Barrymore, Leo G. Carroll, Maude Adams, Laurette Taylor, Carl Benton Reid, and Peggy Wood. When Perkins' garage, later the Ogunquit Square movie theatre, that he had built into a theatre and opened in 1933, became too small for his successes, he bought a tract of land from Henry Weare that stretched from Route One to Shore Road, and built a marvelously ahead-of-its-time Playhouse that opened on July 19, 1937, with a production of *Boy Meets Girl*. From the point of view of posterity, the new theatre was probably the town's second big break, the first being Hartwig's arrival.

When Walter Hartwig died suddenly in 1941, there was no question but that his widow, Maude, a dedicated partner in all of his theatrical endeavors, would carry on. So we have Maude Hartwig to thank for the fact that there is a theatre at all. She kept it going through World War II and was there to include John Lane as a young actor in her resident company of 1946.

Then John Lane decided to be a producer instead of an actor, another big break for the town. So he and his wife, Helen, bought the Playhouse from Maude Hartwig during the winter of 1951 – after the hurricane of November 1950 sheared the top off the stage house and smashed it into the auditorium. John and Helen moved to Maine and became wonderful residents of Ogunquit; and he, with her help and support, proceeded to turn the property that Hartwig had built into a showplace. Lane's mission was quality plays, good actors and actresses, a professional backstage operation. He and his staff always treated the talent as if they were honored guests – a tactic that has been well remembered by many of the actors who appeared here, and undoubtedly, contributed to their willingness to return.

Another unusual characteristic of John's management was his meticulous attention to the physical plant as well as the product. When the nature of summer theatre changed to a star package system, he was active in the development of that system, and began to package his own material and arrange for shows that would travel a circuit of five or six theatres during one season. This certainly helped the Playhouse to rein in costs at a time when other summer theatres couldn't keep up with them and still make a profit. Lane's stewardship of the Playhouse lasted from 1951 until 1996 – 45 years, of which the early decades are universally acknowledged now as the heyday of the straw-hat circuit.

The rest of the story is better known to us these days. Henry Weller and Mort Mather, with the help of then-producer Rob Townsend, raised $500,000 as an endowment and John Lane gave the Ogunquit Playhouse to the community to be run by a foundation with a board of directors. Since 1996, when the town bid farewell and thank you to John Lane at a wonderful gala including many of the notable stars who had graced the stage here during the previous 45 years, the Playhouse has continued to flourish. We've had a producer, Robert Townsend, 1998 and 1999, and two artistic directors, Roy Rogosin, who is remembered for his contribution to the children's theatre as well as his last most successful musical season, and now, Bradford Kenney, who joined the theatre as Executive Artistic Director last year – the first year that the season was significantly extended beyond the ten weeks of high summer.

The occasion of the 75th anniversary of the Ogunquit Playhouse will be celebrated in many ways this summer. All of these celebrations should be reminders to us of how fortunate the town has been in the perpetuation of this marvelous theatre.

Ogunquit Playhouse 75

America's Foremost Summer Theatre

The Village Studio. Courtesy of Historical Society of Wells and Ogunquit.

America's Foremost Summer Theatre: A History

The Ogunquit Playhouse long ago earned its place as ***America's Foremost Summer Theatre.*** Celebrating its 75th year in 2007, it is now one of the few professional summer theatres still in existence. This book, a tribute to those 75 years in operation, will attempt to describe, illustrate and highlight some of the memories of this prestigious seasonal theatre.

It would not have succeeded as it did without the vision, inspiration, sheer tenacity and considerable talent of two very different men. The first, Walter Hartwig, created The Ogunquit Playhouse and inspired much of the structure and programming that has persisted to the present. Hartwig was a visionary, a man completely versed in the commercial theatre, an accomplished producer on Broadway and in the "little theatre" movement, who believed that the world outside of New York City was ready for and up to the best theatrical experiences that could be provided to them. He was a professional theatrical producer of the highest quality with years of success under his belt by the time he arrived in Ogunquit.

The second, John Lane, began as an actor at Hartwig's theatre (although Walter had died several years earlier, his widow, Maude, took over the producing reins) and went on to buy the theatre from Maude Hartwig in 1951. John also had a vision, perhaps not as grounded as Hartwig's in years of theatrical production, but nevertheless a vision that he pursued with singular tenacity. During the forty-five years that it was truly "John Lane's Ogunquit Playhouse," he ruled with an iron will and a firm hand. He was determined to present the finest quality theatre, and his perfectionism rubbed off on everyone who worked with him, from star to stagehand. The Ogunquit Playhouse became one of the most sought-after venues for Colony Theatre students, actors at every level, technical crews, administrative and executive staff personnel. It was an honor to be involved in the Ogunquit Playhouse under the direction of John Lane.

Looking ahead to retirement, in 1994, John offered the Playhouse as a gift to the town of Ogunquit, its citizens and visitors. He decreed that in return $500,000 be raised by a nonprofit foundation to maintain the building and grounds, and that a board of directors operate the theatre. The challenge was met and on September 17, 1997, the Ogunquit Playhouse began its third life, delighting audiences with the best musicals, plays, stars and supporting casts available.

The Environment in Ogunquit before Walter and Maude Hartwig

The village had long been a popular spot for artists. With its picturesque boat harbor, its three-mile-long white sand beach and its cliff walk from the village center south to Perkins Cove, artists flocked here to study with Charles Woodbury and later with Hamilton Easter Field.

A quote from *A Century of Color*: [1]

> During these years (1910 through the '20s) artists, writers, actors and all manner of creative spirits joined forces to create a rich cultural summer life in Ogunquit, which made the town a most interesting and attractive vacation spot. Alliances formed at this time between those creative spirits and other summer visitors became the cornerstone of Ogunquit's art patronage, an important aspect of the town's survival as an art colony. Lively weekly seminars on various topics of the day brought people together at the local hotels, as did war relief benefits after 1916. The Sparhawk Hotel presented Saturday evening dances; [2] the Ontio and Lookout Hotels offered "hops," and the Cliff Country Club, which had opened in 1901, drew the plus-fours crowd to its nine-hole golf course.
>
> In 1913, Merry Delle Hoyt, wife of a wealthy St. Louis industrialist, designed and had built the Village Studio on what is now Hoyt's Lane. (They later gave it to the Village Improvement Society.) Each summer from 1917 to 1931, she sponsored art exhibitions and organized forums and amateur theatricals there. Occasional pageants on the grounds of her estate, Fieldstone, and along the adjoining Ogunquit River dazzled with impressive sets and costumes. Local residents joined in the acting, helping with set construction, sewing costumes and doing back-stage chores.[3]

Barbara Hilty, now on the staff of the Ogunquit Museum of American Art, remembers as a child being dressed in costumes to take part in Mrs. Hoyt's pageants, and also recalled several productions staged by Mrs. Hoyt, in which her brother George Smith (who later turned their summer home, Dunelawn, into a hotel whose clientele included Playhouse stars and featured actors in the '50s, '60s and '70s) along with Ted and David Asherman (sons of Ned and Gladys Asherman who first introduced the Hartwigs to Ogunquit) played many parts. David always played the lead. Barbara remembers particularly,

Alice in Wonderland with David wearing a blonde wig as Alice, brother George and Ted Asherman as Tweedledum and Tweedledee. I was the Mad Hatter, and the Dormouse was a little boy named Peter Alfo. None of us wanted to be in the play – we'd much rather have been on the beach. We had to elbow the Dormouse to wake him up, and we used to make him cry. Mrs. Hoyt fired us, but when she couldn't find anyone to replace us she had to hire us back!

Mrs. Hoyt's pageants became more and more fanciful, including American colonists fighting the Indians on the beach. According to Addison Merrick's brother, who was a nephew of Mrs. Hoyt and who wrote in 1990 the following account that he sent to the Historical Society of Wells and Ogunquit,

> Aunt Del had a flimsy log cabin of poles constructed in the hollow of the dunes… suddenly, a scattering of painted Indians wielding tomahawks and uttering war whoops crept over the dunes and descended on the cabin. From the narrow doorway, a screaming settler wife in a shawl and clutching a baby made good her escape. She was followed by her pioneer husband firing a muzzle loader in the direction of the savages. The Indians then set fire to the cabin, which went up in a satisfactory and highly pictorial blaze of flame and smoke. For the final act over there across the water, the Indians crept away, and an oldtimey sort of chap wearing fringed leggings and coonskin cap advanced to the river's edge. He raised a megaphone to his lips and in a stentorian voice plainly heard by the crowd on the opposite riverbank shouted O – GUN – QUIT! And the pageant for that summer was over. But not before Charles Woodbury had captured the burning of the cabin in oil. [4] [See color plate I.]

Again from *A Century of Color*: [5]

> Another year, portrait artist Channing Hare acted the role of Antony with aspiring actress Mary Crandon (Braggiotti) as Cleopatra. As the Egyptian entourage advanced along the river in barges, summer resident, Gladys Asherman, performed "The Dance of the Seven Veils," with the beach dunes glistening as the desert beyond.

According to Mary-Leigh Smart, who, with her husband, Jack Smart, founded Barn Gallery Associates, Gladys Asherman gave an encore of her seven veils dance on stage at the Village Studio and wreaked havoc there when the scenery fell down behind her. There may have been many exotic dances like the dance of the seven veils, because Mary-Leigh Smart remembers another time connected with the performance of *Black Tents*, by Achmed Abdullah.

> One of the things he wrote was a play, *Black Tents*. They attempted that at the Village Studio. Let me see, Tony Mattei was in it, and Mary Crandon was the star. She was

a fine actress, and a star always. And the thing was that somebody, I think Tony Mattei's wife, came out on stage at intermission and did a belly dance, and the scenery fell down.

According to *A Century of Color*:

> At the Village Studio, two one-act plays or a light three-act play were performed each season by an amateur cast consisting of local residents and summer people. These became so popular that, as the years went on, a professional actor/director (most notably Bennett Kilpack who later became a radio star) was hired for the summer and a series of three-act plays was offered. Mrs. Hoyt often produced original stage works by summer resident Dana Burnet, and she premiered famous Russian-born Achmed Abdullah's play, *Black Tents*. [6]

Mary-Leigh Smart remembers:

> Achmed Abdullah was a very famous writer. This woman, whose name I can't remember now, came with him to the Sparhawk. It was a scandal because they stayed in the same room. Well, of course, Jean was his wife, but she was his agent and she had kept her own name. So people in Ogunquit didn't know they were married, and it was quite a scandal.

From *A Century of Color*: [7]

> Local lore has it that film star Bette Davis, who spent summers at Ogunquit working as a waitress [8] and a lifeguard while in college, got her start as an actress at the Village Studio. As the story goes, George Arliss, the famous British actor, was in the audience one night when Miss Davis was performing. He apparently spotted her talent and asked Mrs. Hoyt if he could meet the young actress. From that meeting, supposedly, a legendary career was launched.

This account does not jibe with other recollections. Martha LoMonaco, in *Summer Stock* claims that Marie Glass Currier, the founder of Mariarden in Peterborough, New Hampshire, may have discovered her first. "Currier had the good fortune to enroll talented young students such as Bette Davis, the Bennett sisters (Joan, Constance, and Barbara) and Walter Pidgeon, whose abilities helped to attract audiences to the public performances as well as future students to the school." [9] So perhaps Davis was discovered elsewhere.

Enter Walter Hartwig

Into this climate of creative energy set in a naturally beautiful setting, came Walter Hartwig. He was a childhood friend of Ned Asherman, a New York interior designer who summered in Ogunquit. They had gone to school together in Milwaukee, and later were friends in New York. Mary-Leigh Smart, whose former husband, David, was Ned's son, remembers the connection:

> Walter had the Colony Theatre in Peterborough, N.H., and after Mrs. Hoyt died and the studio was gone, Ned suggested, or maybe it was Gladys, his wife, to the Hartwigs that they come to Ogunquit, look it over and think about either having a branch of their theatre here or moving the theatre here, which they did, opening eventually in the old Perkins garage. It may well have been, too, that Walter visited Ogunquit earlier while Delle was still alive and discovered her active little thespian group.

Other references to this period suggest that Walter Hartwig returned to Ogunquit a number of times and actually took part in several of Mrs. Hoyt's productions. In any case, Ned Asherman gave the job of decorating the lobby and auditorium to son David – 15 at the time. It was stained dark blue and had orange woodwork. When the new Playhouse was built on Route One, the colors remained the same. The summer of 1937 when the new Playhouse opened, performances were continued at the old theatre with David doing the sets.

In Hartwig's obituary, January 18, 1941, *The New York Times* wrote that he had been a theatrical producer, a leader for many years in the Little Theatre movement, and one of the first to organize a summer theatre. He was 61 years old.

> Mr. Hartwig was born in Milwaukee and after he graduated from the Sorbonne in Paris, worked as an accountant…He was associated with David Belasco for a time, and later a director and actor for the Fox Film company. In 1923, he organized the Little Theatre Tournament, which he conducted for the David Belasco Trophy for ten years. During this period Mr. Hartwig organized the Manhattan Repertory Theatre, which began in the middle nineteen twenties with a summer school in Peterborough, NH. It later moved to Bristol, Connecticut and in 1933 Mr. Hartwig built a summer theatre in a garage in Ogunquit, Maine. [10]

The Manhattan Theatre Repertory Company and Mariarden

As chairman of the Little Theatre Committee of the New York Drama League, Hartwig inaugurated, in 1923, a tournament in which small theatre groups from the across the country were invited to enter a competition, preparing a one-act play and presenting it to a group of judges in a Broadway theatre. Judges would choose three plays out of fifteen presented and award them $100 each. These productions would be presented a second time and the winner of this contest was awarded a David Belasco standard signifying distinction which they would hold until the next year's tournament.

In 1926, as Hartwig staged the fifth tournament, his work was applauded by Barrett H. Clark in a story about the success and growth of thousands of theatres in barns all over the country. He wrote:

> How many of these little theatres are there in the entire country? Several otherwise sane persons have been trying to find out...But there is no guessing about the outstanding fact: the little theatre is with us, lusty, noisy, crude, sincere, affected. But I think it is here to stay. No longer a plaything of society or bohemia, it is an integral part of our community life. Fads don't last long, or the Drama League of America – one of the first symptoms of our national awakening to the need for little theatres – would not be celebrating its' sixteenth birthday... nor would Walter Hartwig be turning gray in preparing for his fifth annual Little Theatre Tournament, which opens here tomorrow night. [11]

Indeed, Hartwig was even then planning for the opening of a theatrical camp on a 250-acre property known as Mariarden, adjoining the McDowell Colony in Peterborough, New Hampshire. Opening in 1927, Hartwig declared in the *New York Times*, "The camp will not be a school in the ordinary sense, but rather a workshop of the theatre where practical training will be given by experts active in the commercial theatre."[12]

Martha Schmoler LaMonaco, in her work, *Summer Stock*, explains the origins of the Manhattan Theatre Colony as follows:

> The history of the Manhattan Theatre Colony properly begins at Mariarden, an outdoor stage and summer school of drama and dance just outside Peterborough, New Hampshire. Mariarden was founded by Marie Glass Buress Currier, a retired actress who had married well and could afford to purchase and redevelop the former Four Winds Farm into an outdoor performing arts center. ... She managed to lure Ruth St. Denis and Ted Shawn, whose company then included the young Martha Graham, to Mariarden to set up an Eastern Denishawn School of Dancing during the 1923 season. [13]

Denishawn did not return to Mariarden the following summer citing the difficult commute for its instructors. Currier carried on for several more seasons, but in 1927 chose to rent the theatre to Walter Hartwig.

LoMonaco states:

> Hartwig's eight-week course was designed for advanced students, preferably those who were already working in the profession. (He) set up a comprehensive training program worthy of a university theatre department, plus a professional stock company, which used Mariarden as its base for touring New England. Students declared a concentration in stagecraft, acting and directing, or playwrighting, to which they would devote three hours of intensive work per day. They also were required to take classes in history of the drama, voice control, body control, stage lighting, costuming, makeup, theatrical publicity, and dramatic criticism, as well as in all three specialty areas designated above [14] ... The faculty was quite prestigious: author and drama critic Walter Prichard Eaton taught history; Alexander Wyckoff of Carnegie Institute of Technology taught stagecraft; (It was to Alexander Wyckoff that Hartwig turned in 1937 to design the new theatre he was building in Ogunquit.) Dagmar Perkins, a leading vocal coach and president of the National Association of American Speech, taught voice; John Anderson, of the *New York Evening Post,* taught dramatic criticism; and Hartwig himself taught acting and directing. [15]

In its second summer, 1928, John Kirkpatrick (who was to follow Hartwig for many years and finally become the director of Ogunquit's Manhattan Theatre Colony) would instruct in playwriting, and in 1929, the third season at Peterborough, Hartwig for the first time included plays to be performed for an audience from town.

In 1930, Hartwig moved the Manhattan Repertory Theatre to Bristol, Connecticut, in search of larger audiences perhaps. LaMonaco reports:

> Hartwig moved his camp, now named the Manhattan Theatre Colony, to Bristol, Connecticut, where in addition to the same quality and range of theatre education established at Mariarden, he offered an eight-week professional stock season. The Bristol locale afforded him two fully equipped indoor theatres as well as substantial workshop space for the design and building of sets, costumes, and properties. Bristol allowed him flexibility in staging and, for the first time, the ability to produce a one-a-week stock season. Frequently referred to by critics as a "gentleman of the old school," Hartwig chose his repertoire from traditional favorites of the late nineteenth and early twentieth centuries, such as *Trelawny of the Wells*, by Arthur Wing Pinero and James M. Barrie's *Dear Brutus*, intermixed with the occasional new play presented in the hopes of an eventual Broadway opening. [16]

The second season at Bristol, Hartwig's classes were acting, history of the drama, stage direction, stage craft, lighting, costuming, make-up, diction, playwriting and drama criticism.

Again John Kirkpatrick was part of the teaching staff. Kirkpatrick would remain with the Manhattan Theatre Colony under John Lane, and he was reported to have brought John Lane to the attention of Maude Hartwig as a potential co-producer.

Writing about the explosion of professional summer stock theatres, on July 12, 1931, a *New York Times* article, referred to Hartwig's second season at Bristol this way:

> Likewise ambitious is Walter Hartwig's Manhattan Theatre Colony, now in its second year at Bristol, Conn. Without benefit of the visiting star system, a company of players with Broadway experience opened on June 29th in Maugham's *The Circle*, which was followed by the Kaufman-Ferber comedy, *The Royal Family*. Beginning tomorrow night, the remainder of the season will see presented Philip Barry's *In A Garden*, Barrie's *The Little Minister*, George Kelly's *Philip Goes Forth*, St John Ervine's *The Lady of Belmont*, and Shaw's *Candida* – a typically balanced schedule. A summer workshop and a smaller theatre for the production of comedies and old melodramas are additional features of this colony, which is advertised as "a training base for the arts of the theatre." [17]

From this article, it appears that as early as 1931, there were summer stock houses flourishing in The Newport Casino; Lakewood Theatre in Skowhegan; Berkshire Playhouse in Stockbridge, MA; Cape Playhouse at Dennis; County Centre Repertory Company at White Plains, NY; Westport Playhouse in Connecticut; The University Players at West Falmouth, MA in their fourth season; the Sharon Playhouse in Sharon, CT; The Wharf Players in Provincetown; the Cape May Playhouse, NJ; the Millbrook Theatre, NY; Westchester Playhouse, in Westchester, NY; and at the Surry Playhouse. It also appears that the beginnings of the package system were already at work that year, with several stars moving from place to place.

Hartwigs to Ogunquit

In 1932, the Manhattan Theatre Colony in Bristol, Connecticut, was dark. One could speculate that Walter Hartwig was making plans to move the group to Ogunquit, and was in the process of negotiating the move into Grover Perkins' garage on Shore Road.

He also spent that winter of 1932 bringing the first-prize-winning long play from the tournament of that year, *If Booth Had Missed,* to Broadway with the Shuberts. This was one of only two plays that Hartwig brought to Broadway.

Adrian Asherman, youngest and only surviving son of Ned Asherman recalls that:

> Sometime during the years that Uncle Walter and Aunt Maude ran the theatre camp in Peterborough, they visited my parents in Ogunquit. Probably they were aware of Mrs. Hoyt's theatrical events. I know that when they decided to come to

Ogunquit, Uncle Walter moved a fine old country home from back country and put it on the Ogunquit River just north of our house on Grasshopper Lane. [18]

This house and its rolling lawns above the Ogunquit River became the site of numerous lectures and play readings during the 1934 season. Residing between these two families on the river was the residence of Virginia Paine, Ma Perkins on the radio.

In 1982, on the occasion of the 50th anniversary, Bunny Hart, not then on the Playhouse staff, wrote the following history:

> On the opening night, July 1, 1933, what the building lacked in creature comfort and technical sophistication was compensated by the caliber of the cast. ... In subsequent weeks and seasons to the once-upon-a-time garage trooped Ruth St. Denis, Laurette Taylor, Daniel Frohman, Maude Adams, Ruth Gordon, Margalo Gilmore, Frances Starr and Stiano Braggiotti. Ethel Barrymore starred in Galsworthy's *The Silver Box* which featured Libby Holman. But the Manhattan Theatre Colony was more than a company of actors; it was a training base for the beginner as well as the experienced artist of the theatre and daily classes in stage crafts were held upstairs in the old Ogunquit Fire Station. [19]

Daniel Frohman, Hartwig's business associate and a Broadway producer, vacationed in Ogunquit that season.

Opening program, 1933. Courtesy of the Ogunquit Heritage Museum.

The old Ogunquit Playhouse from 1933 to 1936

In the first playbill for the 1933 season of the Manhattan Repertory Theatre Company, Hartwig announced that his "company of distinguished artists" would include Blanche Ring, Mary Nash, Ruth St. Denis, Mabel Taliaferro, Leo G. Carroll, Hilda Spong, Carl Benton Reid, Hugh Miller, Robert Allen, A.J.Herbert, Fay Marbe, Anne Seymour, Julie Ring, Florence Williams, May Ediss, Daisy Atherton, Joseph Curtin, Lygia Bernard, Cynthia Blake, Leslie Denison and Cecile Wulff. [20]

Even for a man who had produced ten seasons of the Little Theatre Tournaments, and directed numerous benefit performances for the Actors Equity Fund and five previous seasons of theatre with a resident company, this is an awesome list of the actors and actresses of that period. Many were renowned at the time, and many more of them – Leo G. Carroll, Carl Benton Reid, A.J. Herbert, and Florence Williams – would go on to become great mainstays of the American theatre.

Part of the company at Ogunquit, Maine in 1933. One might recognize Daisy Atherton, Hugh Miller, Leslie Denison, Florence Williams, Cecile Wulff, Lygia Bernard, Carl Benton Reid, and Anne Seymour. Down in front with the cigar is Walter Hartwig, director, with Mary Nash over his right shoulder and Hilda Spong over his left. A. J. Herbert is beside him. The Stage Magazine, *September, 1933. Courtesy of Carole Lee Carroll.*

Walter Hartwig and Mary Nash. 1933. Courtesy of Carole Lee Carroll.

Hartwig produced *Stepping Sisters*, by Harry Warren Comstock; *Candle Light*, by Siegfried Geyer, *The Late Christopher Bean*, by Sidney Howard, with Carl Benton Reid, and *The Second Mrs. Tanqueray*, by Sir Arthur Wing Pinero, starring Mary Nash, that first July. August shows included *Adam The Creator*, by Karel and Josef Capek, adapted by Dora Round, with Leo G. Carroll and Mary Nash, and *Monna Vanna*, by Maurice Maeterlinck, with Ruth St. Denis in her first dramatic role. During the week she played in *Monna Vanna*, the playbill announced that Ruth St. Denis had agreed to give one recital of her Exotic Dances, on Thursday afternoon, August 10th at 2:30.

Publicity photo of Mabel Taliaferro.

Leo G. Carroll.

Daniel Frohman and Ruth St. Denis looking at the Monna Vanna *billboard, during the 1933 season at The Ogunquit Playhouse. By permission from the New York Public Library.*

The Stage *Magazine, September 1933. The magazine wrote, "Ruth St. Denis, a noted dancer, appearing in her first dramatic role in the ambitious revival of* Monna Vanna *at Ogunquit."*

Other productions that first season (really the sixth season of the Manhattan Repertory Theatre Company) were *Philip Goes Forth* by George Kelly, *Tomorrow and Tomorrow* by Philip Barry, *Cradle Song,* by Gregorio Martinez Sierra and Maria Martinez Sierra with Mabel Taliaferro.

The 1933 program notes paid tribute to the professionals involved in its productions, noting that:

> The production will be made with the same care and attention to detail that is exercised in the best metropolitan productions. Mr. Alexander Wyckoff in charge of the decors is an established artist in his field. He has to his credit many beautiful productions and has been associated with Mr. Hartwig for seven years. Miss Evelyn Cohen who will assume the responsibility for the correctness and taste in costumes has an equally wide experience in her line having functioned in a similar capacity under Professor Baker at Yale. We have a thoroughly equipped workshop and all our productions will be built in Ogunquit. As a consultant on our electrical effects we have Thomas Wilfred who is probably the most famous lighting expert in the world.

According to an article in the *Portland Transcript* titled "Maine's Newest Theatrical Colony Established in Ogunquit," and dated July 2, 1933, the new Ogunquit Playhouse for Manhattan Players was an artistic addition to a smart summer resort.

> A person really needs to work with Walter Hartwig, director and moving force behind Ogunquit's Playhouse and summer theatre colony, in order to appreciate the keenness of his penetrating mind and never failing sense of humor which never was more needed than just previous to the opening of the new theatre, when, as usual, nothing was going smoothly and a seeming mountain of work had to be accomplished. However, with suggestions here and there, a smile of greeting to new and old friends, plans were made and remade and, gradually out of chaos, emerged the sparkling little theatre in its bright dress of modern colors, designed and executed by Alexander Wycoff of the College of Arts in Pittsburgh. (Wycoff designed the theatre and its productions. David Asherman decorated the interior of the auditorium under the guidance of his father, Ned, according to Mary-Leigh Smart's recollections.) Several years ago, Mr. Hartwig began spending part of his summer at the delightful summer resort so well known in art circles. Several times he was approached regarding a summer theatre, "But," said Mr. Hartwig, "you have no theatre." "That's easy," came the quick reply, "We'll build you one." Plans were then tentatively made and later emerged, from what once was a garage devoted to the sales and repairs of "Lizzies," the complete and beautiful theatre plant that is now in operation. The entire plant was built by Grover Perkins of Ogunquit, from specifications drawn up by Messrs. Hartwig and Wycoff embracing many modern ideas and provisions for staging most elaborate productions. A "Green Room" for the

company off stage and a long row of spacious dressing rooms occupy the space to the right of the auditorium and stage. The "Green Room" is the place members of the profession gather to discuss new plays, players, business, private rehearsals and many other informal gatherings. Several smart shops are planned for each side of the theatre entrance with its sophisticated sidewalk canopy and unique potted garden either side of the doors. A new and distinctive addition to the theatre is the adjoining refreshment garden with its dancing facilities. Here the guests may go for refreshments between acts and after the performances. Dancing is planned nightly. An orchestra is another of the interesting and permanent assets of this extraordinary theatre and will play every night. The Black Friar's Theatre is the fascinating name of the workshop about a quarter of a mile off the main road where all the productions are built under the supervision of Mr. Wycoff. Here is already accumulated a vast storehouse of scenery and properties for use in various productions. Each play has its own complete scale model with every detail worked out in advance. Then it is built by the student crew of apprentices under competent supervision. Each weekend is a busy one at Ogunquit as the old setting must be taken apart and the new one completely set up and arranged, and lighted in time for dress rehearsal Sunday nights. The stage is managed by Carl A. Reed who brings a wide knowledge of road shows and productions that have taken him around the country five times. Another branch of the Colony is the Theatre School under the personal supervision of Mr. Hartwig, where a limited group of theatre-mnded young people gain certain sure knowledge of their adopted career. The staff includes such famous and well known personages as Walter Prichard Eaton, Montrose J. Moses, Hubert Osborne, Mr. Reed, Margaret Prendergast McLean, John Kirkpatrick, Evelyn Cohen, Carl Benton Reid, Mr. Wycoff and Mr. Hartwig.[21]

Scene shop, Agamenticus Road, 1933.

1934; The Second Season

The first production of the 1934 season was *The Curtain Rises* by B. M. Kaye, starring Florence Williams, a member of the resident company, and one who had been involved as an apprentice at the Manhattan Theatre Colony in Peterborough, where she played first in a "laboratory production." Wrote Mary X. Sullivan, the Publicity Director:

We have observed the progress of this talented and charming young actress with great interest, because it justifies the belief we have in her ability ever since she played her first part. After seeing her work in the student plays, the older members of the group assured her that she belonged in the theatre. "But gaining a foot-hold is such a heart-breaking business, and she is such a child!" they said. "Can she survive the struggle for recognition, the disappointments, and the very fight for existence?" The answer seems to be "Yes." [22]

In the second playbill of the season, for *The Sacred Flame* by W. Somerset Maugham with Florence Britton, Hartwig announced the beginning of shows at the Village Studio. "Now that we have successfully launched the Manhattan Repertory Company at the Ogunquit Playhouse, we have also taken over the management of the Village Studio Theatre, the charming, intimate theatre on Hoyt's Lane." [23]

There, in a series called Manhattan Nights, they offered evening performances by Miss Rose Quong, a Chinese Diseuse (French for a reciter); Mr. Jacques Cartier, a famous interpretive dancer; Mr. Bide Dudley and Mr. Vance Campbell: Dudley was a radio drama critic who spoke on the "Stage from a Human and Humorous Angle." Mr. Campbell, a celebrated radio baritone, must have accompanied Mr. Dudley; and finally, what was undoubtedly the *pièce de résistance*, Miss Ruth St. Denis, in a program of her intimate exotic dances.

The 1934 season saw the much heralded appearance of Maude Adams in *Twelfth Night*, by William Shakespeare. On July 16, 1934, Maude Adams opened in a production, directed by herself, with a newly written prologue by William Pritchard Eaton. Ogunquit Playhouse visitors during the '40s and '50s will remember Maude Adams as the imposing profile, almost full-length, in sepia that hung behind the box office in the lobby for a very long time.

Photo of Maude Adams marquee in front of the old Ogunquit Playhouse, 1933. With permission of the New York Public Library.

Maude Adams as Peter Pan, her most famous role. Courtesy of Carole Lee Carroll.

The profile of Maude Adams seen in the lobby of the Ogunquit Playhouse for many years.

Maude Adams in the role of Babbie in The Little Minister. Courtesy of Carole Lee Carroll.

On July 17, 1934, the *New York Times* reviewed Miss Adams, saying:

> She appeared for the first time in a part she had always wished to play, that of Maria. And she did so on the stage of one of the summer theatres that now dot this land from Maine westward. Men and women who had been followers of Maude Adams when she was "Babbie" of The Little Minister, and Peter Pan, came long distances to see her again. On her first entrance they applauded her for several minutes, and during the intermission, they wished the curtain not to be lowered. Miss Adams chose her own cast, and directed the production herself and it was she who thought of the prologue and epilogue. She has been living in Ogunquit for several weeks, quietly, and no one in the village had seen her. The equipment of Mr. Hartwig's Playhouse is good, but it is not Broadway, and there are certain things that in a summer theatre just cannot be done. Miss Adams accepted all the unavoidable limitations cheerfully; getting the play on was all that mattered. If the applause at the end of the evening meant anything, she succeeded....This evening, her friends arrived from as far away as Chicago. Former Governor Alvin T. Fuller of Massachusetts was present and many others of prominence.[24]

An amusing description of that season's goings-on appeared in the *Twelfth Night* playbill, written (or at least authorized) by Hartwig himself.

> If there is anything more amiable than a summer theatre audience except another one we have yet to see it. They have come out for a good time, in the mellowest of humors, and nothing, least of all the play, is going to stop them. They laugh freely over antique lines and greybeard jokes and get big moments out of fustian (i.e., high flown or affected) and sound drama alike. Of course the summer productions, taken as a whole, are of high professional quality. But some seventy-five companies playing a new play each week have meant considerable inequalities, and these have been met with the best grace in the world. Audiences have, at times, been a little incredulous, to be sure. One of Kennebunk's most imposing dowagers couldn't believe that Maude Adams was going to play at this little theatre. "I'll buy a ticket," she said. "'But understand that if Miss Adams does not appear, I shall raise Cain." Up at Portland people said: "You are advertising Peggy Wood and Fay Marbe, but whom will we really get?" Give a summer audience a star, preferably a star in a new arrangement of a garage like Grover Perkins' and the rest is history now. [25]

Written in the following week's "Colony Chatter": "Among the distinguished guests to visit Ogunquit and the Playhouse last week: Ogden Nash, famous author of humorous poetry; Daniel Frohman, dean of Theatrical Producers, Ward Morehouse, columnist on the *New York Sun*, as well as Richard Aldrich and Alfred DeLiagre of the New York producing firm of Aldrich and DeLiagre." The same playbill called "the apprentice colony all agog over the production of *Everyman* for the Fireman's Benefit, Thursday, August 2nd at the Studio Theatre on Hoyt's Lane."

And the playbill let audiences know about the "Maude Adams Tour" this way:

> Visitors at the Playhouse might be interested to know of the adventures that Maude Adams' *Twelfth Night* company has encountered on their record-breaking tour of New England these past four weeks. There was the time the company almost had to use the Camden jail for dressing rooms, and up in Orono, Mickey Mouse in person sat calmly on the footlights and watched a part of the performance, much to the consternation of the ladies of the company. Then there was the night the huge scenery trailer-truck almost toppled off the mountain roads between Brattleboro, Vermont and Bennington, Vermont where construction crews were at work and no guard rail, plus a rough road and a river bed far below gave the driver a healthy scare. This week the production is playing at the Oceanside Hotel Playhouse in Magnolia, Massachusetts. And the following weeks it continues with recently added playing time because of the tremendous response from all over New England for the opportunity to see the great actress again. On Monday and Tuesday, August 28th and 29th, it will play in Wellesley, after that at Concord, New Hampshire and then Bethlehem, New Hampshire. The following week at the Cape Playhouse in Dennis, and the closing week is scheduled for the Casino Theatre in Newport, Rhode Island beginning September 11th.

One of the Asherman boys, Ted, was reportedly among the touring company.

Stiano Braggiotti, a member of the Manhattan Theatre Colony resident company, and Susan's uncle. With permission of the New York Public Library.

Other plays that season included *The Closed Room*, with Peggy Wood in which Susan's uncle, Stiano Braggiotti appeared as well ; *Her Masters Voice*, by Clare Kummer, with Daisy Atherton; *Loose Moments*, by Courteney Savage and Bertram Hobbs; *At Marian's*, a new play by Laurette Taylor with Tullio Carminati; *Obsession* by Martin Berkeley, a new play; *Yellow Sands,* by Eden Phillpots and Adelaide Phillpots; *His Favorite Wife* by George James Hopkins, with Faye Marbe.

The opening of *The Closed Room* starring Peggy Wood, brought this headline from the *New York Times*: "Peggy Wood Scores in *The Closed Room*; Comedy-Drama by Patterson Greene has premiere in Ogunquit, Maine, Theatre." The reviewer went on to say "the three-act play was well received by an audience sprinkled with prominent society figures from Maine and New Hampshire." [26]

The *New York Times* also reported that Laurette Taylor had received:

> an ovation from (a) crowded house in *At Marian's* in Ogunquit. The play, written by Miss Taylor, concerned the struggle of an authoress to escape a

morbid fear of her own dissipation and a recurrence of her attempted suicide. Miss Taylor was supported by Tullio Carminati, former leading man of Eleanora Duse and star of *Strictly Dishonorable*. Miss Taylor plans to take the play to Broadway in the fall. [27]

The *York Transcript*, on September 14, 1934, proclaimed Hartwig's season:

> has in every way been brilliant. Five new plays were shown to the public for the first time. The plays that were revived were among the best that the English drama can boast of. A permanent resident company of the first quality has been maintained …Four of the greatest names in the American theatre were guest artists with the Manhattan Repertory Theatre Company – Maude Adams, Laurette Taylor, Tullio Carminati, and Peggy Wood. In every respect the productions have been of Broadway quality. [28]

In a 1934 playbill Hartwig poked fun at the old Playhouse:

> Here at Ogunquit, things are usually Broadway suave, but acts of God cannot always be controlled. Last year, during *The Second Mrs. Tanqueray*, a record tempest blew up. No one particularly minded the crash of the thunder or the hammer of the deluge on the shingled roof, even when it made hearing most difficult. But when the lights went out right in the middle of a speech by Hilda Spong, things came to a climax. Bravely the show went on in true stage tradition, despite the pitch blackness until finally Miss Spong, at an appropriate part in her lines explained, "This can't go on."

According to Barbara Hilty, and others who went to the old Playhouse in Grover Perkins' garage, on a very warm evening, the gasoline odor would rise from the floor. And it had a tin roof, so when it rained, the show stopped. The actors would stand on the stage, or sometimes, the curtain would be drawn. They really could not compete with the noise.

One might speculate that difficulties with the garage-theatre (its tin roof, its rough interior, its unpleasant odor of gasoline on hot, humid evenings) perhaps led Hartwig to focus his theatrical productions elsewhere and expand them. In 1934, he had announced a program of Manhattan Nights Entertainment; 1935 marked the return of Manhattan Nights at the "newly decorated" studio theatre in Hoyt's Lane. The program included The Yale Puppeteers; Edward Strawbridge, America's Foremost Male Dancer; John Mulholland, the world-renowned magician; and Ruth St. Denis, performing her exotic dances.

Using yet another venue for the first time, Hartwig announced a series of four readings, *Journeys in Arcady,* a new adventure in the realm of drama, poetry, philosophy and fiction, would take place at "Yellow Sands," his residence on Grasshopper Lane in Ogunquit. Under the guidance of Alexandra Carlisle, an eminent actress, a program of literature would be read and discussed. Each session was to last two hours and was offered at the modest price of $5 per session.

Laurette Taylor and Tullio Carminati rehearse for At Marian's. *With permission of the New York Public Library.*

Laurette Taylor and Walter Hartwig rehearsing at the Graham. Courtesy of Carole Lee Carroll.

Plays for the 1935 season included: *Accent on Youth*, by Samson Raphaelson, with Libby Holman and A.J. Herbert; *Tonight or Never* by Lily Hatvany, with Fritzi Scheff; *The Silver Box*, by John Galsworthy, with Ethel Barrymore, directed by Miss Barrymore; *The Farmer's Wife* by Eden Phillpots, with Mitzi Greene (Mitzi Greene was a famous child star of motion pictures, who made her debut in stock at Ogunquit in *The Farmer's Wife* and *Service for Two*); a new play, *Murder with Pen and Ink* by Frederick Jackson, with Florence Reed; *Oliver, Oliver*, by Paul Osborn, with Alexandra Carlisle; *Jane's Legacy* by Eden Phillpots, with Mollie Pearson; *Service for Two*, by Laurence and Alice Eyre, with Mitzi Greene; and *There's Always Juliet* by John Van Druten, with Violet Heming.

And with the first play, the season was off and running. Under the title, "Ovation for Libby Holman," the *New York Times* reported, on July 1, 1935,

Before an enthusiastic first-night audience of summer guests of this section at the Ogunquit Playhouse tonight, Libby Holman, Broadway musical comedy star, made her debut as a dramatic actress and her first appearance as a member of Walter Hartwig's Manhattan Repertory Company, playing the leading role in *Accent on Youth* by Samson Raphaelson. Miss Holman and the entire company took several curtain calls at the close. Miss Holman's understudy this week is Miss Lydia Fuller, Boston society girl and daughter of former Governor and Mrs. Alvan T. Fuller of Massachusetts. [29]

Alexandra Carlisle. With permission of the New York Public Library.

Photo of Mitzi Greene.

Dressing room assignments for Tonight or Never. *Courtesy of Graham Cookson.*

Program for The Silver Box. *Courtesy of Benita Braggiotti Carey.*

Ethel Barrymore. Picture was prominent in the lobby of the Playhouse for many years.
Courtesy of Carole Lee Carroll.

Photo of Libby Holman.

In the August, 1935 issue of *The Stage* Magazine, James Reid Barker wrote the following account of being in Ogunquit for the opening show that season, *Accent on Youth,* with Libby Holman.

Ogunquit, Me, July 5th, The houses are open again, with housewives ready to cook the most wonderful food in the world for the passing traveler. Hooked rugs, made during the winter are for sale. At the Lobster Pound, you pick your own lobster and time it while it cooks twenty minutes, no more and no less over an outdoor fire. (Ogunquit Lobster Pound, perhaps?) Trim white cottages. Perennial borders. Picket fences. Cars moving decorously through the town at twenty miles an hour. The scent of pines and the sea. And the Ogunquit Playhouse, open for the first week of the season. When a summer theatre goes S.R.O. at a midweek performance, it's news. Going on a hunch, I attributed the crowd to this week's bill – Libby Holman in *Accent on Youth.* I was wrong. When she entered the audience was indifferent. Not even curious. The play, not the star, was the draw. Count in the theatre's reputation, too. Libby Holman was a surprise. Assured, warm, humorous. Glowing with animation, she was having a good time with the part. Suddenly the audience began to like her. "Believe it or not, I was ready to go to Finland with you." Roars of delight. The show goes on like a breeze. The party afterward, in a restaurant across the road. (Bessie's) Some people wanting beer, some wanting Shredded Wheat. Everyone examining the design for a permanent Shakespeare setting. (It was in Hartwig's future plans to build this.) Alexandra Carlisle says, "Here's a set. Here's a company. Why wait?" Talking a blue streak, Walter Hartwig re-enacts the long-distance telephone call engaging Ethel Barrymore for *The Silver Box.* Mr. Hartwig trying to fix the date, Miss Barrymore trying to discuss the art of Galsworthy. (Barrymore was promoting the artist in the U.S. at that time.) The waitress who has been promised an introduction to Libby Holman is called over. Introduction performed. Bessie, skeptically noting Miss Holman's old sweater and frayed skirt, decides the actors are playing a practical joke. "Hi Lib," she says blithely, just to show she isn't deceived. "Hi, Bess," says Libby, enjoying the situation. Others come into the restaurant and greet the party, including Libby. Bessie quails. General forgiveness. Everybody shouting from table to table. Excitement. Tobacco smoke. Hilarity. Theatre! 30

Old postcard of Bessie's Restaurant. Courtesy of Carole Lee Carroll.

Bosley Crowther, famed *New York Times* critic for many years, wrote in June, 1935, about the amenities of Lakewood and Ogunquit as locations for their summer theatres in an article entitled, "As Maine Goes –."

> The atmosphere of Ogunquit is in contrast to that of Lakewood. In the former it is the sound of the surf, rolling upon the long beach, which is constantly in one's ears and the sight of sunburned summer residents strolling before one's eyes. Ogunquit, with its large hotels and many guest cottages, its famous artists' colony and fishing village, its Marginal Way along the cliffs overlooking the sea and its healthful beach, is one of Maine's most famous resorts…It is to audiences made up largely of urban vacationists that Mr. Hartwig's company therefore plays.

He ends:

> Whether or not one takes his summer theatres seriously, a visit to Maine spots should prove one thing: they are an actor's paradise. And no child of the sock and buskin, who has been able to spend a month or six weeks on the edge of a clear blue lake, where the sun sparkles brightly by day and the loons cry mournfully by night, or within sound and smell of the long rolling ocean, can return in the fall to Broadway anything but a better man – if not a better actor. [31]

On Friday, June 28, 1935, the editors, Edward Bangs and Frank Bangs of the *York Transcript*, were impressed enough with the Crowther article to run it in their editorial that week under the title, "Mr Hartwig Serves the State." [32]

On August 4, 1935, the *New York Times* ran an article written by Walter Hartwig subtitled: "Rural Theatres Offer Their Patrons a Romance Long Lost by Broadway."

> The continued growth and spread of the Summer Theatres that now function throughout New England, New York, and New Jersey and are beginning to assert themselves in other states, may very well indicate what course the American professional theatre will have to take if it is to reestablish itself and command the attention and respect that it enjoyed before the cinema replaced it in the affection of the masses.

Hartwig reasoned that movie palaces at 40 cents a ticket had replaced what the public used to find in the legitimate theatre – glamour, romance and adventure. The theatre had become too expensive, but that summer theatres could profit from this.

> There is glamour, romance and adventure sold with a ticket to a summer theatre. Most of the summer theatres are situated in romantic settings. The surprise of the unexpected helps. There is a thrill in the experience of getting good or well-known

actors in popular plays and under conditions and surroundings that hardly suggest such an experience. The summer theatre is intimate with its audience from the time the purchaser of a ticket steps up to the box office until the show is over. In Ogunquit at the Playhouse a customer may not only see where his location is on a chart, but very often ticket purchasers—generally nice old ladies – ask whether they may go into the theatre and see just where the seats are. They are always permitted to do so.

He went on to point out that summer theatre audiences can come from quite far away and that:

> a man who drives a hundred miles to see a play makes an adventure out of it, and that is what theatergoing used to be and must be again before the legitimate theatre can regain its lost prestige. …What the summer theatre has to break down now is the feeling among embryo actors, embryo stage artists and mechanics that anything is good enough for the summer public.
>
> As the summer theatre has gradually grown into an institution and the standards among the better ones have been placed higher, the public has become discriminating, so that the best actors and best scenic designers are none too good for the summer theatre.

He doesn't say so, but he alludes to the fact that unions were tying up the metropolitan theatres, while summer theatres "had the advantage of bringing in younger, well-trained mechanics of the theatre from the schools at Yale and Carnegie Tech to handle the lights, properties and carpentering."

> It is just as possible to make an intelligent production of a new play in the summer theatre as it is in the Broadway theatre. (But) a season of all new plays eventually dries up an audience completely. The only draw that can be expected under these circumstances is that which is attracted by a strong name. but even this feature exhausts itself quickly if the play is not a good one and is not presented with intelligence or even finesse. The summer theatre that is striving for recognition and success (this is 1935, remember), must adopt all the best features of the professional theatre so far as the playing and the settings are concerned, and … eventually this may bring about the regeneration of the legitimate theatre in America. [33]

In later years, this very same advice so visionary in its truth, would be championed by the next owner of the Ogunquit Playhouse, John Lane, whose rigorous attention to the appearance, the technical aspects, and the quality of both its productions, and its choices of plays and celebrity players, kept the Playhouse one of the most respected and admired theatres on the summer circuit. This high quality professionalism may have been the most significant factor in the continued success of the Ogunquit Playhouse.

This rather grand announcement was made by Mary X. Sullivan, the Publicity Director during the Hartwig years, who reportedly went on to become a theatre critic for the *Boston Evening Traveller* during the early 1960s!

The 1935 season ended with *There's Always Juliet,* starring Violet Heming. This is a comedy that "sparkles with brittle and amusing dialogue, with none of the artificiality which often afflicts breezy sophisticated comedies – the story of a girl and a man who fall in love at first sight, in spite of their own predictions that such things don't happen. A.J.Herbert, one of the most popular leading men in our company, will play opposite Miss Heming. Charles Campbell, the young English actor who appeared in *The Silver Box* will return for the play, and Daisy Atherton will be the fourth member of the cast [34]

By the 1936 season, Walter Hartwig's enterprise had expanded to include a resident company of 34 "distinguished artists." The reputation of the company had grown so that the *New York Times* called Hartwig's Manhattan Repertory Theatre, "one of the best known in the business." [35] The plays at the old Playhouse included *Three Wise Fools,* by Austin Strong, with Thomas W. Ross, Rosemary Ames and Edward Emery; *Saturday's Children,* by Maxwell Anderson with Ruth Gordon and John Griggs; *Kind Lady,* by Edward Chodorov, with Frances Starr; *Russet Mantle,* by Lynn Riggs, with Morgan

Photo of A. J. Herbert in costume. Courtesy of Barbara Hilty.

Rosemary Ames.

Ruth Gordon and John Griggs in Saturday's Children, The Stage Magazine, August 1936. Courtesy of Carole Lee Carroll.

Farley and Charlotte Walker; *The Wind and The Rain,* by Merton Hodge, with Morgan Farley, Anne Seymour and Rosemary Ames; *Erstwhile Susan,* by Marian de Forest, with Lillian Foster, Joanna Roos, Wilfred Seagram and Thomas W. Ross; *Mademoiselle,* by Grace George and Jacques Deval, with Florence Reed; *The Night of January 16th,* a murder trial in three sessions by Ayn Rand, with Margalo Gillmore*; and *Fresh Fields,* by Ivor Novello, with Margaret Anglin.

*A curious bit of theatre history concerns Mary Nash and Margalo Gillmore, two of Walter Hartwig's guest stars. Nash played Tracy Lord's mother in *The Philadelphia Story,* the movie that starred Cary Grant, James Stewart and Katherine Hepburn. Margalo Gillmore played Tracy Lord's mother, a number of years later, of course, in *High Society,* the movie remake that starred Grace Kelly, Frank Sinatra and Bing Crosby.

The last performance of the 1936 season marked a departure from the usual dramatic works when the Hartwigs brought *The Ballet Caravan,* a troupe of twelve dancers from the American Ballet of the Metropolitan Opera in New York, performing their own compositions. The American Ballet Company was founded by George Balanchine and Lincoln Kirstein and for a while was the resident ballet company at the Metropolitan Opera. In 1936, Kirstein and M.M.Warburg founded another company, *Ballet Caravan,* to encourage young choreographers. Lew Christiansen, Eugene Loring, William Dollar, and John Taras began with *Ballet Caravan*. This company gave employment to dancers when they were off season. [36]

In the 1936 playbills there are numerous references to rotating art exhibits in the lobby gallery of the old Playhouse. Charles Woodbury's collection from the winter before in the Windward and Leeward Islands of the West Indies, for example, was shown early in the season. A later exhibition featured Eliot O'Hara water color paintings, and still later that year, an exhibit of Henry Strater's work featured five oil paintings of cattle ranches in the Southwest completed over the three years before.

In her 50th anniversary history in the Playhouse playbill of 1982, Bunny Hart wrote:

> By the end of the 1936 season, it was obvious that the enormous popularity of both Ogunquit and its Playhouse demanded a larger theatre. Hartwig

From top to bottom, Frances Starr (courtesy of Carole Lee Carroll), Margaret Anglin, Morgan Farley, and Margalo Gillmore.

eyed the Weare farm on Route 1 south of town. He bought a parcel of land and engaged theatre architect Alexander Wyckoff to design the building in keeping with New England tradition. On completion, the new Ogunquit Playhouse had a larger stage than many Broadway houses, a spacious auditorium seating 700 and the most modern technical facilities available at that time…The new Playhouse debuted on July 19, 1937, the fourth week of the season, with *Boy Meets Girl*. Sally Rand followed in *They Knew What They Wanted*. Tickets ranged in price from $.75 to $2.00. In succeeding seasons top stars flocked to the small village, rehearsed with the resident company and brought splendid theatre to audiences who had not and would not see it on the Great White Way. Theatre professionals credited Hartwig for pioneering the Straw Hat Circuit. Cornelia Otis Skinner, Madge Evans, Grace George, Clifton Webb played Ogunquit; Sinclair Lewis starred in *Our Town*; Edward Everett Horton appeared in his perennial vehicle *Springtime for Henry,* the same week in 1939 that young Diana Barrymore portrayed Shakespeare's Juliet in the thriving Junior Manhattan Theatre Colony. [37]

The Resident Company during the '30s

During these years of the resident company, actors who returned each year inevitably built up a following of their own. And the playbills of 1934 through 1939 promoted the attachments between certain actors and the village inhabitants. A column entitled "Green Room Gossip," in 1936 let playgoers know that:

> Rosemary Ames, who lives a mile outside of town, braves the Route One traffic every day to get back and forth on her bicycle; that Stiano Braggiotti returns to Ogunquit, where he has spent many summers to play the leading role opposite Miss Frances Starr in *Kind Lady*; that Ruth Hammond was famous for her charcoal sketches of theatrical and literary notables. Among those who have sat for her are Edna Ferber, Katherine Cornell and Judith Anderson; and that Laurette Taylor had arrived in Ogunquit to spend the summer, while writing a new play; that she had fallen in love with Ogunquit and the Manhattan Theatre Colony when she starred in *At Marian's* the season before. [38]

The New Ogunquit Playhouse

At the start of the 1937 season, the fifth year of the Manhattan Repertory Theatre Company in Ogunquit (and the 12th season, counting the company's years at Peterborough and Bristol), the playbill ran the following news column:

OUR OLD FRIENDS COME BACK

Well, here we are again, and we suddenly realize that this is our fifth year in Ogunquit. We have been greeting our old friends in the streets of the village -- Cecil Perkins, the genial chief of police, Marcus Littlefield at the telegraph office, the girls who see that we get fed, and last but not least, our faithful subscribers. All of them ask, "Who of the old (not in point of years, of course) are back this season?" So here is an accounting of the return to the fold. Carl Reed, the very efficient stage manager, and Lygia Bernard, who is Mrs. Reed in private life, are back again. Miss Bernard has always been a great favorite with our audiences, and she is appearing in the opening play. Carl Benton Reid (we call him Eddie Reid because of the difficulty of the two Carls) who was our leading man the first season here, has returned to us after three years of playing leads in Shakespearean Repertory with the Globe Theatre. Violet Besson, one of the grandest character actresses in America, is with us again, as is Wilfred Seagram, who established a following in the Playhouse last season. Cecile Wulff, another charter member of the Ogunquit Playhouse, made her debut here with Maude Adams, and has given splendid performances in each succeeding season. Bill Swetland, who got his training in the finest theatre outside of New York – the Cleveland Playhouse – came up last year, captivated the audiences with his grand characterizations – and this is *entre nous* – fell in love with our nicest apprentice and brought her back with him this year as Mrs. Swetland. Later in the season other familiar faces will appear on our stage. Rosemary Ames has firmly refused all offers to go elsewhere, and will be back soon, giving us heart failure by riding down Route 1 on her bicycle; John Griggs will be with us again and Ivan Triesault and Morgan Farley have already taken cottages and have been taking advantage of what few sunny days we have had to get a good tan before they are put to work. Our roster of guest stars includes some old friends, too. Frances Starr, who played *Kind Lady* last season; Florence Reed, without whom our season would not seem right; Ernita Lascelles, who will supervise and play in a Greek tragedy; Laurette Taylor, who came up here to play in one production and has become a regular summer resident; we have other stars coming about whom you will read elsewhere in the program. This is merely for the information of those who want to know who's coming back! Now about Daisy Atherton. We miss her as much as you will – yes, it is true that for the first time Miss Atherton will not be here. But with the grand success she is having in the leading part of *You Can't Take It With You* in Chicago we couldn't ask her to come to Ogunquit even if her contract would allow it. The staff looks pretty familiar with Mr. Hopkins back in the box office, and Miss Rosoff, Mr. Hartwig's secretary, straightening everything out, and Sidney Redish designing the scenery, Carl Reed has Maria Coxe as assistant and Giles Wilson, who has been absent for three years, will again assist in the box office and take tickets. [39]

Some of the resident company in front of the Village Studio, 1934 or 1935, including Lygia Bernard, front row; second row: Rosemary Ames, A.J. Herbert, Daisy Atherton; and in back, Carl Reed. Courtesy of the New York Public Library.

As a footnote, Richard Hopkins, who had run the box office for numerous Broadway shows was a close associate of Walter and Maude Hartwig for many years. He and his wife vacationed on Shore Road in Ogunquit every summer for a number of years after he left the Playhouse, as did Betty Rosoff, Walter Hartwig's secretary.

During the spring of 1937, construction on the new Playhouse looked like this:

Construction of the new Playhouse 1937. Courtesy of the New York Public Library.

The season that year was to feature *The White Headed Boy*, by Lennox Robinson, playing at the Colony Theatre. Appearing in the leads were J. Augustus Keogh and Grace O'Malley, both Irish actors with strong Abbey Theatre (Dublin) backgrounds.

The second production at the Colony Theatre (the old Playhouse) was *Hay Fever*, by Noel Coward with Lillian Foster, and on July 12th, the next show was *Libel*, by Edward Wooll with Carl Benton Reid and John Griggs.

The fourth production of *Boy Meets Girl*, by Bella and Sam Spewack, was held with a great deal of fanfare at the opening of the new Ogunquit Playhouse.

Opening night at the new Ogunquit Playhouse, 1937, Boy Meets Girl. Courtesy of the New York Public Library.

Statement by Mr. Hartwig

With this week the Manhattan Repertory Theatre Company begins its eleventh season. The last four years of these have been played in Ogunquit. We acknowledge with gratitude the interest that the public has taken in our theatre and plays and actors we have presented. We have attracted the attention of the theatre going public from Portland to Portsmouth and from the seashore to Dover. This is obviously a compliment that we do not overlook. Our theatre already ranks as one of the five best in the country and Broadway actors are eager to accept engagements at the Ogunquit Playhouse. It can be said without reservation that the most popular Broadway actors appear each season at our theatre. A major event of the 1937 season just starting will be the opening of the new **Ogunquit Playhouse** on the No. 1 Highway just below Ogunquit in the direction of York. This event, as now planned, will take place on Monday evening, July 19th. When the new theatre is opened we will continue to operate the old theatre just as we have been doing for the past four years. It will be re-christened the **Colony Theatre** and the first attraction will be **Cornelia Otis Skinner**, who will come to Ogunquit under our management for **one performance only** on Thursday evening, July 22nd. Miss Skinner will present her six-scene dramatic play, *The Wives of Henry VIII*, which will be preceded by a group of her original character sketches. (Miss Skinner played that one performance to a full house, including her father, Otis Skinner, Laurette Taylor, and Sally Rand.) The first play at the new Ogunquit Playhouse, which will be presented on July 19th, will be the great New York hit, *Boy Meets Girl* with the full strength of the **Manhattan Repertory Theatre Company**. At the new Playhouse our audiences will find many advantages denied them at the old theatre. For one thing, there will be adequate and well constructed parking space. The interior of the theatre has every appointment of a first class theatre. It will be the finest and best equipped summer theatre in America. The bill at the old theatre for next week will be Noel Coward's *Hay Fever*. We hope that you will continue to be with us this season in both the old and the new theatre, and for many seasons to come in the new theatre.

WALTER HARTWIG

Mary X. Sullivan, Publicity Director, talked about the new Playhouse in the July 12th playbill and quoted Elliot Norton, drama critic of the *Boston Post*, following a visit to see the new Playhouse.

Mr. Norton was so impressed with the Playhouse that he devoted much of his Sunday page to an article on Mr. Hartwig and his work. Among other things, Mr Norton had this to say: "His new theatre is at once an adventure and an achievement. It embodies all his own ideas of what a summer theatre should be. What it cost to build, this department does not know, even vaguely. But that it represents a substantial sum of money is apparent. It is also apparent that this new Playhouse on U.S. Route 1, half a mile this side of Ogunquit proper, will be the best equipped theatre in this country. - - - - It is all part of a showman's dream, a dream that came true because the dreamer had iron courage and hard common sense. [40]

Settled into the new Playhouse, the season continued with *They Knew What They Wanted,* by Sidney Howard, with Sally Rand; *At Mrs. Beam's,* by C.K. Munro, with Estelle Winwood; *Criminal At Large,* by Edgar Wallace, with Nance O'Neil and Morgan Farley; *The Queen was in the Parlour,* by Noel Coward, with Frances Starr; *Journey's End,* by R.C.Sheriff with members of the resident company; and *Dearly Beloved,* by Charles Beahan and Robert Buckner, with Jean Muir and Donald Cook.

The Colony Club on School Street, under the new management of Ann Miner, the owner and manager of "The Back Drop," a restaurant on 52nd Street in New York, served lunches and after-theatre snacks to the company as well as Playhouse subscribers. You had to buy tokens at the box office at five cents apiece, sold in packages of twenty.

In addition to the opening of the new theatre, the Hartwig organization also found time that year to sponsor a series of Chamber Music Concerts at the Cliff Country Club featuring the Manhattan Trio that had played between acts ever since the beginning productions in Ogunquit. That group consisted of George Ochner, violinist, a student at the Julliard Graduate School in New York; George Neikrug, cellist; and Harold Bogin, pianist and graduate of Julliard who had twice appeared as soloist at Carnegie Hall in New York. The fifth concert in the series presented fourteen-year-old violinist Marjorie Edwards, who had debuted in New York's Town Hall in 1936.

> From the 1937 playbill: *Hay Fever* is one of Noel Coward's most successful comedies. It is perfect summer or winter entertainment, and when well done always scores a terrific success. It is particularly interesting that in his recent autobiography, *Present Indicative,* Mr. Coward tells the story of how he happened to write it and discloses that it was inspired by the delightful madness of the household of a certain star who plays at the Ogunquit Playhouse and is one of our greatly beloved.* It is the story of a family, all the members of whom are theatrical and amusing. The father is a successful playwright, the mother a retired actress and the two children precocious, artistic, and underneath it just ordinary, normal boy and girl. What happens on a weekend when all of them have guests makes a most amusing evening in the theatre.

*This play is based on the household of Laurette Taylor and her husband J. Hartley Manners.

Laurette Taylor in her most famous role, Peg O' My Heart, *by J. Hartley Manners, 1921. Courtesy of Carole Lee Carroll.*

Old Fashioned Melodrama at the Old Playhouse

The playbill of August 17th, 1937 announced the opening of an English melodrama, *The Lancashire Lass*, by Henry J. Byron, written in 1868.

> We have duplicated the original programs, the old fashioned hand-bill with the synopsis of the play, scene by scene, (and) we are reproducing the production just as faithfully. Some of the strongest members of the Manhattan Repertory Theatre Company are playing the principal roles, and as for scenery and costume, as well as the grandiloquent style of acting which pleased our grandmothers, it will be just the kind of play you might have seen in the Queen's Theatre in London in 1868. John Kirkpatrick, well-known author and playwright who is in charge of our apprentice group, has directed the play, and the settings have been designed by David Asherman. Tickets for *The Lancashire Lass* may be obtained at the Playhouse or at the Colony Theatre. Prices range from fifty cents to a dollar and a half. Come and hiss the villain, and see virtue triumph at the end. [41]

Also at the old Playhouse in 1937, Laurette Taylor and Stiano Braggiotti appeared in *At the Theatre* written by Miss Taylor, and Cornelia Otis Skinner performed monologues she had written called *The Wives of Henry VIII*.

Cornelia Otis Skinner.

That same season, Hartwig presented the Yale Puppeteers, and The Theatre Dance Company at the Ogunquit Square, and apprentice productions of *The Toy Heart*, *The House with the Twisty Windows*, and *Romance is a Racket*, a farce written by John Kirkpatrick.

In 1938, Hartwig decided to experiment with an 11-week season. He brought in a dozen or so new players into the resident company, and Doris Day was one of them, but it was not the same Doris Day that later generations would know from her motion pictures.

The season included *Yes, My Darling Daughter*, by Mark Swan, starring Florence Reed. This was a play with recorded entr'acte music – such pieces as Mendelssohn's *A Midsummer's*

Night's Dream, Guy Lombardo and His Royal Canadians playing "Whistle While You Work," from *Snow White and the Seven Dwarfs*, and the Benny Goodman Orchestra. At midseason, the management also introduced an hour of informal dancing in the lobby for theatre patrons every Tuesday evening.

Note: up until this time, live music had been used. This is the first sign of recorded music.

Lanny Ross.

Other plays of the 1938 season were: *Room Service*, by John Murray and Allen Boretz with Carl Benton Reid; *The Lady from Broadway*, by Fred Ballard with Dorathe Burgess (this was a new play, advertised as prior to Broadway); *Fata Morgana* by Ernest Vajda, with Elena Miramova; *Liliom*, by Ferenc Molnar, with Tonio Selwart; *Susan and God,* by Rachel Crothers, with Frances Starr; *Romance,* by Edward Sheldon, with Cornelia Otis Skinner; *Time and the Conways,* by J.B.Priestly, with Nance O'Neill and John Williams; *Soubrette*, by Jacques Deval, a new play with Else Argal; *Snow Train,* by Edward Childs Carpenter, with Donald Cook and Dorathe Burgess (also billed as a new play, prior to Broadway); and *Petticoat Fever*, by Mark Reed, with Lanny Ross.

Miramova was captured with Miss Elizabeth Perkins (who bequeathed her house and its contents to Old York Historical Society when she died) and Maude Hartwig (in one of the very few photographs of her) under the heading, "Active in Ogunquit Summer Colony," Prominent members of the summer colony at Ogunquit and York Village include, left to right, Madame Miramova, Miss Elizabeth Perkins, who has a summer home at York Village, and Mrs. Maude Hartwig. Miss Perkins is active in plans for "Days of Our Forefathers" to be observed there, August 20 and 21. She was recently a guest speaker at one of the series of "Five O'Clocks" at the Barn Gallery of the Ogunquit Art Association.

The 1939 season carried a very grand list of 44 distinguished actors appearing in the Manhattan Repertory Theatre Company. The season kicked off with *You Can't Take It With You*, the comedy by Moss Hart and George S. Kaufman, in which a young Diana Barrymore took the role of Alice. In the July 31, 1939 issue of *Life* Magazine, Diana Barrymore at the Ogunquit Beach appeared on the cover, and was featured inside.

The following plays were *Burlesque*, by George Manker Watters and Arthur Hopkins, starring Libby Holman and Clifton Webb; *The Firebrand*, by Edwin Justus Mayer, with Douglass Montgomery; *Brief Moment*, by S. N. Behrman with Madge Evans; *The Circle*, by Somerset Maugham with Grace George; *Our Town*, by Thornton Wilder with Sinclair Lewis; *Madame Sans Gene*, by Victorien Sardou and Emily Moreau with Cornelia Otis Skinner, Rosalind Ivan, and a cast of more than 33 people; *Springtime for Henry*, by Benn W. Levy, with Edward Everett Horton (in a role that would carry him through a great part of his career); *With All My Heart*, by Austin Parker with Glenda Farrell; and *Payment Deferred*.

Clifton Webb and Libby Holman in Burlesque, The Stage *Magazine.*

Douglass Montgomery in The Firebrand.

Cast of Madame Sans Gene, *on set designed by Charles Elson, 1939. Courtesy of the Historical Society of Wells and Ogunquit.*

Edward Everett Horton.

Glenda Farrell, With All My Heart, 1939.

1939 season brochure with photos of resident company.

News clipping of Madge Evans elopement.

The *Boston Herald* reported on July 26, 1939, that Madge Evans and Sidney Kingsley had eloped during the run of *Brief Moment*. The news item captured also by the *New York Times*, described the ceremony in York Village as follows:

> Without waiting to change the dress she wore in the final act of the play *Brief Moment* at the Ogunquit Playhouse, Madge Evans, film actress, 30 years old, left the theatre tonight with Sidney Kingsley, 32, Pulitzer Prize winning playwright, and they were married by a justice of the peace. Damian O'Flynn was best man for Mr. Kingsley who had to borrow a wedding ring from him. The couple motored away in a southerly direction. Miss Evans is due back at Ogunquit tomorrow night for her regular performance. [42]

The same season, Douglass Montgomery and Frances Starr appeared in a publicity shot in front of the Lookout Hotel. The photo was used as an advertisement by the Lookout.

The *New York Times* announced in June that Diana Barrymore Blythe, 18-year old daughter of John Barrymore and Michael Strange, would be making her stage debut in *You Can't Take It With You* at Walter Hartwig's Ogunquit Playhouse. The paper carried more news of the young actress on September 12, 1939.

> Diana Barrymore…has been signed for the touring company of *Outward Bound*, which will star Laurette Taylor and Florence Reed, and feature Bramwell Fletcher. Miss Barrymore will have the role acted last season by Helen Chandler, Mr. Fletcher's wife. [43]

Publicity photo of Douglass Montgomery and Frances Starr in front of the Lookout, 1939.

Shortly after this tour, Miss Barrymore also took the real-life role of Mr. Fletcher's wife. This according to the *Portsmouth Herald* in 1942, which reported that

> Playgoers at the Ogunquit Playhouse during the past few seasons would be interested to hear that Diana Barrymore and Bramwell Fletcher, both of whom appeared at Ogunquit during the summer of 1939, have applied for a marriage license. Diana made her debut at the theatre and that same season, Bramwell Fletcher, an English actor, was a member of the resident company under the direction of the late Walter

Hartwig. Miss Barrymore, oldest child of the late John Barrymore and Michael Strange (Mrs. Harrison Tweed), spent that summer at Ogunquit and appeared in several productions that season. (Despite this report, they probably met in 1940, not 1939, as Fletcher wasn't at Ogunquit in 1939. But they were both there in 1940.) [44]

In the 1939 playbills for the Ogunquit Playhouse, several of the backstage crew were highlighted. Carl Reed was described this way:

> Carl Reed, whom you rarely see away from his vigilant post in the wings, offstage right, has been Walter Hartwig's stage manager since the latter's first year in Ogunquit – and for two seasons before that, when the Manhattan Repertory Theatre Company was operating in Bristol, Conn. In between those summer stretches he has stage-managed for practically every topflight star in American theatre.

Charles Elson, who was to become a legend among set designers, was credited thus:

> Charles Elson, under whose directorial artistry Ogunquit Playhouse settings are built each week, is one of the country's best known stage designers not identified with Broadway. He expects to hurl himself on that glittering boulevard very shortly, having prepared amply for a place there. Mr. Elson was born in Chicago, where he attended school before going to the University of Chicago and obtaining his B.A. and Ph. D. degrees. He then spent a year in technical work at the Goodman Theatre in Chicago, and from there went to Yale for three years, earning a Master's degree in Fine Arts for achievements in the famed "47 Workshop" where he studied under Prof. George Pierce Baker, Donald Oenslager and Stanley McCandless. He designed and lighted two huge ice carnivals for Sonja Henie during those Yale days.

Diana Rivers at one of the clam bakes she gave for cast and crew. In the background, Betty Dixon with Carole Lee and Gale. 1945. Courtesy of Carole Lee Carroll

Elson remained at Ogunquit Playhouse until 1945, designing 44 productions in all. As a teacher and designer with hundreds of set designs nationally and internationally to his credit, Elson became something of a legend in the theatrical design world. His design of the set for *Madama Butterfly* at the Metropolitan Opera in New York, was used for more than twenty years. Elson also wrote several volumes of technical writing on stage design. He was married to Diana Rivers, an actress, and Carole Lee and Betty both remember they lived one year in a cottage where the Riverside cottages are now, and near the bridge to Perkins Cove.

They were very artistic and they would decorate their place differently for each month. When they entertained, they often invited cast and crew to a traditional shore dinner at a nearby cove, closer to the Cliff House, digging holes to put lobsters, clams and corn in – a real clambake.

Bolton Wilder, the lighting designer, had been responsible for the design and installation of the very elaborate stage lighting system in the new Playhouse. Working with McCandless and Kirk, famous lighting consultants in New York City, he had been involved in the job of floodlighting Rockefeller Center the year before, and had worked on thirty of the buildings at the New York World's Fair. At Yale Drama School, he studied under Stanley McCandless and Donald Oenslager, two of the biggest names in theatrical lighting and design respectively.

The playbills that year also talked about the music director:

> You know, of course, that the Playhouse has a music director. Yes, Mr Alden Asherman, an expert on program arrangement, who knows all the symphonies backward, has served you before, between and after the plays, and whether you care for music or not, Mr. Asherman has done his job well.

The following article published by The York Press ran in the *Wells Ogunquit Compass* on September 8, 1939.

> In 1933, there was many a weather eye turned on the (Hartwig's Playhouse). Ogunquit had never been identified with a professional theatre, so where, in this little village, even with its summer visitors, was an audience to come from, large enough to support so pretentious an undertaking. Although there was considerable excitement around the old garage that summer, there was no audience large enough to support the new venture. Hartwig lost five thousand dollars in Ogunquit in 1933. Nearly everybody expected there would be a loss, even Hartwig. Local opinion was more or less unanimous that to try to make a go of a theatre such as his in Ogunquit was like having a hen sit on a door knob – nothing would ever hatch out. With the red ink of 1933 staring him in the face, (Hartwig) came right back in 1934 with the same enthusiasm and more courage to try it again. There were more people who came to his theatre that year – enough more so that the 1934 loss was a paltry thousand dollars. And the doubters increased in number. But Hartwig figured it differently. To him the difference between a loss of $5,000 in one year and only $1,000 the following year meant a potential profit of $4,000. A conservative financier would call this cock-eyed, but Hartwig is neither conservative nor a financier -- he is a showman. So 1935 found him back again to take it, either on the chin or in the pocket. Lo and behold, 1935 turned a profit – a hundred odd dollars and some cents. Just as the tide was turning for success on the enterprise the roof began to leak in the old garage. You couldn't sell it as an open air theatre for all its leaky roof. The stars that Mr. Hartwig engaged to play for him drew a smart limousine audience, but they would only come once. They didn't feel happy in the quaint old garage even if Ethel Barrymore was trying to entertain them on the stage. But Hartwig had a five year lease, so the trick was to try to convince the audience that the performances were so good that no matter what discomfiture you were obliged to put up with, it was worth it. Those who could afford to pay for good entertainment went along

with Hartwig on this basis for a limited time and even more limited patience. Then the enterprise faced a crisis. Fame had overtaken the venture. Success was waiting at the door but not at the door of the dear old garage. York, which has always contributed a large portion of the audience at the Ogunquit Playhouse, saw its opportunity and made Hartwig a flattering offer to transfer his theatre there, but that would have meant changing the name. Hartwig had told the world from Nova Scotia to San Diego that Ogunquit was the place for the best summer theatre in America and it would have been too costly to tell the world all over again that now it was York Village – only eight miles away. [45]

There are probably many errors in this version of Hartwig's adventures, but several of the assertions have been challenged by other reports. It is claimed but not confirmed that Hartwig had a friend in York, Morton Stearns Frye, who offered to buy the field across from the present-day York Chamber of Commerce for the Playhouse, but that the York selectmen turned it down. [46]

Barry Sullivan.

Perhaps the most outstanding event of this very eventful season was the appearance of Sinclair Lewis in Thornton Wilder's play, *Our Town*. Lewis played the Stage Manager to Diana Rivers' Emily and John Craven's George. Sinclair Lewis, a very famous author, was the first American novelist to win the Nobel Prize for Literature in 1930. Born in Minnesota, the author of such classics as *Arrowsmith*, *Main Street*, *Babbit*, and *Elmer Gantry*, Lewis appears to have taken a few years off to try out acting. Some accounts say that he did this to research the summer theatre for a future novel or play. In any case, it was certainly a coup for the Ogunquit Playhouse and the Hartwigs to have him in the resident company for two years.

The 1940 season began with Jimmy Savo, a mime, in *Mum's The Word*, written by himself. Next came *The Guardsman*, by Ferenc Molnar. Members of the Manhattan Repertory Theatre Company who appeared in the play were Bramwell Fletcher, Rhys Williams, Lygia Bernard, Doris Dalton, Bert Tanswell, and a very young Barry Sullivan

Outward Bound by Sutton Vane, with Laurette Taylor, Louis Hector, Barry Sullivan, Bramwell Fletcher, Muriel Starr and Rhys Williams came next, on a set by Charles Elson. It was followed by *Biography*,

Biography *playbill. Courtesy of Carole Lee Carroll.*

an S. N. Behrman play with Cornelia Otis Skinner, Carl Benton Reid, Rhys Williams, Barry Sullivan, Arnold Korff, and Grace Briscombe; *The Greeks Had a Word for It,* by Zoë Atkins, with Madge Evans, Diana Barrymore, Bramwell Fletcher, Barry Sullivan, Carl Benton Reid, and the young Betty Furness; and *No Time For Comedy*, by S.N. Behrman, with Frances Starr.

In August 1940, the resident company was seen in *Amphitryon 38*, by S. N. Behrman, *Design for Living*, by Noel Coward, *The Hottentot*, by Victor Mapes, *Elmer the Great*, by Ring Lardner, with Buddy Ebsen and his sister, Vilma. Sinclair Lewis was featured again when at the end of that 1940 season he appeared in Eugene O'Neill's *Ah Wilderness*, with other members of the resident company.

Betty Furness.

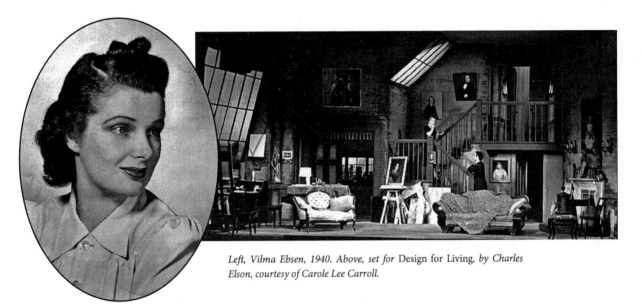

Left, Vilma Ebsen, 1940. Above, set for Design for Living, *by Charles Elson, courtesy of Carole Lee Carroll.*

A 1940 publicity announcement from the Playhouse to the *Portsmouth Herald* claimed that:

> The most ambitious production ever staged in any summer theatre will be presented at the Ogunquit Playhouse Monday when director Walter Hartwig raises the curtains on that gigantic laugh production, *Amphitryon 38* (a play by Jean Giraudoux, adapted by S.N. Behrman) starring such notables of stage and screen as Michael Strange, John Lodge and his beautiful wife, Francesca Braggiotti. The added scoop is that of seeing Michael Strange in her only appearance of the season on any stage.[47]

> **The Playhouse Team to Raid Camp Langdon**
>
> Buddy Ebsen's Ebb Tides, a softball team till recently unheard of, will play the Camp Langdon team tomorrow afternoon at the Camp baseball field. Ebsen, a noted stage and radio comedian, has organized the stagehands at the Ogunquit theatre into what he claims, a softball team with latent power. Ebsen will pitch for the Tides and although his pitching record for the year has never been published, rumor has it that he is pretty good. It is quite possible that Ebsen started the rumor, though.
>
> Any local softball teams that would like to play the theatre team are welcome to do so. Mr. Ebsen can be reached at the Playhouse and wants games. [48]

During his two seasons at the Ogunquit Playhouse in the resident company, Buddy Ebsen played a lot of softball. This was attested to by a rather bizarre announcement seen in the *Portsmouth Herald,* August 11, 1941:

Paul Mason, now on the board of the Restoration Committee of the Ogunquit Heritage Museum remembers a game Ebsen put together with "townies" like this:

Buddy Ebsen and cast behind the playhouse in Elmer the Great, *1941. Courtesy of the New York Public Library.*

> Sometime in the 30s, (actually it was 1940) Buddy Ebsen was in Ogunquit and I remember he was here for longer than just week (He was in the resident company for two seasons.) Anyway, we got together a small group of townies and friends. I remember Bessie Sideris' brothers, Tony and Nick, played and there were others. One time, we played in the Colony field against a group from the Playhouse. Buddy Ebsen was the pitcher for their side, and I was pitching for the townies. He walked up to me and said "Name's Ebsen," and I said, "Name's Mason." We had a fun game and I will never forget it.

Joe E. Brown was another famous actor who loved to play softball. Bunny Hart remembers games that he put together

Joe E. Brown, while playing in Elmer the Great *in 1939, at the Cape Playhouse with some of his softball players. Bunny Hart is second from left. Courtesy of Bunny Hart.*

America's Foremost Summer Theatre 47

Buddy Ebson seated beside the Playhouse with a dog, 1940.

Below, Vilma Ebsen and Walter Hartwig beside the Playhouse. Both photos come from an album in which Frederica Going, recorded her summer in Ogunquit in 1940. Courtesy of the New York Public Library.

Maude Takes Over

Walter Hartwig died on January 18, 1941. That could have been the end of the Ogunquit Playhouse, but Maude Hartwig, Walter's widow, didn't hesitate for a moment. With lots of support around her, she moved into the 1941 season without a pause. But the opening playbill of the 1941 season carried this message from Jack Kirkpatrick:

> The theatre is a gay place, a festive place and in these days usually wears the mask of comedy. When sorrow enters it, we call it tragedy. For whether comedy or tragedy, it must still fulfill its mission and purpose – the reflection of life. Conversely when sorrow comes into this life which the theatre mirrors, perhaps we should view that, too, as part of a large tapestry composed of the comic and the tragic and not allow personal grief to overshadow the happy moments which the footlights and grease paint have provided us. Anyway we feel sure that Walter Hartwig, whose love of the theatre was so inspiring to all those who worked with him, would have felt this way and we feel sure that from some place in the great proscenium arch of the universe he approves our determination to carry on the work which meant so much to him.

The plays offered during the 1941 season were *Something Gay,* by Adelaide Heilbron, starring Betty Furness; *By Your Leave,* by Gladys Hurlbut and Emma Wells, with Dorothy Sands; *One Sunday Afternoon,* by James Hagan, with Fay Wray; *Nancy's Private Affair,* by Myron Fagan, with Anna Sten; *Ladies in Retirement,* by Edward Percy and Reginald Denham, with Fritzi Scheff and Estelle Winwood; *The Male Animal,* by Elliot Nugent and James Thurber, with Conrad Nagel; *The Poor Nut,* by J.C. and Elliot Nugent, with Buddy Ebsen; *Her Cardboard Lover,* by Jacques Deval, with Tallulah Bankhead; and *Our Betters,* by Somerset Maugham, with Elsa Maxwell and a little-known bit part player named Ricardo Montalban. The last play of the 1941 season was *Kiss The Boys*

Maude Hartwig photographed for an article in the Boston Sunday Globe, *1949.*

Goodbye, by Clare Boothe Luce, starring Anita Louise. According to an article in the *Portsmouth Herald*, dated July 15, 1941:

> *One Sunday Afternoon*, the movie which brought Fay Wray into prominence, serves as the vehicle for her appearance at the Ogunquit Playhouse this week. Making her first appearance at the Playhouse last night, she enacted a different role than she did in her movie appearance. In the film version she portrayed the flirt, who menaces the lives of the characters, while in the production at Ogunquit her role is that of the warm-hearted youngster who catches Biff Grimes on the rebound and eventually makes him thankful that he chose her. Her acting won the approval of the audience. The role of Biff Grimes was enacted by Barry Sullivan, one of the favorites of 1940. Sullivan left New York, where he had been playing in *The Man Who Came to Dinner*, and arrived in Ogunquit Sunday morning. With one day's rehearsal he went behind the footlights last night and presented an assured performance. He had learned the part during his last week at New York. [49]

In 1942, Mrs Hartwig announced that the Playhouse would operate, but that plays would be presented by the Junior members of the Manhattan Theatre Colony under the direction of John Kirkpatrick.

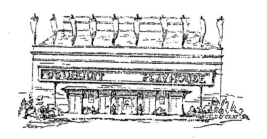

MRS. WALTER HARTWIG

Takes pleasure in announcing that while certain conditions prevent her from operating the Ogunquit Playhouse under the same policy as formerly, at least at the beginning of the season, she is nevertheless enabled to continue her service of providing there entertainment which she believes will appeal to you.

Beginning on July 9th, Mrs. Hartwig will present the Junior Members of the Manhattan Theatre Colony in a series of plays to be announced later.

Productions will be under the direction of John Kirkpatrick.

Performances will be given on the evenings of Thursday, Friday and Saturday, (July 9, 10, 11) with Matinees on Friday and Saturday (July 10 and 11). Evenings at 8:30 – Matinees at 2:30.

For these performances the price will be 50¢ (plus tax) for unreserved seats; $1.00 (plus tax) for reserved locations.

Telephone: Wells 70

YOUR PATRONAGE IS SOLICITED

Maude's announcement for 1942.

The Ogunquit Playhouse was closed in 1943. Betty Dixon remembers:

> Maude had a very difficult period. The war started in 1941 and there were blackouts because Ogunquit was near the ocean. But she did continue during that time, she went to Portsmouth with the students. I think they performed at the Music Hall. We were all grounded. When she could open, and did, people don't realize, but we were allotted two gallons of gas a week, unless you were a nurse or a doctor, so we couldn't drive long distances. So she had those worries and transportation worries. And a lot of the people that had worked for her had to go into the army. But there was always a certain group who were very loyal to her and were with her in Ogunquit.

In 1944, Mrs. Hartwig managed to put on *Having Wonderful Time,* by Arthur Kober, with Eugenia Rawls, Ned Payne, Clarence Derwent and Elfrida Derwent; and *The Luck,* by Reginald Denham and Edward Percy, with James Ganon, Augusta French, Eugenia Rawls and Clarence Derwent. The company staged *Arsenic and Old Lace,* with Daisy Atherton, Arthur Jarrett and Bruce Adams; *The Late Christopher Bean,* by Sidney Howard; *The Bat,* by Mary Roberts Rhinehart and Avery Hopwood; *Three Cornered Moon,* by Gertrude Tonkonogy; and *French without Tears,* by Terence Rattigan, with Francis Compton. Most of these productions were under the direction of Jack Kirkpatrick.

Poster of Dough Girls. *Courtesy of Carole Lee Carroll.*

In the 1944 playbills, Maude Hartwig addressed the following message to her patrons:

> To the Patrons and Subscribers
> of the Ogunquit Playhouse
>
> Much has transpired in the world since last it was our privilege and pleasure to entertain you, away back in the summer of 1941. We have missed you as we hope you have us. Now after two years we again take pleasure in presenting plays and players for your entertainment. Many of the actors who have graced our stage and the technicians who have built the fairylands are scattered over the globe: from the jungles of New Guinea to the shores of France, and they travel the airways of the world. God speed them in their missions. They and we cherish the hope that they return ere long from the world of grim reality to the world of make believe. So let's carry on.

In 1945, Maude and her stalwart resident company succeeded at mounting nine productions. For starters, there were *George and Margaret, Three's a Family, Blithe Spirit,* and *Doughgirls,* by Joseph Fields, in which Leora Dana, a Colony student, made her first appearance.

The second half of the season was taken up with *White Wings*; *Kiss and Tell*, directed by Katherine Alexander; *Roseanne*, with Mary Morris and Curtis Cooksey; *Snafu*; and *Dear Brutus*, by James M. Barrie, with Neil Hamilton. In *Dear Brutus,* Leora Dana was chosen from the junior group to play the role of Margaret. Her performance was remembered by everyone who saw it. She returned in the resident company in 1948, after which, Dana went on to make her Broadway debut in *The Madwoman of Chaillot*, for which she won the Clarence Derwent Award. In 1973, she won a Tony Award for her role in *The Last of Mrs. Lincoln*. A graduate of the Royal Academy of Dramatic Art in London, Leora Dana had a very successful career in television and film as well as on Broadway.

1946 marked both the twentieth anniversary of the Ogunquit Playhouse and the return to full normalcy of the Playhouse and its resident company, the Manhattan Theatre Colony. Mrs. Maude Hartwig was in charge. There were 30 well-known actors and actresses in the resident company, including a few that would become quite a bit more famous in the future – Dennis King, Jr., Tom Ewell, and John Lane (for a different reason).

The plays they presented included *That's Gratitude*, by Frank Craven, directed by John Kirkpatrick and featuring many of the resident players; *Autumn Crocus,* by Dodie Smith, also known as C.L.Anthony (the next time this play would appear at Ogunquit, in 1954, it would star the daughter of the 42nd U.S. president, Margaret Truman.); and *The Late George Apley*, by John Marquand and George S. Kaufman, with Leo G. Carroll. Nancy Marchand, a junior member of the Manhattan Theatre Colony appeared in this production, and later became a very well-known actress, and still later, the mother of troubled Tony Soprano in the HBO hit *The Sopranos*. She died during the taping of the fifth year of that series.

Tonight at Eight Thirty, a set of three one-acts by Noel Coward, with Lilian Harvey came next, then *Angel Street*, by Patrick Hamilton, with Viola Keats and Charles Quigley, directed by Jack Kirkpatrick. *The Hasty Heart,* by John Patrick, directed by John Kirkpatrick, starred one of the younger members of the resident company, John Lane, in the role of Lachlen. This role would be thought of later as his best, in this, his first season. People for years afterward remembered John in *The Hasty Heart*, but not much else of his acting career. *Ten Little Indians*, by Agatha Christie, with Nicholas Joy, Jane Middleton and Charles Quigley was the last show of the 1946 season.

One of the most memorable events of the 1946 season was the world premiere of *Balloon*, a play by the famous Irish playwright from the Abbey Theatre, Padraic Colum, directed by Michael Myerberg, who had previously staged *Lute Song* and *The Skin of our Teeth* on Broadway. Ask any of the old timers about *Balloon*, and they will tell you it was a giant fiasco. And yet it was a monumental production that included four mobiles onstage created by the famous sculptor, Alexander Calder.

Carole Lee Carroll says, "My father was on the crew then and he was engaged to go down to Calder's studio and pack up these mobiles. And Sandy Calder took him on a tour, and that was a highlight for him. He enjoyed that so much, it was just wonderful."

Balloon had a cast of sixty, and was a departure from the plays then being seen because it was abstract. Asked which productions she remembers the best, Mary-Leigh Smart said:

> Well, yes, we all remember the Calder production, *Balloon*, everybody remembers that. People from all over town and all the Colony players were in it. It was memorable, but I can't remember what it was about. We all drank and had dinner before we went to the theatre and everything was a happy haze.

When you mention *Balloon* now, everybody laughs. Speaking of her late husband, Jack Smart, famous as "The Fat Man" on radio and television, Mary-Leigh continued:

> It was produced by Michael Meyerberg. You know, he did the first production of *Waiting for Godot,* and my Jack was in that production down in Florida, and it made him ill. It was Alan Schneider who directed it. Jack was diabetic to begin with and he went to Joslyn Clinic from down there. Schneider was a mad man. He did awful things. He kept changing how he wanted them to do it. And you know how difficult *Waiting for Godot* is, you flub one line and nobody knows where they are because it's quite repetitive. Well, anyway, he was changing things up to the dress rehearsal. He was sending them yellow sheets of paper telling them to change this and do that. Oh, he was a terror.

One curiosity of the three Myerberg productions put on at the Ogunquit Playhouse, first *Balloons* in 1946, then *Dear Judas* in 1947, and finally *The Frog Pond* in 1965: each of those productions had sculpture prominently figuring in the set. The first sculpture was by Alexander Calder. The *Dear Judas* set featured a fig tree sculpture by the studio of Robert Laurent, a leading artist in the Ogunquit art scene and the director of the Hamilton Easter Field school in Perkins Cove. The last sculpture, called "Albatross," was made up of found objects, and was the creation of J. Perry Fitzhugh, a sculptor who worked in the area in the '60s.

The end of that season saw productions of *Mr. Pim Passes By*, by A.A. Milne, with Katherine Alexander and Daisy Atherton, and *Cradle Snatchers,* by Russell G. Medcraft and Norma Mitchell, also with Daisy Atherton. The junior players were more active that year than they had been in the past, producing and appearing in eight productions, staged at the Playhouse as matinees with evening performances on Friday evenings at Wentworth-by-the-Sea in Portsmouth, or in the new outdoor pavilion (later to become the home of the Colony), and even one production that was exported to The Barn Theatre in Hampton, NH.

The staff for the 1946 season included a young lighting director by the name of Bob Barry who became in later years a very well-known lighting director at CBS. He began in the early days of television and continued working into the sixties. In the recently re-broadcast Barbra Streisand specials *My Name is Barbra* (1965) and *Color Me Barbra* (1966), Barry's work is visible. *Color Me Barbra* was one of the first big specials telecast in color, which presented new and difficult lighting problems for the lighting professionals pioneering this new medium. Bob Barry was a leader in utilizing the new technology.

Because the final plans for the student theatre were put on hold by the death of Hartwig, for the 1946 season, Mrs. Hartwig had constructed a pavilion in the meadow behind the Playhouse that was used for a number of outdoor productions by the apprentices. The first of these productions was *A Midsummer Night's Dream*. Carole Lee Carroll remembers seeing that production in the original pavilion.

> I was just a child, we all sat outdoors on the ground and they performed in the pavilion without any tent, it was all open air. And they performed *A Midsummer Night's Dream,* that I will never forget. There were sprites coming out of the trees, and everybody was leaping up and down off the platform, and people were coming in and out of the forest. We sat on the ground and watched this amazing thing. It was fantastic. I was enchanted.

Maude Hartwig wrote about the junior players in the first playbill of the 1946 season:

> A junior membership in the Colony is designed for those who want training and experience in some particular department of the theatre. It is an opportunity for the potential actor to act, for the potential director to acquire the necessary technique, for the designer, the lighting technician, for all, in short, who plan a career in the theatrical world to broaden their knowledge and experience in their chosen fields. All the work of the junior membership is practical; there is no abstract theory taught.

Registration for the Colony Players that year was the largest it had ever been, due in some measure to the return of G.I.s. The Colony that year was accredited by the U.S. government, which allowed openings to be filled by G.I.s on the G.I. bill. Mention is made that year of the fact that as soon as building restrictions are lifted, the new student theatre and snack bar would be constructed on the same property that the Playhouse occupied.

In 1947, Maude Hartwig leased the Ogunquit Playhouse and the Manhattan Theatre Colony to her friend, the very famous producer, George Abbott, and wrote the following announcement to her patrons:

> Welcome to George Abbott
>
> In this the twenty-first year of the Manhattan Theatre Colony, and our fourteenth year at the Ogunquit Playhouse, I take pride in announcing as my new associate, New York's most distinguished playwright producer, Mr. George Abbott.
>
> So many Broadway hits have been launched under the George Abbott banner that space prevents listing them all, but you well remember *Boy Meets Girl, Three Men on a Horse, Room Service, Brother Rat, What A Life, Pal Joey, Kiss and Tell, Best Foot Forward,* and *Barefoot Boy With Cheek.*
>
> The traditions of the Ogunquit Playhouse have been high. Over the years Walter and I did all in our power to bring the highest in entertainment to you, our patrons. Summer is a time for relaxation and laughter. In George Abbott, Broadway's genius of stage entertainment, I feel I am introducing to you someone who will live up to the ideals we have tried to establish during our twenty-one years.
> My confidence is with him, as I know yours will be.
>
> > Sincerely,
> > Maude Hartwig

Actually, George Abbott came to Ogunquit only once that season, to see the production of *The Little Foxes*, with Ruth Chatterton. He hired Robert Fryer as Managing Director to run the theatre, and it appears that his interest in Ogunquit stemmed from a desire on the part of his wife, Mary Sinclair, to try her hand at acting.

Daisy Atherton, 1947.

Because she starred in the first production of *Years Ago*, by Ruth Gordon, Daisy Atherton's picture was featured on the cover of the first playbill.

Productions under George Abbott's leadership included *The Little Foxes,* by Lillian Hellman, with Ruth Chatterton, and *The Late Christopher Bean,* by Sidney Howard, starring Zazu Pitts (in which a young actress by the name of Nancy Davis appeared as Susan Haggett; Miss Davis would go on to become the future Mrs. Ronald Reagan). Other plays that season were *State of the Union*, starring Faye Emerson who was, in private life at that time, Mrs. Elliott Roosevelt; *Best Foot Forward,* a George Abbott musical; *Joan of Lorraine,* by Maxwell Anderson, starring Judith Evelyn and Richard Widmark; *Dear Judas*; *The First Mrs. Fraser*; *Caprice,* by Sil-Vara, with Ruth Chatterton; *The Marquise,* by Noel Coward, with Lillian Gish; and *The Fatal Weakness,* by George Kelly, starring Peggy Wood.

The playbill for *State of the Union* proudly announced:

> George Abbott's invitation to Miss Emerson to portray the role of the wife of the idealistic presidential aspirant marks a milestone in astute casting. In a sense it adds to the basic satire of the Lindsay-Crouse play for, although Miss Emerson has achieved stardom both on the stage and on the screen – solely as a fine and sensitive actress, she holds a unique advantage over any other actress in essaying the part. Her married name, more than any other in the country, connotes "Democrat," yet, in the play she portrays the wife of the Republican presidential candidate. In private life, she is Mrs. Elliott Roosevelt.

And it was reported, in fact, that Mrs. Eleanor Roosevelt was in the audience for one of Miss Emerson's performances.

In presenting the next attraction, *Best Foot Forward*, a hit musical that George Abbott had produced on Broadway, the management claimed Abbott was setting a precedent in Ogunquit.

> The limitations of summer theatre have heretofore presented a seemingly insurmountable obstacle to musical comedy, with its large professional casts, extravagant scenery, and full musical complement.

Indeed, Abbott pulled out all the stops, hiring Hugh Martin, who had written the original score with Ralph Blane for not only the New York production but for the motion picture version starring Lucille Ball as well, to sing at the Playhouse and direct the music. It turned out to be a major production.

For *Dear Judas*, adapted and staged by Michael Myerberg, Maude Hartwig took over the producing reins. In all the puffery written about the play in the playbill, two things are worth noting: that *Balloon*, at the Ogunquit Playhouse the season before had been acclaimed by the critics and held over for a second week, but also that Myerberg had produced some successful shows – *Skin of Our Teeth,* and *Lute Song,* starring Mary Martin.

Ruth Chatterton dining with Harold Cail and others.

Dear Judas, with E. G. Marshall, was advertised as prior-to-Broadway and did open in October 1947 in New York. The play ran for 16 performances, after being advised by the Catholic Church not to come to Boston. Members of the Catholic congregation objected to the play because of the sympathetic portrayal of Judas. It is interesting that due to recent translations of biblical literature, this seems to be a treatment of Judas that many theologians now subscribe to.

Ruth Chatterton was signed to return to the Playhouse midseason and star in *Caprice*. Chatterton's performance in *The Little Foxes* had "broken all previous attendance records established here in the fourteen year history of the Playhouse," claimed Mrs. Hartwig's press representatives. Her biggest stage hit had been as Judy Abbott in *Daddy Long Legs*, and her subsequent career in talking pictures had seen her in 13 films. When she returned from Hollywood to the stage, she starred in *The Constant Wife*, and as Liza Doolittle in Shaw's *Pygmalion*.

Lillian Gish starred next in Noel Coward's *The Marquise*, and Jane Cowl starred in The *First Mrs. Fraser*. According to the playbill, Elliot Norton, the drama critic for *The Boston Post*, had written:

> Miss Cowl makes the first Mrs. Fraser a charming, witty, and altogether admirable woman. Her Mrs. Fraser straightens out the troubled marital problems of her bumptious first husband with adroit skill and wit. Miss Cowl is cool and regal about it all. She lends the Lady Fraser her dark beauty and sly wit.

The 1947 season closed with Peggy Wood starring in *The Fatal Weakness*, by George Kelly. Playgoers learned that Peggy Wood had begun her career as a singer and had acquired early stardom on the musical stage.

1948 opened with *Apple of His Eye*, with Robert Burton and many of the resident company, and *John Loves Mary*, with Oliver Thorndike, and Leora Dana in the title role of Mary.

Mrs. Hartwig announced the inauguration of the 22nd season of the Manhattan Theatre Colony, on June 28th saying:

> One of the oldest and most famous Schools of the theatre will begin classes this week. Students from every section of the country from California to Washington, D.C. and from Michigan to Texas make up the enrollment this year…young hopefuls who come for training in every branch of the theatre. John Kirkpatrick will assume the duties of General Director. And Mr. George Fluharty, of the faculty of Princeton University will be Director of Speech. Miss Lygia Bernard will conduct classes in make-up and Mr. Jerome Andrews will be in charge of dancing and body control instruction.

Other plays that season included *The Corn is Green*, by Emlyn Williams, the Welsh playwright, with Frances Starr; *Is Zat So?* by James Gleason and Richard Taber; *Excursion*, by Victor Wolfson, with Carl Benton Reid; the premiere of *Ting Ling*, a musical by Ignatz Waghalter and Richard Diamond, with Lois Hunt and Frank Rogier; *And So To Bed*, by James Bernard Fagan, with Eugenie Leontovich and Rhys Williams; *The Gentleman From Athens*, by Emmet Lavery, with Anthony Quinn; *The Legend of Leonora*, by James M. Barrie, with Lillian Gish; *For Love or Money,* by F. Hugh Herbert, with Anton Dolan; and *Juno and the Paycock*, by Sean O'Casey, with Sara Allgood.

A jewelry exhibit by Hilda Kraus, of Handmade-By-Hilary, a workshop in Perkins Cove, was featured in the lobby at one point during the season. The new set designer that season was Robert MacKichan, one of the most talented of the scenic designers at the Playhouse. He became a West Coast television designer, and was best known for the mini-series *Roots* and *The Thornbirds*. Ralph Holmes, the lighting director that season became a CBS lighting director in New York in the early days of television. He was revered and respected by all who knew him – a true show business legend. Also in 1948 Colony staff children, Carole Lee Dixon and Mary Fay Compton, appeared in *Excursion;* Joan Bower, a former junior member of the Colony became the assistant stage manager; and the program announced during *The Legend of Leonora* that:

> The role of Leonora is admirably suited to the dainty, sympathetic personality which has endeared Miss Gish to her public. She is of the same Dresden china pattern as Maude Adams who according to reviewers of the day, "interpreted the role of Leonora beautifully, delicately, daintily."

Lillian Gish agreed to lecture at the Ogunquit Art Association on the subject of D.W. Griffith, the famous film producer with whom she had been associated for such a long time.

Sara Allgood, left, gives a party for cast and crew of Juno and the Paycock *at the Graham. Courtesy of Carole Lee Carroll.*

Wes McKee, director, at the Allgood party.

The Playhouse presentation of the Abbey Theatre's Sara Allgood in *Juno and the Paycock* by Sean O'Casey was another highlight of the 1948 season. The playbill offered this description of the Abbey Theatre in Dublin, Ireland:

> They were the first to do away with the grand manner of acting, to institute naturalism for the first time and establish a new tradition for the theatre. The star system was unknown at the Abbey. The players were all used in repertory in which they would play leads one night and walk-on bits the next. Thus they developed a quality that made their visits to England and America an exceptional pleasure to connoisseurs of acting.

Lygia Bernard and Edward Everett Horton, stars of Present Laughter.

During the 1949 season, Maude produced *Present Laughter*, by Noel Coward, with Edward Everett Horton; *Charm*, by Jack Kirkpatrick with Daisy Atherton; *The Time of Your Life*, by William Saroyan, with Eddie Dowling, directed by Noel Leslie; *Made in Heaven*, by Hagar Wilde, with Richard Arlen; *An Inspector Calls*, by J.B.Priestley, with Carl Benton Reid, directed by Noel Leslie; *Strange Bedfellows*, by Florence Ryerson and Colin Clements, with Donald Cook and Nydia Westman; and *Of All Things*, a new musical revue by Ken Welch, directed by Wes McKee. Junior member, Carolyn Jones, who had a small part in this production, went on to star in television and motion pictures.

Other productions included *The Voice of the Turtle*, by John Van Druten, with Marcia Walter, Boyd Crawford and Helen Harrelson; *Accent on Youth*, by Samson Raphaelson; *A Highland Fling*, by Margaret Curtis, with Francis Compton, Noel Leslie and John McQuade, directed by Wes McKee; *Love from a Stranger*, by Agatha Christie, with Helmut Dantine, Signe Hasso and John Newland.

Donald Cook, Strange Bedfellows.

It is thought that Jack Kirkpatrick provided Maude Hartwig with her next producing partner. However that came about, for the 1950 season, Hartwig was sharing producing credits with John Lane. The first 1950 season playbill announced:

> Manhattan Theatre Colony
> Ogunquit Playhouse
> Under the Management of Mrs. Maude Hartwig
> With John Lane
> Presents
> Stuart Erwin
> In
> *Harvey*
> By Mary Chase

The second show that season was *Born Yesterday,* by Garson Kanin, and the cast list offers the first reference to a junior player by the name of David Janssen. In this production he appeared as The Barber. He would play in four of the productions that summer and even dance with a young Lee Remick in *Just Around the Corner.*

Mike Todd produced the next show, a world premiere called *The Live Wire*, written by Garson Kanin and directed by the author. Some of the lesser names in this production were Scott McKay, Jack Guilford and Peggy Cass.

Just Around the Corner was another world premiere, this time a musical. With music and lyrics by Joe Sherman and Langston Hughes, and book by Abby Mann and Bernard Drew, and with choreography staged by Fred Kelly, *Just Around the Corner*, in addition to its two young dancers, Lee Remick and David Janssen, had a cast of thousands. Both Dixon girls, Francis Compton's son and daughter, Monty and Mary Fay, and Susan's cousin, Benita Braggiotti, were in it. Imagine how exciting that week must have been: Fred Kelly, Gene Kelly's brother, choreographing and Langston Hughes, one of America's earliest and most famous African-American poets, visiting, as Carole Lee Carroll remembers it "that week was so special, it was thrilling to be there."

John Lane and Mike Todd on the set of Live Wire, *1950.*

John Lane played Reverend Watson in *The Silver Whistle*, by Robert E. McEnroe, and the same production featured Don Doherty, longtime member of the repertory company and Doro Merende.

John Lane as Rev. Watson in The Silver Whistle, *1950. All three images courtesy of Carole Lee Carroll.*

Don Doherty in The Silver Whistle, *1950.*

Daisy Atherton and Doro Merande, in The Silver Whistle, *1950.*

John Golden's production of Leo G. Carroll in a new play, *Once An Actor,* by Rosemary Casey, was the next show in 1950. *Happy Birthday,* by Anita Loos, starred Imogene Coca, and was a very fitting vehicle for a company-wide birthday celebration for Maude Hartwig. Peter Woodbury, curator of the Littlefield Library at the Ogunquit Heritage Museum remembers it this way:

> My brother and I were ushers in 1950 and I kept a journal. We did *Born Yesterday, Live Wire, The Silver Whistle, Once An Actor,* that had Leo G. Carroll in it. The last one we did was *Happy Birthday,* with Imogene Coca. And that happened to be the same week that we had a birthday party for Mrs. Hartwig. I remember she gave us each a $5 bonus for working hard.

Peter also remembers house manager Dick Franklyn tap dancing during the plays. Peter and Chris Woodbury also directed traffic for Mrs. Hartwig.

> One time I was out on Route One directing traffic and my father came by. Of course, he went straight to Mrs. Hartwig and said, "My son cannot be directing traffic on Route One." So after that, we stayed in the yard. We had a wonderful time. 1950 was the time when Mrs. Hartwig was still there, but John Lane was coming on board, and he sort of shadowed Mrs. Hartwig and went everywhere that she went.

The last play of the 1950 season was *His French Wife,* starring Edward Everett Horton, with Natalie Core, Francis Compton and Stephen Elliot. David Janssen was one of the "Bobbies." David Janssen produced a sweet poem at the end of the season in which he included the titles of every play they had done.

It Happened in 1950, by David Janssen

Harvey's girlfriend *Miranda* wasn't *Born Yesterday.*
In fact she is a real *Live Wire,*
Her boyfriend who lived *Just Around the Corner* was *Once An Actor,*
And every Saturday night, he blows *A Silver Whistle*
Because it reminds him of his *Happy Birthday.*
Actually, he does all this just to *Light Up the Sky*
For *His French Wife.*

When Maude Hartwig said her goodbye to the Playhouse patrons that season, she could not have foretold that a hurricane in November would change all of her plans for the next year.

Maude Hartwig: the Link between the Old and the New

Because of her determination to carry on with her husband's plans, we have Maude Hartwig to thank for the fact that there is a theatre at all. She kept it going through World War II and was there to include John Lane as a young actor in her resident company of 1946.

But Maude Hartwig should be remembered for more than just that. She was an avid believer in repertory theatre; she was passionate about the junior players at the Manhattan Theatre Colony. For a tiny person, she carried a huge weight during the years between Walter's death in 1941 and John's takeover in 1951.

Here's how Betty Dixon remembers her:

> Maude was a petite person, very composed always. She never lost her composure. I never heard her raise her voice. I remember one time, we had a terrible dress rehearsal that went on and on, and I said something to her like "How are you?" And she said, "Well, I'm not very happy." Even when she was annoyed, she didn't get flustered, or lose her composure. She never made remarks about anyone. When the actors and the actresses weren't pleased or happy, they could go to her, and she would listen, but she didn't take sides. She would just solve the problem.

About the Manhattan Theatre Colony and the junior players, Betty notes that Maude was very nice with the students. That was a big focus of hers.

All along Stearns Road and Ledge Road, there were many guest houses. You could stay in a guest house, and maybe have a little place in the refrigerator for something. But they also expected you home at a reasonable hour each night. When the students came, they chose to live either in the Maxwell House, or at these guest houses. The girls always stayed in the guest houses. Stearns Road and Ledge Road were near the field which made it easy for the students to get to classes at the Colony.

The Maxwell House, where many students of the Manhattan Theatre Colony and staff at the Ogunquit Playhouse rented rooms for the summer. Courtesy of the New York Public Library.

In 1949, Elliot Norton wrote that there were four women who would be running summer theatres that year.

> None of the four is a novice; they have all done it before with credit to the theatres and to themselves. They have also managed to show a profit in other years, which is more than some of the gentlemen have done.

He went on to describe Mrs. Maude Hartwig this way:

> Small, slim and seemingly fragile, with snow white hair, Maude Hartwig was a Wall Street investment counselor before she came into the theatre and her friends say she was good. From a private office in Manhattan, she gave advice to a select group of investors, and you can take the word of some friends that her clients emerged from the crash of 1929 without losing their shirts. Although she insists now that "Walter was a fine business man," some show folks will tell you that she was really the "business man" of the Ogunquit Playhouse. 50

John Wm. Riley wrote about Maude Hartwig in the *Boston Sunday Globe* in 1949:

> Mrs. Walter Hartwig is a tiny, birdlike woman well past middle age, who looks more like your favorite grandmother than the operator of a highly successful summer theatre. But she is the sole owner of the Ogunquit Playhouse which has been under the same management longer than any other summer theatre in the country. And all the reins of its management she keeps firmly in hand. "You have to play fair with the public," says Mrs. Hartwig. Her assistants say she is a careful manager, but doesn't spare expense to put on a good show (about $3000 per show).

Riley goes on to quote Bessie Johnson:

> "I love Maude dearly," said Bessie Johnson, which shows how the local people feel about Mrs. Hartwig. Bessie practically grew up with the Playhouse. Her family, the Siderises, have long run a small restaurant in Ogunquit. Called Besssie's Restaurant, it's right in the middle of town and is, as always, a sort of center for theatre and town folk.

Maude Hartwig photographed in the box office of The Ogunquit Playhouse, for an article in the Boston Sunday Globe, *1949.*

Riley offers another view of how the Hartwigs got started in Ogunquit:

> Walter and Maude Hartwig came to Ogunquit early in 1932 and rented an old garage just off the Main Stem. They got a five year lease in return for remodeling the place. They stayed there five or six years before they had put together enough money to build the handsome, now famous 700-seat Ogunquit Playhouse in a former cornfield just outside of town on Route 1. They spared no expense to make it efficient and comfortable. "Most of the money," says Mrs. Hartwig, "came out of the box office. Mr Hartwig did borrow $12,000 – $3,000 from each of four people – on a mortgage to be amortized in four years. But he paid it off in three years. The building cost $50,000 and most of it came out of our earnings. We have no backers. So we take all the profits, and all the losses, too."

When Mrs. Hartwig was asked by Riley how she and her husband could make such a success of Ogunquit, while other summer theatres regularly changed management and ownership, Mrs. Hartwig had this to say:

> First of all, playing fair with the public. Then you have to keep it impersonal. Too many summer theatre managers are encumbered with too many friends – actors, managers and backers. We run it all ourselves. [51]

Endnotes ~ Chapter I

1. *A Century of Color 1886-1986,* by Louise Tragard, Patricia E. Hart and W.L. Copithorne (Barn Gallery Associates, Inc, 1987), pg. 38.
2. Susan Meffert remembering: "The maple dance floor was salvaged by my father, George Smith, when the old Sparhawk was torn down, and given to me to use in my house on River Road."
3. *A Century of Color,* pg. 38.
4. Anecdote recalled by Addison Merrick's brother, written in 1990 and sent to the Historical Society of Wells and Ogunquit.
5. *A Century of Color,* pg.38,
6. Ibid.
7. Ibid.
8. Sydney Henderson, whose husband, artist Eliot Henderson, was very involved in the art scene in Ogunquit during those years, confirms that Bette Davis worked as a waitress at the Beachmere Hotel in her teens.
9. *Summer Stock,* LoMonaco, Martha Schmoyer, Paulgrave McMillan, 2004 pg. 49.
10. *New York Times,* January 18, 1941.
11. *New York Times,* May 26, 1926, "America and the Little Theatre: The Revolt on the Road."
12. *New York Times,* May 28, 1927, "Theatrical Camp to Open in Summer."
13. *Summer Stock,* LoMonaco, Martha Schmoyer, pg 49.
14. Ibid., pg. 52
15. Ibid., pg. 52
16. Ibid., pg. 53
17. *New York Times,* July 12, 1931 "The Summering Drama Goes To the Country Again."
18. On October 28, 2006, the Ogunquit Heritage Museum hosted an oral history called *Do You Remember, Part 5: The Ogunquit Playhouse.* Adrian Asherman spoke about his recollections, as did a number of others who will be quoted often in this history.
19. From the Playbill, Ogunquit Playhouse, 1982 Season, 50th anniversary, written by Bunny Hart, Publicity Director at the Ogunquit Playhouse from 1963 to 1970 and from 1985 to 1999.
20. Notes from the 1933 playbill.
21. *Portland Transcript,* July 2, 1933, "Maine's Newest Theatrical Colony Established at Ogunquit." From the vertical files, Maine State Library, Augusta.
22. 1934 Ogunquit Playhouse Playbill, program notes for *The Curtain Rises* by B.M. Kaye.
23. 1934 Ogunquit Playhouse Playbill, program notes for *The Sacred Flame.*
24. *New York Times,* July 17, 1934 ProQuest Historical Newspapers.
25. 1934 Ogunquit Playhouse Playbill, program notes for *Twelfth Night* by William Shakespeare.
26. *New York Times,* July 17, 1934, ProQuest Historical Newspapers.
27. *New York Times,* July 17, 1934. Ibid.
28. *York Transcript,* September 14, 1934, from "Summer Theatres," vertical file at Maine State Library, Augusta, Maine.
29. *New York Times,* July 2, 1934, "Ovation for Libby Holman," pg. 24 ProQuest Historical Newspapers.
30. Quoted in the playbill from *The Stage* Magazine, August, 1935. Courtesy of Carole Lee Carroll.
31. *New York Times,* June 1935, Bosley Crowther, As Maine Goes…"
32. *York Transcript,* June 28, 1935.
33. *New York Times,* August 4, 1935, an article written by Walter Hartwig subtitled: "Rural Theatres Offer Their Patrons a Romance Long Lost by Broadway."
34. Ogunquit Playhouse, Playbill, Mary X. Sullivan excerpt, 1935.
35. *New York Times,* May 2, 1936, ProQuest Historical Newspapers, pg. 10.

36. *New York Times,* June 28, 1936, and background information on The Ballet Caravan courtesy of Carole Lee Carroll.

37. Ogunquit Playhouse, Playbill, summer, 1982, "Fifty Seasons, The Prologue," by Bunny Hart.

38. Playbill, 1936, "Green Room Gossip."

39. Playbill, June 28, 1937.

40. Playbill, July 12, 1937.

41. Playbill August 17, 1937.

42. *New York Times*, July 26, 1939, ProQuest Historical Newspapers, Evans elopement.

43. *New York Times*, September 12, 1939, ProQuest Historical Newspapers.

44. *Portsmouth Herald,* 1942.

45. *York Times/Wells Ogunquit Compass* September 8, 1939 courtesy Maine State Library, Augusta and Maine Historic Preservation Commission, Augusta Maine.

46. Linda Frye recollections.

47. *Portsmouth Herald,* August 3, 1940, "Saturday Evening."

48. *Portsmouth Herald,* August 11, 1941, "The Playhouse Team to Raid Camp Langdon."

49. *Portsmouth Herald,* July 15, 1941.

50. *Boston Post*, Elliot Norton, 1949.

51. *Boston Sunday Globe*, John Wm. Riley, 1949.

Daniel Frohman, 1935. All photos courtesy of the New York Public Library.

The John Lane Years

In 1946, Maude Hartwig invited a young actor and U.S. Army veteran of World War II, John Lane, to join the resident company of the Manhattan Theatre Colony. That season, he was seen in *The Hasty Heart,* and as Anthony Marsten in *Ten Little Indians.* He appeared in *Balloon, Mr. Pim Passes By, Cradle Snatchers,* and *Charley's Aunt,* but it was the role of Lachlen in *The Hasty Heart* that was his best according to everyone who remembers. He was not as well thought of as an actor in his other roles that year.

John Lane's obituary said:

> He was born in Greensboro, N.C. His love of theatre began at an early age, and he came north to enter the American Academy of Dramatic Art. After only one term, he made his first professional appearance in the revival of a play called "White Cargo." After several other appearances, he traveled to London and attended the Royal Academy of Dramatic Art, where he was instructed by John Gielgud, Laurence Olivier, and Ralph Richardson, among others. Upon his graduation, he stayed in England several more years and acted in plays until World War II called him home. After five years of military service in the Army, he returned to the theatre and made his first appearance at the Ogunquit Playhouse as an actor in 1946. By then, his entrepreneurial spirit was taking hold and he bought a summer theatre in Fairhaven, Massachusetts, that he operated for four seasons, serving as his own producer and appearing in a number of roles. In 1950, Mrs Hartwig invited John to assist her in running the theatre. By then, he was married to Helen Macmillan Lane, a portrait artist, and had established a home in New York City. He accepted Mrs. Hartwig's offer and came to Ogunquit as co-producer for the 1950 season and after that, the Lanes moved to Maine and John bought the Playhouse from Maude Hartwig in 1951.[1]

John Lane, early publicity photo

John and Helen Lane in Helen's New York apartment with their dogs, Randy and Sieglinda

Photos of hurricane damage, November 1950

A 1951 midwinter bulletin of the *Ogunquit Breeze* claimed that

> the greatest damage was done to the famed Ogunquit Playhouse. The winds blew the roof right off the stage and fly loft and tossed the rear wall into the front seats of the auditorium. However, the day after the storm, the wreckage was being cleared away, rebuilding started and it is expected that the new and reinforced eastern end of the theatre will be completed by mid-April. John Lane, co-manager of the Playhouse with Mrs. Maude Hartwig, has been making frequent trips to Ogunquit from New York to supervise reconstruction. The Playhouse expects to open its 19th season, June 25.[2]

Though John and Maude Hartwig had a contract to co-produce at the Playhouse for three more years, the Thanksgiving hurricane of 1950 probably caused Mrs. Hartwig to sell out sooner, so that John Lane's first season as sole producer, 1951, was probably his most difficult year. Henry Weller, John Lane's General Manager for many, many years, remembers that he and John went to see Maude the winter of 1951 to work out the repairs. Maude was a frugal producer, and did not have any extended coverage on the Playhouse. Extended coverage would have perhaps covered the hurricane damage. Instead, Maude expressed no interest in continuing, so Helen Lane sold her apartment in New York, and that became the down payment for the Playhouse, which John and Helen bought for approximately $63,000. While struggling with repairs through the winter, John continued planning for the season to follow, and he opened the theatre on time with *Springtime for Henry*, starring Edward Everett Horton. The 1951 season went on to include appearances by Basil Rathbone, Lillian Gish, Melvyn Douglas and Arthur Treacher.

1952, the twentieth anniversary season of the Ogunquit Playhouse, led off with *Season with Ginger*, a world premiere of a new comedy by Ronald Alexander, starring Melvyn Douglas, who hoped to take the play to Broadway in the fall after its tryout on the straw-hat circuit, as

---

The Council of Stock Theatres

John Lane was one of the originators of the Council of Stock Theatres, a coalition of primarily New England "Straw Hat" theatres. The alliance provided opportunities to share productions among the member theatres and bring otherwise unaffordable stars to the mostly smaller venues. It was to succeed as a system that allowed marvelous theatrical talent to be brought to the region for more than four decades.

he had with *Glad Tidings*, a play in which he had co-starred with Signe Hasso in Ogunquit in 1951. (*Glad Tidings* ran for three months on Broadway the winter before.)

Lane had booked 12 productions instead of the usual ten or eleven for the anniversary season and they included *On Your Toes*, a new version of the popular Richard Rodgers musical. (Rodgers had raided the casts of his other musicals, *The King and I*, *Oklahoma*, and *South Pacific* for his principals in *On Your Toes*: Katherine Sergava. Bill Callahan, and Yvonne Adair.) Next came *An Evening with Beatrice Lillie*, with Reginald Gardiner, and *Here's Mama*, Frank Gabrilson's new play based on the CBS-TV show transferred from television to the Ogunquit stage, with Peggy Wood, Kenny Delmar, Judson Laire, Rosemary Rice, Robin Morgan and Dick Van Patten, directed by Ralph Nelson. *Gramercy Ghost*, by John Cecil Holm, the third production of the season, inspired Harold Cail, drama critic for the *Portland Evening Express*, to write:

Robin Morgan and Rosemary Rice on stage in Here's Mama, *1952.*

> *Gramercy Ghost* as presented at (Ogunquit Playhouse) with its old favorites and local talent is a welcome change from glamour, and a thoroughly amusing evening's entertainment. Guest stars are the frosting in the summer theatre, but a good resident group is the cake itself. Most effective support was afforded June Dayton and Dean Harens by Daisy Atherton and Francis Compton, veteran Ogunquit favorites, and Don Doherty who is becoming one of the same. [3]

The next attraction was *Old Acquaintance*, by John Van Druten, with Ruth Chatterton and Margaret Bannerman, directed by Noel Leslie, followed by *Kiss Me, Kate*, the wonderful Cole Porter musical, starring Arthur Maxwell and Juliana Larson; *Ballet Variante*, an evening of ballet with Mia Slavenska, Frederic Franklin, and Alexandra Danilova; *Theatre*, by Somerset Maugham with Kay Francis; *The Man*, by Mel Dinelli with Dorothy Gish and Oliver Thorndike.

Perennial favorite, Edward Everett Horton appeared with Marta Linden and Christopher Plummer in *Nina*, a French comedy by Andre Roussin.

Alexandra Danilova in Ballet Variante, *1952..*

Juliana Larson and Arthur Maxwell on the set of Kiss Me, Kate, *1952.*

Dorothy Gish and Oliver Thorndike on the set of The Man, *1952* >

∧ *Edward Everett Horton, Christopher Plummer, Marta Linden on the set of* Nina, *1952.*

And John Lane ended his second full season with this letter to his audience:

> To Our Patrons:
>
> On Saturday evening the curtain will fall on the Twentieth season of the Ogunquit Playhouse. The actors, crew, staff and myself have participated in the problems and rehearsals which the theatre requires; but, we have also participated in that grand element which the theatre is fast losing – Fun !
>
> We sincerely hope that as the evenings grow longer you will occasionally enjoy with us the memory of an evening with Beatrice Lillie, June Dayton and Dean Harens, Edward Everett Horton, Daisy Atherton, Kay Francis, *Kiss Me, Kate*, Melvyn Douglas, the CBS-TV *Mama* family, Francis Compton, Dorothy Gish, Mia Slavenska, Frederic Franklin, Alexandra Danilova, *On Your Toes*, Ruth Chatterton and others. Your laughter which encouraged Beatrice Lillie to encores, your cordiality which stimulated many members of the *Mama* family to return to Ogunquit for vacations, your friendliness which prompted Dorothy Gish to stay a few days after her show, are all a part of the pleasant tales of summer.
>
> Your enthusiastic and record-breaking support has made duties a pleasure and work a delight giving all of us a summer filled with joy.
>
> Thanking you for your patronage and anticipating a gala season for 1953, I am,
>
> Sincerely yours,
> John Lane (signature)

The John Lane Years 71

Like Maude Hartwig, Helen Lane was an active partner in the early days of John Lane's tenure. During the 1950s, Helen was a tireless helper, hosting gatherings for the Playhouse, and entertaining visiting stars. Though separated from John in the late 1950s and later divorced, her support of the Playhouse continued, and she is remembered by all as a generous silent partner for many years. She also became deeply involved in Ogunquit's various artists' organizations, and continued to pursue her own impressive career as a portrait artist.

Helen Lane in her New York apartment with Randy and Sieglinda, 1951.

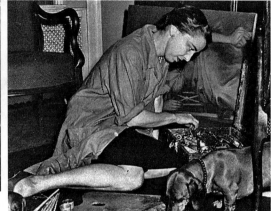

Helen Lane painting in Ogunquit

Betty Dixon remembers hearing how Helen and John met. They had mutual friends in New York who said several times that they should meet each other. John's first response was, "I've spent years getting rid of a southern accent, I certainly don't want to get it back." When they met, of course, they clicked.

Helen and John were married before the war. They lived in Atlantic City at one point, because he was stationed in New Jersey. Betty Dixon, who met Helen when John was acting in Maude's resident company, recalls her friendship with Helen this way:

> She was a dear person. I have lots of memories of her that are very lovely. I thought a lot of her and miss her very much. She had exquisite taste. When she and John first had an apartment on Ledge Road, she painted this beautiful water scene all around the wall of the bathroom. She had such a flair.

Helen was one of the founding members of the Barn Gallery and of the Ogunquit Art Association. When John gave the land at the edge of the Colony field to the Barn Gallery Associates for their building, he reminded everyone that it was a gift from both him and the Ogunquit Playhouse, and in that context, the Ogunquit Playhouse meant Helen.

Helen Horn, who became her good friend though they were years apart in age, remembers Helen Lane this way:

She was gracious and warm, and a lovely southern lady. That's all you can say, she was a lady and it was a privilege to know her. In later years I remember that John bought one of the Woodbury houses up on a promontory overlooking Narrow Cove. One night, Helen was having dinner with us, and she looked up at his house and said, "I don't understand what he's doin' up there." And we said, "Why, Helen?" She said, "You know the world has two kinds of people, there are the cliff dwellers and there are the cave dwellers. John is a cave dweller." I just want to say that when Helen had cancer, John was very sweet to her. He would take her to Portland every week for treatments. They had a good relationship after the divorce. He called the day she died, and he was very broken up. So I just wanted to say that there were many sides to John. [4]

Dunelawn; the Right Place at the Right Time

Without a doubt, one of the contributing factors to the success of the Playhouse during the first three decades of John Lane's stewardship – the '50s, '60s, and '70s – was the opening of George Smith's family home as an elegant hotel overlooking the Ogunquit River and the beach. Called Dunelawn, the manor house could accommodate roughly 14 people elegantly and some 7 or 8 others less so. In fact, each year in the early days of the hotel found at least one staff member from the Playhouse staying in the "servants" quarters for the entire season. The hotel provided John with inexpensive but fabulously luxurious housing for the stars in plays that he packaged in New York and toured to Ogunquit and several other summer theatres then operating on the east coast circuit. John and Helen Lane were good friends of Harriet and George Smith, the owners of Dunelawn. The hotel was in its infancy, so the opportunity to put up celebrity guests was undoubtedly an appealing idea for the Smiths. But as new hotel owners, the Smiths were not astute managers and so John was able to persuade them to provide this wonderful setting for his actors at well below the going rate. Claiming that Actors Equity Union required him to find housing for as little as $30 or $45 a week, he was able to fill up the hotel each week at the beginning and the Smiths were able to have a full house even though the rents were not enough to make a living from. And for almost two decades, this worked for everyone involved. Rents for the front rooms that looked out at the river and the beach were from $90 to $150 per day. The actors and actresses from the Playhouse paid as little as $45 and as much as $150 per week. When actors claimed that their favorite summer theatre was Ogunquit, they were often

Harriet and George Smith on the lawn of Dunelawn. Courtesy of Susan Meffert.

referring to the warm welcome they received at Dunelawn and the kind of care they got there. It was a wonderful, cozy but elegant, private home with 22 rooms in all and for the early years, an American plan hotel offering breakfast and dinner, all of which was prepared by Harriet Smith herself. And she was a very good cook.

In 1959, Shirley Booth opened the Ogunquit Playhouse season with *Nina*, and the June 25th *Wells-Ogunquit Compass* carried this story by Paula Lawrence, the director's wife:

> **Dunelawn – or how to Rehearse In Luxury**
> Thanks to our wonderfully warm-hearted and generous hosts, Harriet and George Smith, this past week has been a dream of what working in summer theater should be and never is. Of course, the fact that we arrived before the season started was a big help to the Smiths and to us. In any case, my husband, Charles Bowden, who is directing *Nina,* and I, plus our cat, Noelie (born the night my husband's production of *Fallen Angels* opened on Broadway, and named for the author, Noel Coward, by Miss Lynn Fontaine) and Mr. Douglas Watson, our leading man, were delighted to find ourselves living in baronial and solitary splendor amidst the Georgian elegance of Dunelawn. Our star and cherished friend, Miss Shirley Booth, plus her two white miniature poodles, Prego and Grozl, happily took up residence in Dunelawn's carriage house, newly renovated and complete with kitchen, where Miss Booth prepares meals for them which we all envy. Our advance director, Mr. Wayne Carson, together with Miss Booth's supporting players, Mr. Leo Lucker and Mr. Robert Wilkins gleefully settled into Dunelawn's Rose Cottage. Then as luck would have it Mr. Paul Foley, Ogunquit's resident stage manager, and Ogunquit's scenic designer (Bill Ryan) became the next tenants. So John Lane, who is the Ogunquit Playhouse, had the brilliant idea of holding rehearsals in the music room at Dunelawn, to which the dear Smiths agreed. Since *Nina* employs a giant cast of four and utilizes only one set, this was ideal. The grass was so green, the trees were so leafy; the ocean so close; the birds sang so sweetly; the Smiths were so endlessly accommodating – we longed to share our good fortune. Doug Watson rushed to the telephone and insisted that his wife, Genie, join him immediately, and sent a roundtrip plane ticket to Portland to cinch it. The next day we persuaded my husband's partner, Ridgely Bullock, to fly up here with his three-year-old daughter, Muffie (our goddaughter) and her nanny. So here we are, all living and working in these idyllic and paradisical surroundings, full of life-giving minerals derived from Maine lobsters, and all I can say is, if John Lane weren't such a stick-in-the-mud, we would cancel the rest of Miss Booth's tour and he would cancel all his other bookings and we could all stay here in Shangri-la for the rest of the season and maybe happily ever after. [5]

John Lane and Shirley Booth in front of the Playhouse, 1953.

Alexis Smith, Bell, Book & Candle, *1953 publicity photo.*

In 1953, Alexis Smith made her first appearance at the Ogunquit Playhouse with Victor Jory in *Bell, Book and Candle,* by John Van Druten. Although this photo was a publicity photo with a Siamese cat of unknown origin, the Piewacket who actually performed that week was a tortoise tabby cat named "Chaucer" who was a good friend of John Lane's. As Helen Horn related the story:

> Mike and I lived in the icehouse (at Perkins Cove) at the time and we had a cat named Chaucer. He was sort of a tortoise shell cat. He roamed freely around Perkins Cove and would come into the restaurant. John came often with celebrities from the Playhouse and that was quite exciting. We loved that. He would come with Burgess Meredith, or Faye Emerson, and Chaucer seemed to know whenever John was around. So he would come over, and John would feed him tidbits and stroke him. And one time the Playhouse was putting on *Bell, Book and Candle,* and it had a cat in it -- Piewacket. John asked if Chaucer was available for a role in the play. Every day, he would send Brewster's Cab over to Perkins Cove to pick up the cat and then he would bring him back after the performance. Then it would be twice a day on matinee days.

June Dayton and Dean Harens, The Moon is Blue, *1953.*

Cedric Hardwicke and Lili Darvas in *Island Visit,* a new play by Andrew Rosenthal, came next. Then Zachary Scott appeared with June Dayton and Dean Harens in *The Moon is Blue,* by F. Hugh Herbert. (His daughter, Pamela Herbert Chais, would go on to write the comedy, *Jack Be Nimble,* that starred Betsy Palmer at Ogunquit Playhouse in the 1966 season and went on to Broadway.) Ellie Asherman, a Colony student in 1953, recalls how the students all responded to Zachary Scott: "Zachary Scott! He was so suave. He had a very fancy Hawaiian shirt and white pants and white sneakers. And he had a *diamond* in his ear!!!"[6] Asherman also recalled:

> Alexis Smith, in *Bell Book and Candle.* She was one of the people who led me away from the theatre. She had left two children to go on tour for the summer, and she was so anxious about those kids. And another one was Barbara Cook (who came with *Carousel* the next week). On the most beautiful summer day when everyone else was at the beach, she was in the theatre rehearsing. She was so dedicated. I figured then that this might not be the career for me.

The woman that Ellie Asherman was referring to was a little-known soprano by the name of Barbara Cook who appeared the next week in the role of Carrie Pipperidge in *Carousel*. And indeed, her hard work paid off for her. Cook starred the next year, 1954, as Carrie in the New York City Center revival of *Carousel*. By 1956, Cook had starred as the original Cunegonde with Robert Rounseville as Candide in Leonard Bernstein's musical, *Candide,* opening on Broadway in December, and she went on to star as Julie Jordan in a second revival of *Carousel*, at New York City Center, in 1957. Following her amazing Broadway career, starring as Marian, the librarian in *The Music Man*, and as Amalia Balash in *She Loves Me*, Cook turned to cabaret and then continued as a successful concert singer. She has gone on to coach opera singers on how to cross over into popular music. Barbara Cook has become a legend; she was the first popular singer to ever have a concert at the Metropolitan Opera in New York.

The backstage crew of *Carousel* took a breather during the run to "play" on the set. Present and enjoying themselves were Francis Dixon, William Flynn, Linda Roberts, Paul Dozier, Martha Wadsworth, and Blair Nesbitt.

Crew on the set of Carousel, *left to right: Francis Dixon, William Flynn, a Colony student, Linda Roberts, Paul Dozier, Martha Wadsworth, and Blair Nesbitt. Both images this page courtesy Carole Lee Carroll.*

1953 saw the appearance of Wally Cox, television's Mr. Peepers, in the John Cecil Holm and George Abbott comedy, *Three Men on a Horse*. This was one of the first times that a television performer was enlisted to appear in a production at the Ogunquit Playhouse. There would be many more to come. Appearing with Wally Cox was Walter Matthau, who would become a very famous motion picture actor. *Island Visit*, a new play by Andrew Rosenthal, with Cedric Hardwicke and Lili Darvas, came next.

Island Visit, *set design by Jock Purinton.*

Mr. Roberts, *1953, set design by Jock Purinton. Courtesy of Carole Lee Carroll.*

John also brought to Ogunquit that year an original revue that had been touring the west coast, *One Thing after Another*. In August, 1953, *Mr. Roberts,* the Joshua Logan comedy hit, opened with Richard Arlen, Dick Van Patten, Rosemary Rice and James Broderick. Carol Shuttleworth, a student at the Colony in 1953, remembers Dick Van Patten:

> Dick Van Patten and Ellie and I got to be in *Mr. Roberts*, and Dick Van Patten was a hoot. He had a cousin who was a jockey at Scarborough Downs. He kept winning, so I said, "this is unfair, why aren't you taking my money to bet on the horses?" One day, he said he had a sure thing and I gave him $20. Well, of course, the horse placed instead of winning. So to this day, I don't gamble.

Ezio Pinza appeared next in *The Play's the Thing*, by Molnár. Pinza had just starred in the Rodgers and Hammerstein blockbuster *South Pacific,* opposite Mary Martin. In Ogunquit, he stayed at Dunelawn and there had the occasion to meet a summer resident, Brinton Lucas, who was his exact double. According to Barbara Hilty, the two became good friends and kept in touch for a long time.

In 1954, the twenty-second season of the Playhouse, the program cover changed to a sketch of patrons arriving at the Playhouse in green set against a pale green and white background. Also, the driveways in front of the theatre were paved in the middle of the season, as John said, "to eliminate irritable dust." At the end of the season, John Lane wrote this farewell message to his subscribers:

Margaret Truman and George Voskovec in Autumn Crocus, *1954. Reprinted with permission from Getty Images.*

It has been a happy season here at the Ogunquit Playhouse, thanks to you thousands of theatre-going friends who have preferred our special form of entertainment and manner of presentation. "America's Foremost Summer Theatre" can only hold that title because you have made it so.

1954 saw the arrival of Margaret Truman, starring in *Autumn Crocus* with George Voskovec. The play called for a little girl, Minna, the Crocus-Gatherer, and Barbara Hilty remembers John asked if her daughter, Toni, could appear. Since Barbara was busy at her restaurant, the Lobster Bar, Henry came each night and matinee to fetch Toni and bring her back home afterward. She of course loved it, because, as Barbara tells it, one of her pieces of business was to eat pudding during each show. So beforehand, the properties mistress would ask her what kind of pudding she wanted, and that's what she ate, six nights and two matinees. The same season, Margaret Truman was featured in a *Life* Magazine cover story about the growth of summer theatres. (August 2, 1954).

Cornelia Otis Skinner returned to Ogunquit for her fifth time in *Paris '90*, a review of monologues that she had written herself about characters reminiscent of Paris in the 1890s, with an emphasis on the various women portrayed in the posters and canvasses of Toulouse-Lautrec. In costumes designed by Helene Pons, Miss Skinner seemed to emerge from the artwork itself.

Then came *Jenny Kissed Me*, starring Rudy Vallee and Lee Remick as Jennie. Remick had rather recently begun acting at the Cape Playhouse and in Ogunquit, and she would go on to become a very well-known actress. A young James Broderick was featured.

Howard Atlee, the Publicity Director in 1954, wrote little snippets of news about the Playhouse in each of the playbills. Audiences were treated to information about Bette Davis and her husband Gary Merrill, for instance, living in Cape Elizabeth and coming to the theatre to see Tallulah Bankhead in *Dear Charles*. He also reported that Mr. and Mrs. Richard M. Nixon, the vice president and his wife, had been recent guests at the theatre. On July 5th, his first month wedding anniversary, Henry Weller was hit by an automobile in Ogunquit village, leaving him hobbling around the Playhouse in a plaster cast.

A different sort of disaster struck in September that year, while Tallulah Bankhead was appearing in *Dear Charles*, a new play by Alan Melville that was slated to go to Broadway directly afterward.

Tallulah Bankhead was always a source of stories, but during the week of *Dear Charles,* she didn't have to provide any pranks because a hurricane took out the power at the Playhouse and left the theatre dark for one performance. Henry Weller remembers:

The John Lane Years 79

Cornelia Otis Skinner in Paris '90, *1954.*

Rudy Vallee on the set of Jennie Kissed Me.

John and I were sitting in the box office refunding money. You know how Actors Equity is, no show, no dough, so Tallulah agreed to do an extra performance, but we had no lights. The fire department loaned us a generator, but that wouldn't do anything. So I went up to Portland to Edwards and Walker, and I bought 6 or 7 Coleman lamps and 5 gallons of white gasoline. We filled those lamps up with it. But the best thing, the thing that made it most impressive was that I got candelabras from the undertaker, you know six candles up and across. Everybody seemed to like the show.

In fact, Carole Lee and others remember that *Dear Charles* by candlelight was a magical experience. During the same storm, Barbara Hilty remembers:

Miss Bankhead was staying at Dunelawn, and she had a woman who had been with her for many years as an assistant to her. She was staying in the main house, and for some reason, the power was out in the main house but not in Rose Cottage, so my brother, George, the owner, came to her assistant, Rose, to tell her that Miss Bankhead could go over to the Rose Cottage to take a bath because there was hot water there. And Rose said to him, "Oh my God, Mr. Smith, do you want her running stark naked across your garden? Don't tell her!"

There were two musicals presented in 1954, *The Boys From Syracuse*, by Rodgers and Hart, and *Song of Norway*, a musical written about the life of Edvard Greig. A young Jack Cassidy, former husband of Shirley Jones and father of Shaun Cassidy, starred as one of the twins in *The Boys from Syracuse*.

Steve Cochran and Patricia Peardon rehearsing Heaven Can Wait.

Steve Cochran starred with Noel Leslie and Patricia Peardon in *Heaven Can Wait*, the play that later became a motion picture starring Warren Beatty. Murial Williams, Bunny Hart's step-mother, also appeared, and the playbill notes claimed that the remainder of the cast was formed of resident members of the Ogunquit Playhouse and the Manhattan Theatre Colony.

Daisy Atherton has been with us since the inception of the organization. Like Mr. Leslie and Mr. Doherty, she ranks among the top of Ogunquit's favorite players. Harry E. Lowell, back for his second season as Stage Manager, makes his first appearance this season as the Doctor.

He is one of the most capable mainstays of the backstage organization and has been in the theatre 32 years. From the Colony: Vivian Dowling comes from Tarpon Springs, Florida, and is a student at Wellesley College. Katherine Pappas has acted in stock in New Jersey, Indiana and Illinois. Henry Hasso is the son of actress Signe Hasso and is making his debut on a professional American stage with this performance. Ken Starrett is a scholarship student from the Children's Theatre in Portland. Merrill Dollar was born in Maine and attended Bangor High School and Hudson College.

Even Francis Dixon, Carole Lee's father who was the Technical Director, and other members of the crew made an appearance in this production.

In August of 1954, John Lane offered a special benefit performance of *Ada Beats the Drum*, a play written by his Director of the Manhattan Theatre Colony, John Kirkpatrick. The entire admission went to benefit the local chapter of the National Foundation for Infantile Paralysis (If you recall, an outbreak of polio in the fifties led to the creation of the Salk vaccine, but not before a large number of children were affected.)

During the 1955 season, the Playhouse announced the two most spectacular engagements "in its twenty-four year history. Never have two such magnificent stars played successive weeks in any summer theatre in America." It was referring, of course, to the appearance first of Ethel Waters in *The Member of the Wedding*, and then, of Claudette Colbert in *A Mighty Man is He*.

Claudette Colbert.

Ethel Waters.

A young Steve McQueen.

Lee Remick.

Eva Marie Saint and Mark Richman on the set of The Rainmaker, *1955.*

Two Fingers of Pride, Gary Merrill, Tamara Daykarhanova, Margaret Feury.

Cast and set of The Rainmaker, *1955.*

The same year, John staged *Wonderful Town*, the musical based on *My Sister Eileen*, with music by Leonard Bernstein; *Champagne Complex*, with Donald Cook back for a third season; Eva Marie Saint in *The Rainmaker*, by N. Richard Nash; Jeffrey Lynn and Stephen Elliott in *The Caine Mutiny Court-Martial*, by Herman Wouk; and *The Great Waltz*, with music by Johann Strauss and Johann Strauss Jr. It was also the season that John produced the world premier of *Two Fingers of Pride*, by Vincent J. Longhi, starring Gary Merrill, with Tamara Daykarhanova and Margaret Feury. Steve McQueen appeared in a minor role as a very young actor.

Henry Weller tells a great story about Bette Davis visiting during that week:

> They were rehearsing *Two Fingers of Pride* for Broadway. Bette sat at John's desk every performance and I sat at my desk. And I remembered that she had been in the office with another actor some time before and they were having a heated argument about something political. This time, she began taking the reverse position. I said to her, "Bette, are you sure? The last time you talked about that you took the opposite view." "No, that's impossible," she said. "Well, I'm pretty sure you did. You were talking with so-and-so." "Oh well, I didn't like him. So naturally, I didn't agree with what he was saying."

The Ogunquit Playhouse production of William Inge's Pulitzer Prize comedy, *Picnic*, featured three who would go on to success on Broadway, movies and television: Sandra Church, who later appeared as Gypsy Rose Lee in *Gypsy* on Broadway, Lee Remick, who had a too-short but very successful career in all three mediums, and Robert Webber, later a television actor who achieved great success.

In 1955, Celeste Holm visited Ogunquit, stayed at Dunelawn, and saw her son, Ted Nelson's performance as Barney MacKean in *The Member of the Wedding*. Ted is also the son of Ralph Nelson, the director of *Picnic*, which had played at the Playhouse the week before.

Eva Marie Saint starred in *The Rainmaker*, and was so delighted by the Playhouse and Ogunquit that she expressed a desire to return in 1956. Supporting her were Will Geer, Mark Richman and Sidney Armus.

Billie Burke and Elaine Swan in The Solid Gold Cadillac, *1956.*

Before the 1956 season, a new air ventilation system had been installed and the theatre redecorated. The 1956 season opened with Billie Burke in *The Solid Gold Cadillac*, by Howard Teichmann and George S. Kaufman. Julie Strong, the daughter of Dr. Osmond Strong of Concord, New Hampshire, and a student at the Manhattan Theatre Colony, won the role of Miss L'Arriere.

In June that year, Harold Cail, drama critic for the *Portland Evening Express*, ran a bit of gossip in his *Two on the Aisle* column to the effect that he had heard from a reliable source that:

> Art Carney, "Norton" of the Jackie Gleason television show, is coming to the Ogunquit Playhouse in *The Seven Year Itch*, I'm not sure of the date, but believe it will be in August. Brett Somers, local actress, is going to be in it, I'm told. If you want to see Art Carney, make your reservations now.[7]

Proclaiming the Ogunquit cast of *Bus Stop* a Big-Town cast, Harold Cail wrote: [8]

> Anyone who feels the Ogunquit Theatre production of *Bus Stop* is as good as Broadway's is on solid ground for five of the eight performers are out of the Big Town company. There's Barbara Baxley and Elaine Stritch, who are starred, and Howard Fischer, Patricia Fay and Graham Denton, who are featured.

With the cast of *Bus Stop* housed at Dunelawn, we can remember a party put on by Elaine Stritch in the Rose Cottage, and remember too that she enjoyed her stay at Dunelawn so much that she came back in the fall with her then boyfriend Ben Gazarra for a quiet little vacation.

Following a week of *Ballet Theatre*, starring Nora Kaye and John Kriza, Lane brought *Anastasia*, starring Delores Del Rio and Lili Darvas to the Playhouse. When the *Portland Evening Express* ran Del Rio's picture on July 24th and a description of her beauty secrets, "moderate exercise, good food and lots of rest have retained Miss Del Rio's natural beauty," [9] the kitchen help at Dunelawn were not surprised: as far as we could tell, Miss Del Rio slept every day, almost all day. No wonder she was so beautiful.

Harold Cail wrote in his column, *Two on the Aisle*: [10]

> As much as the next one I like to be entertained when I go to the theatre. But equally important also is to come away with something to remember. *The Seven Year Itch*es are fine, as are the *Anniversary Waltz*es and the *Tender Trap*s, but for something worthwhile give me *Saint Joan*, with Katherine Cornell; *Winterset* with Burgess Meredith; *Time Limit*, with Arthur Kennedy; O'Neil's *Strange Interlude*, *The Lark* with Julie Harris; *Man and Superman* with Maurice Evans or *John Brown's Body*, with Raymond Massey and Tyrone Power. Now add to these, *Anastasia* which has two more performances to go at the

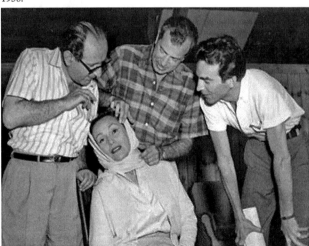

Anastasia, *Delores Del Rio, with Martin Balk, Stephen Elliott and Paul Stevens, 1956.*

The John Lane Years   85

John Lane with Delores Del Rio and Nicky Neshamkin.

Delores Del Rio as Anastasia, 1956.

Ogunquit Playhouse and I wish I could see both of them. Here certainly is the highlight of the season in dramatic quality and exquisite performances by Miss Lili Darvas and Miss Delores Del Rio.

Harold Cail told this story of having dinner with Lili Darvas and Harold Shaw (then Publicity Director at the Playhouse) [11]

> Having dinner with Miss Darvas the other evening provided me with two of my most pleasant hours in galloping around from one show shop to another. Not only this year, but ever. Miss Darvas entertained Harold Shaw and myself with her experiences with "television's 26-year-old geniuses," who sit with their feet on the table deciding whether she can fill a certain part or not. When one told her he'd have to think it over, she replied "Well think fast, I'm leaving tomorrow." For Miss Darvas doesn't have to wait on the gray flannel suit set. She crossed the country nine times last year for film and TV appearances. She's on a two-month tour in *Anastasia* and her husband's estate contains play rights to a musical version of *The Guardsman*. Interest in this probably was touched off by the success of *Pygmalion* being made into *My Fair Lady*.

Anniversary Waltz, by Jerome Chadorov and Joseph Fields and starring Carol Bruce and Edmon Ryan, was the fifth attraction in the 1956 season. Jeannette Pomeroy, reviewing for the *Portland Evening Express*, noted that local fans would be interested in two bit parts played by John Fitzgerald and Arthur Dishavo, students at the Manhattan Theatre Colony. "They managed to make relatively bit parts noticeable." [12]

The New York papers picked up on the next production, *The Golden Egg*, by Philip King. The play had run in London for two years and was being taken to Broadway in the fall, starring Donald Cook, a leading comedy player, in a rewrite by Donald Cook's wife, Gioia. Unfortunately, *The Sanford Tribune and Advocate's* Isabel O'Connell panned the play saying that "Donald Cook was the only thing keeping the production from being an egg!" And Arthur Gelb, writing for the *New York Times*, on July 23, 1956, noted that:

> An old musical and two new plays are about to be placed in the summer-circuit incubator in possible preparation for Broadway. The new plays that will be getting their pre-Broadway tryouts are *A Sudden Spring*, starring Celeste Holm, and *The Golden Egg*, starring Donald Cook, Muriel Kirkland and Patricia Peardon. *A Sudden Spring* is slated for Broadway production by Alfred de Liagre Jr. (one of Walter Hartwig's guests in Ogunquit during the 1930s) and Henry T. Weinstein (producer of Westport Playhouse during the 50s) The story deals with a girl's school and what happens to the student body when spring and the circus arrive simultaneously in the small town. [13]

There are lots of stories about Art Carney in Ogunquit then and in later seasons. But one in particular is very instructive of who the man was. Staying at Dunelawn, Art became quite friendly with Harriet and George Smith, the owners. One evening in 1973, while he was playing at the Ogunquit Playhouse, a large gathering of the Barn Gallery Associates was being hosted in Dunelawn's music room. The dinner went on for a very long time. Meanwhile, in the kitchen, the wait staff and the Smiths were chatting with Art Carney and wishing that the Barn Gallery folks would finish up and go home. Art told the Smiths that he could get them to break it up. As Mike Horn, on the Barn Gallery board and a guest at the dinner, tells it:

> We were all very elegantly dressed. And suddenly this guy appears in a tee-shirt and he was mopping the floor. You couldn't see his face because he had his head down, and he just kept mopping the floor. People were starting to get upset and looking for George to come and get him out of there, when he lifted his head up, and it was Art Carney as Ed Norton.[15]

> **Harold Cail:**
>
> There's nothing phoney about Art Carney. I met him briefly Monday night and again in mid-week. The second time, he was rehearsing a scene from *The Seven Year Itch* with Miss Rawn Harding who succeeded to the role of "the girl" when Lee Remick got a picture offer that took her off to Hollywood. Rawn was selected from more than fifty young actresses who auditioned.[14]

Art Carney and Rawn Harding rehearsing The Seven Year Itch, *1956.*

Carney made many brief visits to Dunelawn, with Jean, his wife who had been his high school sweetheart. In 1973, when he was playing Ogunquit in *The Prisoner of Second Avenue* by Neil Simon, he appeared with his second wife, Barbara. Later, he came back again after he had remarried Jean. His son, Brian, came to the Manhattan Theatre Colony during the season of 1964. Ian Compton, the youngest son of Francis Compton and also a Colony student that year, recalls that he and Brian hung out together and they both played the guitar.

Carney had joined the Jackie Gleason Show, *The Honeymooners*, in 1951, and would be returning to tape the next season as Ed Norton, on September 29, 1956.

The 1956 season ended with Beatrice Lillie in a new review *Beasops Fables*, and the critics raved. Boston Post artist, Donald Stone even drew his views of the extraordinary comedienne on the Dramatic Page of the *Boston Sunday Post*.[16]

The Straw Hat Circuit of summer theatres was in its zenith during the fifties and sixties, and Sylvia F. Porter of the *New York Post* wrote about the phenomenon.

It just doesn't seem possible that in only a few years, Broadway-In-the-Sun has zoomed from an impromptu, haphazard affair run by stage-struck amateurs to a multi-million-dollar business. Less than a decade ago, there weren't more than a couple of dozen successful summer theatres and these were concentrated in the more "arty" areas of New England and the West Coast. This June, July and August there will be more than 300 theatres, musical tents, Shakespeare festivals and pageants active every night in the week in 39 states. That's about 30 times the number of theatres that will be open on Broadway this summer. Today, the straw hat circuit is highly professional in acting and production and most of the big theatres operate year-round – planning in fall and winter, negotiating for properties and casts in spring, putting on productions daily in summer. An estimate is that last summer the theatres grossed over $15 million, a whopping half of the gross of the Broadway season, and the conviction is 1957 will top this. "You really don't know until Labor Day, but it looks very good for 1957," says John Lane who operates the Ogunquit Playhouse in New England.[17]

Janus, *1957. Joan Bennett, Donald Cook and George Voskovec.*

Of course, when she said that "in only a few years, Broadway-in-the-Sun had zoomed from an impromptu, haphazard affair run by stage-struck amateurs to a multi-million-dollar business," she was wrong in regard to Ogunquit where for almost three decades sophisticated audiences had been enjoying first-rate theatre put on by well-known and highly professional actors and actresses, thanks first to the Hartwigs and later to John Lane.

Joan Bennett, the star of *Janus,* John Lane's first play of the twenty-fifth season, 1957, traveled to Portland to have dinner with critic Harold L. Cail at the Lafayette Hotel, where Miss Bennett learned for the first time that her father, the late well-known actor, Richard Bennett, had spent some of his early acting days at the Gem Theatre on Peaks Island. The theatre which had been built in 1884, burned down in 1934.

Lane's second attraction in the twenty-fifth season was a pre-Broadway play, *The Man in the Dog Suit,* by William R. Wright and Albert Belch, under the direction of Melvyn Douglas and starring Hume Cronyn and Jessica Tandy, one of the theatre's most talented husband-wife teams.

Hume Cronyn and Jessica Tandy, publicity shot.

When the Manhattan Theatre Colony staged *Yankee Fandango*, a play written by longtime Colony director, Jack Kirkpatrick, that season, the *Portland Evening Express* picked up on the premiere and on Daisy Atherton who was seen in a role written especially for her by Mr. Kirkpatrick. Daisy, a fixture in Ogunquit for many years, was at that time the drama coach at the Colony.

And the production of *Witness for the Prosecution*, starring Basil Rathbone, brought back a number of early Colony players. Noel Leslie and Claude Horton, along with Claude's wife, Jean Cameron, were summer residents but had also appeared in the Ogunquit Playhouse resident company under Walter and Maude Hartwig.

Elliot Norton, writing for the *Boston Daily Record*, reported that the most popular play on the summer circuit was probably Agatha Christie's *Witness for the Prosecution*.

> Last week, the company headed by Basil Rathbone sold out every evening performance at Ogunquit after seven other semesters of similar success in major theater centers. In Philadelphia's municipal Playhouse-In-the-Park they triumphed over a heat wave that kept one actor's pocket thermometer between 105 and 118 degrees for nine successive nights. This play is really hot! There is a good performance of the curiously boyish defendant by Peter Brandon and an amusing one by Guy Spaull as the prosecuting attorney. This is an excellent summer show.[18]

Cast of Inherit the Wind *during a performance in Saratoga, NY. Julie Strong is seated stage left behind Ed Begley who is gesturing toward the judge.*

Inherit the Wind, the play by Jerome Lawrence and Robert E. Lee, based on the actual Scopes trial which was held in Dayton, Tennessee in the summer of 1925, came to the Ogunquit Playhouse directly from a long run on Broadway. It brought Ed Begley playing the leading role of Henry Drummond. Begley had spent two seasons on Broadway playing the secondary role of Matthew Harrison Brady, the dramatist's moniker for William Jennings Bryant, to Paul Muni's Drummond, the attorney who was in real life Clarence Darrow. In New York, when Muni was forced to leave the show, Herman Shumlin, producer and director, conceived of the idea of swapping Ed Begley from one role to the other. According to an interview with Harold Cail at the *Portland Evening Express,* Begley said he would be up for the challenge of doing both roles – say three days a week for each.[19]

Inherit the Wind at the Ogunquit Playhouse stood out for another reason. It was the play in which a total of 18 Colony students and townspeople, more than any other show, took part in the production, Susan's grandfather Harry Cassell and Carole Lee's mother Betty Dixon included. There were very few people left to serve as the audience!

On August 22, 1957, Harold Cail ran the following story in *Two on the Aisle*:

Cathleen Nesbitt, 1957.

The Cinderella factor in the theatre struck last week at The Ogunquit Playhouse. Evelyn Mando, who played the role of Mrs. William Jennings Bryan in *Inherit the Wind* was stricken ill Thursday. Julie Strong got up in the part in the afternoon and was letter-perfect at the evening performance. Not only did she continue the role there but was taken with the cast to Falmouth, Mass., and so far as is known, will continue to Saratoga, NY, for the final week. Miss Strong hails from Concord, N.H. She spent two years with the Manhattan Theatre Colony of the Ogunquit Playhouse, and this season was working backstage. It's the sort of thing that gives the theatre its magnetic attraction. One can never tell when the "lightning" will strike or where. [20]

Next in the 1957 season was *The Chalk Garden,* with Vivica Lindfors and Cathleen Nesbitt. And Harold Cail wrote:

> Edgar A. Guest once wrote a poem to the effect that it takes a heap o' livin' to make a house a home. After last season's viewing of *The Chalk Garden* I felt it would take a "heap o' acting" to make it at all interesting at a second sitting, this time at the Ogunquit Playhouse. But that's what happened. The acting is there. And for the first time, *The Chalk Garden* really means something. [21]

Elliot Norton, esteemed drama critic of the *Boston Daily Record,* and a professor of dramatic criticism at Boston University (Carole Lee studied under him in the late 1950s) wrote about Ogunquit's Tradition:

> John Lane has kept up the standards at the Ogunquit Playhouse and in its 25th season it ranks with the best and most popular of the summer theaters. In an atmosphere of comfort and informality, Mr. Lane follows the tradition of the late Walter Hartwig, bringing the best of Broadway to Maine. Walter Hartwig was among the pioneers, a showman of New York with an enormous capacity for hard work and a fervent conviction that summer visitors to Maine would support the best actors in the best plays. He made his point and, in so doing, focused national attention on Ogunquit. Walter's first theater was a made-over garage in the center of the town. Stars of high and mighty reputation were glad to act there under his management. He persuaded Maude Adams to appear for him and since she was something of a legend in the theatre, her appearance created the kind of sensation which can only be achieved in the emotional world of Show Business.
>
> Ethel Barrymore starred in this old theater once, and became a frequent and imposing visitor to the colony of celebrities, many of them magnificently temperamental, whom Walter attracted. Laurette Taylor was one of that colony for several years. Walter Hartwig and his wife, Maude, sheltered that magnificent star when Laurette was in a dreadful period of decline and dissipation, trying without much success to break away from alcoholism. Later, Laurette found herself and returned to the theater to give one of the greatest performances of the modern American theater in *The Glass Menagerie.*
>
> At Ogunquit, she acted occasionally, taught students in the Playhouse school and had the comfort and consolation of being accepted among actors and actresses in a period when every producer on Broadway was afraid to employ her because of her drinking.
>
> Although Water Hartwig leaned back to the theatre of the past, the drama of the Frohmans and Belasco, with whom he had associated, he looked ahead, too, and was always alert to the importance of publicity. He gave the young Diana Barrymore her chance to act for the first time on any stage, and kept her on as an apprentice actress long after Diana had demonstrated that she had more temperament than talent or good will. Diana's presence at the Ogunquit Playhouse focused the national spotlight on the theatre, as Walter knew it would. In the interest of showmanship, on the one

hand, and because he admired her father, John Barrymore, and her amiable mother, Michael Strange, Walter allowed Diana to act on his stage and tolerated her bad acting offstage as long as anyone could. Twenty years ago, Walter Hartwig built the new Playhouse on Route One and moved out of the garage into a theatre which is almost unique in the country for comfort, convenience and fine equipment. Most of the summer theaters are housed in buildings that were originally used for some other purpose. The Cape Playhouse, at Dennis, was once a church. In Gilford, NH, the Lakes Region Playhouse was a dairy barn for 65 cows. At Westboro, the Red Barn Theater is as the name suggests, a Playhouse made from a barn. The Ogunquit Playhouse, however, was built as a theater and designed to present comfortably almost any attraction that can play Broadway. If it were of stone instead of wood, it could be used permanently. John Lane took over the operation of the theater from Walter Hartwig's widow. A former actor, a showman in the newer tradition, he has held on to what was good in the Hartwig plan but has gone ahead to adjust to the changing picture in the summer theater. This is why Ogunquit still ranks with the best of the theaters in 1957; it has not been allowed to live on tradition or on past success.

Since it is now difficult to originate all the shows of a summer season, as Walter Hartwig did, John Lane has accepted the tradition of traveling package shows. In order to make sure that these are as good as they should be, he has originated some of them himself. The touring company of *Witness for the Prosecution,* which is playing around the wheel now with Basil Rathbone starred, was produced before the season began by John Lane.

Daisy Atherton at the Graham Hotel. Courtesy of Betty Dixon.

The young producer was one of the first summer showmen to recognize and do something about the great drift of the American show-going public to musicals. When some of the other managers decided that they couldn't present musical comedies because the cost of an orchestra was too high, he experimented successfully with productions that used only two pianos as accompaniment. In his present schedule, three of ten shows are musical comedies. Under John Lane, the twenty-fifth season of the Ogunquit Playhouse will probably be the most popular of all because his program is geared to the show-goers' pleasure in 1957.[22]

Then came *Pajama Game*, the musical written by George Abbott and Richard Bissell with music and lyrics by Richard Adler and Jerry Ross, and to end the season, Peggy Wood returned in *Jane*, and received a warm response from audiences and critics alike.

In May of 1958, Harold Cail published an interesting account of the problems that were beginning to face summer theatres all over the country.

King-Size Headache

As mentioned earlier in the week, but briefly, we dined with John Lane and Harold Shaw of the Ogunquit Playhouse when in New York recently. John was headed that night for a meeting of the summer theater operators who are trying to arrange schedules and solve problems. One of these is the astronomical prices the "name" performers are asking. In some cases new promoters are fouling up the situation, Lane said, by offering 'em too much to begin with." I noted evidence of this in a column I read on the way home.

Some dope had offered Donald O'Connor $10,000 a week. This is absolutely ridiculous, unless one is operating on a State Department budget and nobody is, except Huntington Hartford who has the A&P stores' millions back of him. Incidentally, he has diverse theater interests but Hartford isn't running a summer theater.

If anyone were foolish enough to pay O'Connor $10,000 a week, the expense of a supporting cast, stage crew, house staff, advertising and other costs would add from $3,000 to $5,000 more to the "nut" (operating costs). Let's call it $15,000. Lakewood Theater seats nearly 1,100. They'd have to completely sell out eight performances at $1.50 for every seat, front, middle and rear, orchestra and balcony, just to pay the bills. The Ogunquit Playhouse, with 700 seats, would have to get $2.50 for every seat in the house, eight performances. A 400-seat theatre, about the size of Kennebunkport Playhouse, would have to charge around $4.50 for every seat and sell out for eight performances. If one went into scaling the house in the usual manner, best seats would be up around Broadway prices, without providing any profit for the operators. And who's running a summer theater for his health? [23]

Claude Dauphin, 1958

The lineup for 1958 included *Dulcy*, with Dody Goodman, known for her television work with Jack Paar; *Triple Play*, with Jessica Tandy and Hume Cronyn; a new comedy, *The Third Best Sport*, by Eleanor and Leo Bayer; *The Waltz of the Toreadors*, with Claude Dauphin and Lili Darvas; *Maggie*, with Ella Logan; *The Remarkable Mr. Pennypacker*, with Burgess Meredith; *The Happiest Millionaire*, with Victor Jory; and *Holiday for Lovers*, with Don Ameche. Comedy was the key for this Ogunquit season, and Elliot Norton predicted it would be enormously prosperous.

Local reviewers noted that Celeste Holm was here for the second season in a row. Harold Cail pointed out that a young performer named Mickey Calin, who had played in *A Sudden Spring*, in 1956 with Celeste Holm, had come back in 1957 as a singer-dancer in *The Boyfriend*, and that during the winter of 1958 he had really made a name for himself in *West Side Story*, and now he had been signed by Columbia Pictures and his name had been changed to Michael Callan.

Lili Darvas, The Waltz of the Toreadors, 1958

Later in the 1958 season, Cail wrote under the title *Budding Thespians:* [24]

Patricia Mortimer has a small role in *Holiday for Lovers* at the Ogunquit Playhouse, as a French maid, but it's fairly important as such roles go because of the French that must be spoken. Pat's a member of the Manhattan Theatre Colony. It's worth passing on that Don Ameche, guest star, has said she's the best they've had in the part on their summer tour. She was in *Waltz of the Toreadors* earlier in the season and in *Jane* last year. Also from John Lane, Ogunquit's impresario, comes word that Jean Armstrong, the Pond Cove youngster there on scholarship from the Children's Theatre of Portland, has one commendable quality. "She's lively," says he. "Vitality is an important asset in a performer. Too many hopefuls don't have it. Jean has shown promise in her first year at the Colony," says Lane.

Harold Cail wrote about Daisy Atherton:

This, to be exact, is Miss Atherton's 26th season at Ogunquit. In other words, she came with the Playhouse, so to speak, since it observed its 25th anniversary last year. Such is her popularity that guest stars have received less applause on an initial entrance than has Miss Atherton, even though her role was a small one. Over the years, Miss Atherton has appeared here and on Broadway with the best of them, Lillian Gish, Leo G. Carroll, Cornelia Otis Skinner and Dennis King to name a few. For several seasons now she's been on the staff of the Manhattan Theatre Colony, imparting to young hopefuls some of the experiences she has acquired in a long successful career. Many happy curtain calls, Miss Atherton.[25]

Ann Harding.

Gig Young and Ann Harding appeared next in Daphne Du Maurier's romantic comedy, *September Tide*, and The Ogunquit Playhouse racked up its first Monday night sellout of the season. "Credit this welcome situation to the magic of the names – the stars as well as the playwright," said Harold Cail.

Wendell Cory appeared with his wife of twenty years, Alice Wiley, in a comedy, *Goodbye Again,* in the next to last show of the 1958 season, followed by *Fallen Angels,* starring Hermione Gingold and Carol Bruce.

1959 and the summer theatre circuit was truly in its heyday. Going into that season, Elinor Hughes of the *Boston Sunday Herald,* proclaimed

More theatres are open, more actors working, and, it seems more than probable, more people going to the theater than in any other 8-week period of the regular season. From Maine to Virginia, the flags are flying, the box-offices jingling, and the playwrights are counting their royalties. [26]

The stars that would be featured in those 168 theaters were as diverse as the theater locations. John Geilgud, Siobhan McKenna, Jason Robards; Margaret Leighton, doing classical theater in Cambridge, Mass; Frankie Laine, Anna Maria Alberghetti; Genevieve doing the musical tents; Rosemary Harris, Joan Fontaine, Barry Morse, Gloria Swanson, Buddy Rogers, Eli

Wallach, Anne Jackson, Shirley Booth, Lloyd Bridges, Elaine Stritch, Joe E. Brown, and the list went on and on. Everyone who could get into the summer season in some way or other did so.

Shirley Booth opened the Ogunquit Playhouse season that year in *Nina*. Faye Emerson came next in S.N. Behrman's comedy, *Biography*, about an internationally famous artist who is under pressure to publish her biography and the way she chooses to handle that. Harold Cail quickly arranged an interview on the subject of Miss Emerson's prior marriage to Elliott Roosevelt, son of President Franklin Roosevelt, and her plans to write a memoir about it. This led to an Associated Press dispatch claiming that "Faye Emerson's memories of six years of marriage to Elliott Roosevelt are not for sale." [27]

Betsy Palmer, who would become one of the most frequent and popular visitors to the Ogunquit Playhouse stage, appearing more than 11 times, and acting as mistress of ceremonies for the 1996 Gala, *"Thank you, John Lane,"* put on by the Playhouse Foundation as a celebration of Lane's 45 years in the theatre, made her first appearance in Ogunquit in 1959 with Kurt Kasznar in *Once More With Feeling*. At that time, Palmer was best known as a panelist on *I've Got a Secret*, but her star was rising, and in a *Newsweek* feature story the previous fall, Dave Garroway was quoted as saying "when she's around things sparkle and sound good. She's young, pretty, gentle, and a lady." [28]

Palmer's popularity was immediately apparent. John Lane, faced on Tuesday morning with a theatre sold out for the entire week and an incessant demand for tickets, arranged a special Saturday twilight matinee of *Once More With Feeling*, a very unusual occurrence which was directly attributable to the popularity of Betsy Palmer alone.

Faye Bainter, a great actress of the American stage with a resume of 61 years in the business, and Ann B. Davis, who became famous as television's "Shultzy" on the *Robert Cummings Show*, appeared together in the next production, *The Girls in 509*, a Howard Teichmann comedy that had a successful run on Broadway in 1958. (Monty Compton, a Manhattan Theatre Colony student, and the son of Francis Compton, one of the resident company members under Walter Hartwig, appeared in this production.)

Faye Bainter.

The next week, the legendary Gloria Swanson, called a Glamour Queen by all of the local press, arrived in Ogunquit, having flown to Maine from Saratoga, New York. But her chauffeur and car arrived much later. Betty Dixon recalls that John certainly knew how to treat stars, and she mentioned Arthur Treacher, Basil Rathbone, "even Gloria Swanson, who came with a chauffeur and a black car. He insisted that they have china for their tea, and flowers in the dressing rooms."

Henry Weller recalled a birthday party put on that week at Dunelawn in honor of Mary Pickford, Buddy Rogers' wife.

Harriet had a birthday party and Kurt Kasznar, Gloria Swanson, and Buddy Rogers, were there to celebrate Mary Pickford's birthday, but she was in California. Everybody knew her and so at 12:30 p.m. which was California time, Mary Pickford got a phone call, and after everyone had offered their best wishes, someone handed me the phone and said, "Here, talk to Mary Pickford." So I did.

Susan's sister, Elizabeth, working at Dunelawn at the time, recalls that Gloria Swanson shared her best beauty secret with her: a tablespoon of vinegar and a tablespoon of honey every morning. Ciba (Elizabeth) was so impressed with the results that she has never forgotten the advice.

Ben Gazarra, in Epitaph for George Dillon, *1959.*

Ben Gazarra, who was then starring in the movie, *Anatomy of a Murder,* with James Stewart, Orson Bean and an Ogunquit regular, Lee Remick, was the next attraction at Ogunquit, appearing in *Epitaph for George Dillon.*

On July 5, 1960, Harold Cail reported "Summer theaters are off to a great start with the Ogunquit Playhouse having "less than a score of empty seats on its first Saturday night."

During that 28th season, Howard Keel played the young Franklin Delano Roosevelt in *Sunrise at Campobello,* and Edward Mulhare, Rex Harrison's replacement as Professor Higgins in Broadway's *My Fair Lady,* brought a new play, *Memo for a Green Thumb,* to the Playhouse. *Memo* was a production of Elliot Martin, John Lane and Charles Mooney. Kurt Kasznar directed. The play was pretty much panned by Elliot Norton of the *Boston Daily Record*, and didn't make it to Broadway that fall.

Harold Cail wrote: "Something in the nature of a surprise attraction will be Howard Keel in *Sunrise at Campobello.* Keel's movie background, his switch to dramatics, and this particular play in an election year make this a stand-out offering."[29]

Two other movie stars, Dana Andrews and Shirley Booth, were also slated to appear at Ogunquit – Andrews in *Two for the Seesaw,* and Booth in the revival of *The Late Christopher Bean.*

For Dana Andrews, it would be a return to the part he had played on Broadway. Elliot Norton wrote, "Henry Fonda and Anne Bancroft originated this warm and winning comedy of romance on Broadway. When Fonda left, Dana Andrews succeeded him and had been playing the role of lonely Jerry Ryan for a year."

Andrews and his co-star, Gerry Gedd, had been together two weeks before in Andover, N.J., and would go on to Laconia, N.H., Lakewood, Me., and Falmouth, Mass. Norton went on to say, "At Ogunquit, they reached a pitch of playing perfection which made the play seem every bit as stimulating and, somehow, just a touch warmer, more touching than the Broadway production." [30]

Harold Cail noted:

> Hugh O'Brien was in Friday's matinee audience of *Two for the Seesaw*, riding over from Kennebunkport where he is playing the same role as Dana Andrews. Betty Field, whose daughter, Judy Rice, is at the Colony Theatre, apprentice adjunct to the Playhouse, was an opening nighter. [31]

It was Judy Rice's second season at the Colony.

The Playhouse production of *Two for the Seesaw* also starred a new jackknife stage. The new stage was installed to handle more complex productions. Designed and executed by David Hale Hand, this innovation was meant to become a permanent fixture at Ogunquit. Jackknife stages had two full stage wagons about 12 feet deep and the full width of the stage. When one was in use, the other was stored off-stage, perpendicular to the footlights. Each wagon had a pivot on the on-stage/down-stage corner that allowed it to swing on or off the stage in very little time. At that time, only three other theatres in the country were equipped with "jackknife" stages. Unfortunately, it was removed in later years.

John Vivyan and cast of The Second Man, *sign autographs on the set.*

As for television stars that year, John Vivyan, TV's "Mr. Lucky," starred in *The Second Man* making his first stage appearance following his overnight success as Mr. Lucky on the television series.

Byrne Piven and Gerrianne Raphael starred in West Side Story *in July to rave reviews.*

In early July that year, Betsy Palmer returned to Ogunquit for her second appearance, this time with Paul McGrath, in a new comedy by English author, Leslie Storm, *Roar Like a Dove*. Leslie Storm came from England that week to see Betsy in her play.

Set of Roar Like a Dove, *design by Don Jensen, 1960.*

Gloria Nelson, Patrick Horgan and Betsy Palmer on the set of Roar Like a Dove, *1960.*

In August 1960, Joan Fontaine appeared in *Susan and God*, by Rachel Crothers. In the cast was Lily Lodge, daughter of John Davis Lodge, American Ambassador to Spain, and niece of Henry Cabot Lodge, Republican nominee for vice president. Both Lily's parents had appeared at the Playhouse under Walter Hartwig, in *Amphitryon 38* during the 1940 season.

Harold Cail reported:

> Last night's opening performance (of *Susan and God*) seemed to present more than the play's usual message. The theater was hotter than the home of the horned man in the red suit, as if to suggest what would happen to those who failed to respond to Susan and her teachings. It was equally hot on stage. While the audience suffered for the players as they pretended to be cool and comfortable, the players in turn felt sorry for the audience packed in like sardines.[32]

Full air conditioning was installed in 1968.

At the end of the 1960 season, a trade publication, *Show-Business*, carried a story by Ray Yates entitled, "Maine Turning Back the Clock Toward More Resident Summer Stock Companies."

Packages and stars have brought good business to Maine Playhouses this summer. But this has not meant profits for most of the managements due to high prices paid for "name" attractions. A return to resident stock companies was indicated by producers interviewed. One exception seems to be the Ogunquit Playhouse where Howard Keel in *Sunrise at Campobello* did top box office. Producer John Lane was cheerfully counting his money even in the face of orbiting star costs.[33]

The Playhouse withstood the onslaught of rising costs longer than many of its neighboring theaters, but the costs would catch up with it eventually, and this was but a small warning of what was to come.

The 1960 season closed with Maine's own Bette Davis in *The World of Carl Sandburg*. Davis had toured the play with her husband, Gary Merrill, and later with Barry Sullivan, for the entire previous season, and was bringing this production to Ogunquit as a pre-Broadway trial, co-starring Leif Erickson, a charming man who stayed at Dunelawn, and taught everyone there to pronounce his name "life, not leaf." Miss Davis had had a highly successful tour with the show, which was adapted from the writings of the illustrious poet by Norman Corwin, who also directed the Ogunquit production. The play was deemed a highly successful climax to a fantastic and exciting season.

The World of Carl Sandburg, *Bette Davis, Leif Erickson, 1960.*

Captain Brassbound's Conversion, *Siobhan McKenna and Zachary Scott, 1961.*

Captain Brassbound's Conversion led off the 1961 season, starring Siobhan McKenna and Zachary Scott. Reginald Denny also starred in the production and was interviewed by Harold Cail on the occasion of his 70th anniversary. Born in England, he had been on the stage from the time that he was 8 years old.

Celeste Holm returned to star in *Invitation to a March* with Louise Latham, Wesley Addy and Winifred Ainslee. Celeste had married Wesley Addy in 1960. Holm, whose son, Ted Nelson, had spent several years in the Colony sometime before, took time to meet with Colony students and offer advice and support. Myrna Loy and Claude Dauphin appeared in *The Marriage Go Round*. It was Myrna Loy's first appearance on the stage, and Elliot Norton found her performance flawed.

Barbara Smith Hilty and her daughter, Toni. Both photos from a Portland Evening Express story about families who were regulars at the Playhouse.

The Smith family at the Playhouse: Susan Milburn, Elizabeth Milburn, Harry Cassell, Harriet Smith, George Smith, and Harry Milburn.

Next, Susan Oliver, Scott McKay, and William Redfield starred in *Under the Yum Yum Tree*.

When Faye Emerson and Reginald Gardiner opened in *The Pleasure of His Company*, the *Portland Evening Express* wrote that Richard Rodgers of the famed Rodgers and Hammerstein duo was coming to Blue Hill, Maine to collaborate with Samuel Taylor on a new musical, *No Strings*, that would star Diahann Carroll and Richard Kiley. Taylor had authored such plays as *Sabrina Fair* and co-authored *The Pleasure of His Company*, playing at that moment in Ogunquit.[34]

Julia Meade, who appeared with Orson Bean in *Send Me No Flowers*, was at that time best known to television viewers for her commercial announcements for eight years on the *Ed Sullivan Show*. Her mother, Caroline Meade, had been a repertory star of the 1920s and had inspired Julia to choose the theater also. Julia and her husband, Warsham Rudd, later came to Ogunquit to vacation, and it was while Sylvia Rubin, a resident who entertained a number of the Playhouse stars over the years, was showing Julia around that she discovered property near the Cliff House and went on to buy a vacation home here. Caroline also spent time in Ogunquit and eventually taught classes at the Colony for two seasons.

Herbert Marshall and Zamah Cunningham starred next in *A Majority of One*, followed by Jane Wyatt and Tom Helmore in *O Mistress Mine*, also starring Billy Gray. Gray was Miss Wyatt's television son and he made his stage debut in Ogunquit that week.

Martha Scott starred with Donald Woods in *Future Perfect*, a political story that some reviewers identified as similar to the career of Margaret Chase Smith, the Maine legislator who served in Washington for so many years.

Craig Stevens and Alexis Smith closed the season in *Critic's Choice*, by Ira Levin, and in an interview with Harold Cail, Stevens noted that after having completed 48 films and 18 plays in his long career, he had achieved his greatest personal success as television's toughest private eye, Peter Gunn.

"Lane Saves the Best for Last," Cail wrote on August 24, 1961 in *Two on the Aisle.* "This week's play, *Critic's Choice* is the cherry on top of the season's parfait."

Another critic writing for *The Tourist News* on August 23, 1961 claimed:

> A packed house watched the opening performance of the play. It seems that the tradition of a good play with big names at Ogunquit has held the box office in a happy turmoil throughout the season, and this final production is no let-down.

Harold Cail noted at the beginning of the 1962 season that whereas Ogunquit had not staged any musicals the season before, the 1962 season would present two musicals. They were *Bye Bye Birdie* and *The Music Man.*

Tallulah Bankhead returned to Ogunquit in 1962 starring in *Here Today,* by George Oppenheimer. Elliot Norton described Tallulah "at her blockbusting best."

> Watching her dazzle her way through three acts is like watching a great fencer demonstrate his entire repertory…All exhibited with a sense of sheer joy. She finds it fun.35

Pat Finley in Bye, Bye, Birdie.

The play to open the next week as a "World Premiere," *There Must be a Pony,* starring Myrna Loy and Donald Brooks was in Ogunquit rehearsing the week that Tallulah was there. Jim Kirkwood, author of *There Must be a Pony,* was a great friend of Bankhead's so it was a very glamorous and exciting week for everyone backstage. Carole Lee Carroll, who was the Scenic Artist that year, remembers there were animals and birds in the new play including someone's pet ocelot, a kinkachoo, and Javanese love birds, and that this caused a good bit of chaos. The love birds, for instance, were let out of their cage behind the Playhouse and flew away. She remembers the play as quite interesting, if not completely evolved.

Elliot Norton called *Pony* a soap opera, not a drama and panned it. James Kirkwood was the son of James Kirkwood, "once a towering hero of the movies" and Lila Lee, also a movie actress. The play was written by him out of his own Hollywood background as the son of two stars.36

On the other hand, there *was* a successful try-out that summer that *did* make it to Broadway and did enjoy a very respectable run. *Cradle and All,* starring Paul Ford (Col. Hall to Phil Silvers' Sgt. Bilko in the popular television series), Maureen O'Sullivan, and Orson Bean, opened on Broadway in November of 1962 under the new name of *Never Too Late,* ran until April of 1965, and was regarded by all who saw it as a very funny play.

Martha Scott and Walter Pidgeon appeared in 1962 in T*he Complaisant Lover,* by Graham Greene, also starring Murial Williams, Bunny Hart's stepmother. Bunny remembers that while Walter Pidgeon was ensconced at Dunelawn, Martha and Murial, with visiting Bunny, had rented Pearl Hanson's house on Shore Road across from the Ogunquit Museum of American Art. But Martha came with many relatives, so many that Murial and Bunny had to quickly make other arrangements. They wound up at Dunelawn for the week. The play had been cut from three acts to two acts, so that an intermission was cut out. Bunny, in the audience, discovered at the last moment that the program didn't reflect that. So there was pandemonium about that.

Curious Savage, *Spring Byington and Murial Williams, 1963. Courtesy of Bunny Hart.*

The 1963 season opened with Spring Byington in *The Curious Savage,* a comedy by John Patrick. Of special interest to Maine theatergoers was the supporting part played by Linda Lavin, who is a Rumford, Maine, native. Murial Williams was also in the cast.

The Portland papers played up another Maine connection that season. Phyllis Thaxter, who starred with Art Carney in *Time Out for Ginger,* also starred opposite Margaret Ellen Clifford, with whom she had been life long friends. They summered together for many years at Cushing's Island, and both graduated from Wayneflete School. Miss Thaxter had been a student at the Manhattan Theatre Colony in 1937 and had made her first stage appearances that year in the new Playhouse's production, *Boy Meets Girl,* and in Laurette Taylor's play, *At the Theatre.* She went on to appear at Ogunquit many times thereafter. For the entire week, the papers referred to her continually as "Maine's own Phyllis Thaxter." Art Carney received glowing reviews including this from Elliot Norton at the *Boston Record American*: [37]

Carney is almost heroic in the way in which he allows the younger ones to use him as a foil. As an expert technician, he could upstage any one of them, but he stands his ground mutely, while they bounce the funny lines off his chest. Is there any other comedian who would do this?

What else was going on in Ogunquit that summer? Well, George Towar was giving a lecture on the Marginal Way about the "Rocks of Ogunquit," there was a block dance at Wells Beach with Richardson's Combo Band, an Ogunquit Village Concert at the Firemen's Hall with Frances Archer, Beverly Gile and the Balladeers. There were three square dances, and four "Forbes" Record Hops at Wells Beach.

Romanoff and Juliet brought Walter Slezak to Ogunquit at the end of July, 1963, along with Marie Powers, an actress who was in real life a countess. That led to a flurry of news stories. She used her own $250 Paris original hat as a prop in the show; it was one of the 350 hats that she kept in a wardrobe at her home on the Côte d'Azur near Nice! She claimed that she knew about Grace Kelly and Prince Rainier before anyone else and that she was front and center in the cathedral at that famous wedding. At the end of the week, Marie was off to visit an old friend, Helen Leadbetter, in the "oldest house in Fryeburg." [38] The set for *Romanoff and Juliet* was designed by Lynn Pecktal.

Walter Slezak in a scene from Romanoff and Juliet, Holiday Inns Magazine, *August, 1963.*

Next came *She Didn't Say Yes* by Lonnie Coleman, starring Joan Caulfield and Peggy Cass, with newcomers Joan Hackett and William Redfield, directed by Hal Prince.

In 1964, Harold Cail wrote about the perennial popularity of Bessie's. As mentioned earlier, a reviewer wrote about the place after the opening of Libby Holman in *Accent on Youth* in 1935. Early Colony students, Carol Collery Shuttleworth and Ellie Asherman, remembered trekking to Bessie's to buy fig bars, and we know that when the old Playhouse was at the Ogunquit Square, Bessie's was a draw after the theatre. So, not surprisingly, in 1964, thirty years later, the institution known as Bessie's was still going strong:

< In 1963, at the Ogunquit Playhouse, the lobby looked like this. From Ogunquit-by-the-Sea, by John D. Bardwell, after 1994. Courtesy of Dwight Bardwell. The rest of the images on this page courtesy of Carol Lee Carroll.

∧ Edwin Grant served as properties assistant to Properties Mistress Cathy Dunham, 1963.

< David Harper was Stage Manager, and Robert Gray was Electrician, 1963.

∧ Walter Dolan worked as Technical Director with Tim Smith, his production assistant, pictured at the cutawl.

∧ Lynn Pecktal was the Production Designer and Carole Lee Dixon was his Scenic Artist.

Opening night at the Ogunquit Playhouse also means for me, opening night at Bessie's. The popular eating emporium for the after theater crowd was open a month, to be sure, before the Playhouse went into action. Bessie was in high spirits, welcoming old friends and making new ones. More than ever, as she related some incident in her animated manner, she reminded me of Anna Magnani. [39]

From the worlds of television and the movies in 1964 came Merv Griffin in *Broadway*, by George Abbott and Philip Dunning; Van Johnson in *A Thousand Clowns*; and Lloyd Bridges in *Anniversary Waltz*. The two big musicals were *My Fair Lady* and *The Sound of Music*, both of which did extremely well according to end of season reviews. The old timers that year were outstanding thespians Cyril Ritchard, Cornelia Otis Skinner, Helen Hayes and Hermione Gingold.

Harold Cail wrote "Bunny Hart, attractive, busy and knowledgeable press agent for John Lane's Ogunquit Playhouse, paid her first call of the season yesterday. A real bright spot in one's first day back at work."[40]

The 1964 season began with a replay of *The Constant Wife* by W. Somerset Maugham, and immediately the critics were reporting on the challenge of Barbara Bel Geddes playing the same role, on the same stage as other greats of the theatre. Harold Cail wrote, "She will be treading in the footsteps of Ethel Barrymore, who created the role in 1926, and Katherine Cornell, who starred in a production of the play in 1951." [41]

One of the biggest problems that John Lane and later executive producers would face was a lack of good material and Bel Geddes in *The Constant Wife* gave a first glimpse of that. Elliot Norton, who could usually go to the heart of the matter in his theatrical criticism, and didn't suffer less than first quality productions gladly, wrote:

John Lane with a friend in North Carolina, from Palm Beach Magazine.

Although it's been trimmed and tailored, and to a certain extent, updated, Somerset Maugham's old chestnut, *The Constant Wife,* is still an old chestnut and all the art, the charm and the personal appeal of Barbara Bel Geddes cannot conceal either its age or its ailments. Lines that once glittered with the high shine of epigram are now for the most part sadly sophomoric. [42]

Barbara Bel Geddes.

Bel Geddes took all of that in stride and wound up being one of the favorites among the Playhouse staff. The play was directed by her husband, Windsor Lewis. She was quite familiar with the Ogunquit Playhouse, as her daughter, Suzy Sawyer, had been a Colony student in 1961. That opening week also marked Carole Lee Carroll's first set as Designer at the Ogunquit Playhouse, and it was well received by all, including both Bel Geddes and Windsor Lewis.

Merv Griffin followed Bel Geddes in *Broadway*, by Phillip Dunning and George Abbott, a play of the roaring 20s with a few songs and dances added. And on opening night, the Playhouse threw a birthday party for Griffin on the set designed by Carole Lee Carroll.

Van Johnson, starring in *A Thousand Clowns* the next week, decorated his dressing room in his favorite color, red, and hung clown dolls around the mirrors. The Playhouse staff even helped him by putting down red carpet and painting the back of the door red. Carole Lee Carroll's set was sufficiently jam-packed as his tiny one-room apartment in New York.

A Thousand Clowns, set by Carole Lee Carroll, lighting by Ray Caton, 1964. Courtesy of Carole Lee Carroll.

For the most part, summer visitors as well as town folk tended to treat incoming movie and television personalities with respect, and allow them space to enjoy themselves. But as Barbara Hilty recalls there were two instances where she had to intervene with an overzealous fan.

> If the stars stayed at Dunelawn, they ate at my restaurant. I became friends with a great many of them. My employees would have been fired if they ever asked for an autograph, but we couldn't stop the public, and Art Carney and Van Johnson were the only two that were just so bothered by fans that I finally sent them over to my house to eat. The boys just loved taking their food over, because they got great big tips. I only remember those two stars being pestered. Mostly, people left them alone. With Van Johnson, he had just had a bout of cancer, and a woman came up to him in the restaurant and asked "how's your cancer?" I just whisked him away to my house after that. But I was in Bloomingdales some years later and a voice said, 'boo!' and Van Johnson popped up from behind a counter.

Van Johnson.

Johnson is remembered by all who saw him at the Playhouse for his red socks.

When Lloyd Bridges came in *Anniversary Waltz,* he brought his son, Jeff, to play his son on stage. Bridges was then America's best known skin diver thanks to his long-lived television series, *Sea Hunt.* Bridges' co-star Eloise Hardt brought her daughter, Marina Habe, to play the on-stage daughter in the same play.

My Fair Lady, having just completed its long run on Broadway, played in Ogunquit for two weeks and was one of the biggest hits the Ogunquit Playhouse had ever produced. The show played to sellout crowds nearly every night for two weeks.

Cornelia Otis Skinner, whose portrait had graced the lobby of the Ogunquit Playhouse for many of the Hartwig years, returned in August 1964 with Cyril Ritchard in *The Irregular Verb to Love.*

In his "Season in Review," Harold Cail wrote about Ogunquit's season this way:

> *Sound of Music* was the best single week at the Ogunquit Playhouse, *My Fair Lady* might have been first had it too been confined to a single week, but it played two. At that, it was a virtual sellout. Cyril Ritchard and Cornelia Otis Skinner, teamed in *The Irregular Verb to Love*, gave Ogunquit its third best week. Van Johnson and Lloyd Bridges were neck and neck behind *Verb*. New records at the Ogunquit Playhouse are next to impossible. The seating capacity is just about ideal in the upper 700s and sellouts occur frequently, and have for many years since John Lane got rolling. The season as a whole was slightly behind 1963. [43]

Eve Arden.

Eve Arden opened the 1965 season in *Beekman Place*, by Samuel Taylor, who also wrote *Sabrina Fair* and *The Pleasure of his Company*. He lived in Blue Hill, Maine, and had collaborated with Richard Rodgers, during the summer of 1961 on *No Strings*. *Beekman Place* brought Eve Arden (AKA *Our Miss Brooks*) and her husband, Brooks West, to Ogunquit that season.

Hans Conried, who played to standing-room-only audiences in *Take Her, She's Mine* in 1963, returned this year to the Ogunquit Playhouse in a new comedy, *Absence of a Cello*, by Ira Wallach. In the cast that week were Michaele Myers and James Karen.

Walter Pidgeon arrived at the end of July, 1965, to appear with Murial Williams in *The Happiest Millionaire*. The cast also included Eileen Bennett and her real son, Nicholas Hammond, 15, who would go on to appear with Julie Andrews in the motion picture of *The Sound of Music*. Pidgeon had also starred in the original Broadway production of *The Happiest Millionaire*.

The company of *Camelot*, coming in next for a two-week stint, needed a sheep dog to walk on with King Pellimore. Since it was hard to travel with one, they picked up a new dog at each theatre. In Ogunquit, as Harold Cail tells it,

> The company started out with a St. Bernard who had pulled a lying down act at rehearsal and since there was just no moving him until he was ready, it was decided not to take a chance on his temperament when show time came. So Thumper, a French poodle owned by Richard Perkins, was brought in at the eleventh hour. He got the star treatment, being driven to and from the theater in regal style by Bill Traber, the theater's business manager. Somehow it seemed as if Thumper sensed the end when he was returned home on the second Saturday night. Traber says he just sat there with a resigned expression that said, "You mean to say I'm done?" [44]

Also, in Camelot, the man who played King Pellimore, Alexander Clark, turned out to be the son of Alexander Clark who had been a leading singer in Gilbert & Sullivan operettas for many years. The Alexander Clark appearing in *Camelot* had been born in a theatrical boarding house in Times Square, at the corner of Broadway and Forty-Third Street, according to Harold Cail. And he had been to Ogunquit several times before, with Lillian Gish in *Miss Mabel*, and with Ezio Pinza in *The Play's the Thing*.

Camelot had the distinction of being the musical that had played nine weeks in five of the six summer theaters in Maine. It played in Ogunquit for two weeks, and was sold out for the entire engagement. Speaking of selling out, the seat prices at the Ogunquit Playhouse that year went to $3.50 from $3.00 for matinees, and for evening performances, there were no longer $3.00 seats, only $4.00 and $3.50!

And then there was the Michael Myerberg production of *The Frog Pond*, which was a world premiere but which also was the play that everyone universally remembers as the worst play they ever saw at the Ogunquit Playhouse. Carole Lee Carroll, who was the Set Designer that year, remembers the set as unusual, with a fireman's pole that people had to slide down and a huge piece of junk sculpture. Bunny Hart remembers that during performances of the play, she, John and Henry would hide in John's office in the dark in order to avoid having to talk to anyone about the play. This was the third Myerberg production at Ogunquit. His earlier world premiere in 1946, was *Balloon*, that Mary-Leigh Smart remembers as being a very large production that was not very good, and in 1947, *Dear Judas*, which raised the ire of the Catholic Church. *The Frog Pond* starred Mindy Carson, Rita Gam and Betsy von Furstenberg and was already slated for Broadway, to open at the Brooks Atkinson Theatre on September 30, 1965.

Kevin Kelly in the *Boston Sunday Globe*, August 15, 1965, wrote "Miss Scott (Georgette Scott was the author), to be as kind as I can about it, is a writer of appalling ineptitude and *The Frog Pond* is a fitting tribute to her talent." [45] Fritzi Cohn, drama critic for WCSH-TV, Portland, called for:

> ...drastic surgery if it's to make its Broadway unveiling. It was a strange evening that started out with a capacity crowd and ended, not much before midnight, with a depressingly half-full house. A perfectly beautiful set could not be improved upon. At this point in its labor pains, *The Frog Pond* doesn't seem to have a prayer but if the dialogue is cut by one solid hour and the actors by a whole half, well perhaps Gene Frankel can pull a miracle out of his most capable hat. Good luck! [46]

So, the journalists weren't kidding when they headlined *Diplomatic Relations* with Anne Baxter and Gene Raymond as "bringing fun back to Ogunquit." Baxter had already won two academy awards for *The Razor's Edge* and *All About Eve*. During that week, a York Hospital Benefit performance organized by the Women's Committee of York Hospital raised over $4200.

Mrs. Dally Has A Lover, by William Hanley, starred Arlene Francis, Ralph Meeker and Robert Forster. Of the four new plays at Ogunquit during the 1965 season, this, like *The Frog Pond*, had been booked for Broadway, scheduled to open at the John Golden Theater early in the New York season. Elliot Norton expressed grave doubts that it would be worth

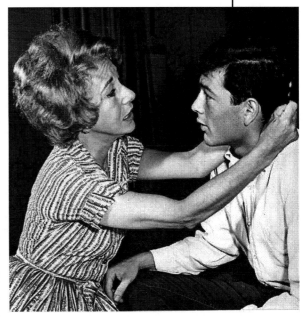

Mrs. Dally Has A Lover, *Arlene Francis, Robert Forster, 1965.*

the effort, and claimed Arlene Francis far too sophisticated and confident to be effective in the part of Mrs. Dally.

In 1966, John Lane opened the season with a musical, which might have been risky in the past, but he enjoyed one of his best first weeks ever. The musical was *How to Succeed in Business without Really Trying.*

Other shows that year included Gertrude Berg in *Dear Me, The Sky is Falling,* Dennis Weaver, known to millions of television fans as Chester on *Gunsmoke,* appeared in a comic mystery, *Catch Me If You Can,* Vivian Vance starred in *Time of the Cuckoo,* Julia Meade and Scott McKay played in *Mary, Mary* by Jean Kerr, Alexis Smith returned to Ogunquit with Gabriel Dell in *The Coffee Lover,* and Betsy Palmer starred in a new comedy, *Jack Be Nimble,* written by Susan Herbert Chais. This was her third appearance at the Ogunquit Playhouse.

The second musical that year was *Oliver,* and the stage manager in 1966 was newcomer, Mort Mather, recruited by John Lane from the Lambertville Music Circus. Although Mort was to remain backstage at the Playhouse for only three years, he would become a major player almost thirty years later as John's health began to fail.

The 1968 season opened with Allan Ludden and Betty White, real-life husband and wife, in *Once More, With Feeling,* by Harry Kurnitz, and directed by Porter Van Zandt, who had staged *Wait Until Dark* and *The Odd Couple* at the Ogunquit Playhouse in 1967. *Once More, With Feeling* had been done at Ogunquit with Kurt Kasznar and Betsy Palmer in 1959. Allan Ludden was known in those days as the host of the television game show *Password.* Betty White, was then a popular television actress who later became even more famous as "Sue Ann" on the *Mary Tyler Moore Show,* and "Rose Nylund," one of the *Golden Girls* with Bea Arthur.

In 1968, two of the backstage staff, Barbara Jones and Mort Mather, met each other for the first time. It was Mort's second year as stage manager and Barbara was technical support and became properties mistress in 1969. Mort had come from a background of summer stock in Lambertville, New Jersey, at the Lambertville Music Circus, which was the first tent theatre in-the-round in the world. He had worked there five seasons and had gotten his Equity card as an assistant stage manager and then stage managed the last show of that season – *Springtime for Henry,* with Edward Everett Horton. Mort remembers:

> Well, John was really great to work for. He was great and he was awful. The good part, when he offered me the job, he came to me because somebody had said to him, you need to have Mort, or at least, that is the way he presented it to me. But that made me feel very special. He sold me on coming up to Ogunquit, and he took me

out to lunch innumerable times. And when I got there, he treated Paul Bertelson, the designer, and me like royalty. It was as if we were kind of the stars of the show as far as John was concerned.

Mort continues:

> He was very demanding but what I was fond of telling other people was that there was no backstage of any theatre anywhere in the world that was as clean as the Ogunquit Playhouse. Actors and technicians loved to come to work at the Playhouse because they were treated well, they were respected, the place was clean. That was John's number one thing, keeping the place clean. The stories about John working on the grounds were some of my favorites. He would be out there, digging around and trimming hedges and somebody would come up and ask where John Lane was, or get into some kind of conversation with him thinking that they were talking to the grounds keeper, and I remember he would really get a kick out of it when they would start saying how well they knew John.

Mort's tale of how he arrived in Ogunquit that year bears repeating. He had been rehearsing *Once More, With Feeling* in New York, and was due to fly to Boston on the shuttle where John was meeting him. But let him tell it:

> My second year there, 1968, I was dating a married woman at the time who had told me that she was getting a divorce and I had asked her to marry me. We were rehearsing Allan Ludden and Betty White in *Once More, With Feeling.* The last day of rehearsal in New York, I was to be all packed with the props and go directly from rehearsal to the shuttle and John was going to pick me up in Boston. When this woman went out that morning to walk the dog, she never came back. My bags were packed and I was just about to go to rehearsal when I got a phone call from her at work. She said that when she got down to the ground floor her husband was waiting for her, so she kept walking and went to work with the dog. Apparently the husband had followed us back to the apartment the night before, and had spent the entire night there between the doors. So then the next phone call I got was from him and he told me things that made me see that she'd been lying to me. So I went to rehearsal and on the lunch break I met this guy for lunch and he told me more. I went back to rehearsal, packed everything up and got on the shuttle. John met me in Boston, and the fiberboard box that had all the props including a break-away violin and the sound-tape for the show did not arrive in Boston. So I arrived there without the props, without the sound-tapes, and without half of my mind. Well, I got to the Playhouse and the sound system was not working. And the only tape that we had to test the sound system was a toilet flush, just one little piece of tape. I had a technician from Adams Radio and Televison in town, and it was Joe Hill. And Henry. And Joe Hill and Henry and I were trying to get the sound system to work, with nothing more to play through it than the brief sound of a toilet flushing.

Barbara, now married to Mort, adds, "That was the summer we called him Murky Mort. That was his name for the summer." Mort responds:

> Why? Because my mind was gone, I was in tough shape. I missed cues like crazy. I would miss doorbells and telephones. It was just awful. My mind was just gone and I couldn't hang on to it. Well, John was really wonderful to me. He didn't throw me out for the mess that I was making of the show. And he tried to console me and was very helpful.

To the audience, *Once More, With Feeling* appeared to run without a hitch. And it was followed by Rosemary Prinz, known to the world as Penny Baker for the past twelve years on *As The World Turns,* in *A Girl Could Get Lucky*. She was followed by Joan Fontaine as Amanda in Noel Coward's *Private Lives* with Michael Allinson, and by the musical *Sweet Charity*.

Barbara Jones came to the Playhouse in 1968 rather than go to her first choice, Falmouth, because John paid everyone. She was in college that first summer and it was her mother who made the decision for her based on the fact that the backstage staff at the Ogunquit Playhouse had paid positions.

> He paid everybody. Nobody worked for nothing. And in a lot of places, then, people were called apprentices, and worked for nothing, whereas we were technical assistants. I remember that I was paid something less than $40 per week. I know that my rent at Dunelawn was $18 per week which was considered very high at that time, but it was Dunelawn. I shared a room in the old servants' quarters on the third floor. And I had money left over to occasionally go to Bessie's or Dicky Dare, or get breakfast at My Sister and I.

Barbara remembers that John was a demanding person but he was also very, very giving. For her, the job of doing props was an easy job, first of all, because John had so much in stock, but also borrowing things was easy because people were very happy to lend the Playhouse furniture and props.

Press coverage in 1968 refers to the newly air-conditioned Ogunquit Playhouse. During the run of *Sweet Charity*, reviewer Franklin Wright said

> Producer John Lane has a lot going for him on the stage at the Ogunquit Playhouse this week – a scintillating star, a smooth production of a bright musical comedy, a well-balanced cast, and air conditioning! [47]

John Lane's production of *The Little Foxes,* in mid-season of 1968, was one of the more daring attempts he made at serious drama. Lillian Hellman's powerful drama of a decadent

Southern family, had been revived by Mike Nichols the year before at New York's Lincoln Center and John booked the national tour of the play with an all-star cast headed by Geraldine Page and Betty Field. Ogunquit Playhouse releases announced "This important one week engagement offers Maine theatre-goers the rare opportunity of seeing some of this country's finest actors together in one of the truly genuine classics of the American theatre." [See color plate XVIII., set design for *The Little Foxes*.] And with the opening of *Show Boat*, the next attraction at the Playhouse, Harold Cail wrote: "The summer theater season at John Lane's Ogunquit Playhouse has come alive with two smash hits in a row. *Show Boat*, which opened last night, is as stunning musically as *The Little Foxes* was dramatically last week." [48]

Years later, when Stuart Nudelman, longtime Ogunquit resident and current company photographer at the Playhouse, approached John to congratulate him on his production of *Dancing at Lughnasa*, in the 1990s, Stuart remembers,

> I saw it and felt that it was a fantastic performance, better than the New York performance that I had seen earlier. I walked up to John and said, "I commend you and thank you for putting on this excellent play." He said, "Thank you very much. You know this play, like one play every season, I put on for myself. I lose money on that play every year, but I do it for me." It was important for him to produce plays as works of art even if he lost money on them. Everything had to be perfect with this man, but there was one part of him that felt a responsibility to present good theatre to the public.

The Little Foxes in the 1968 season was John's play for himself. Rich Latta, who came to the Playhouse as an electrician in 1985 and has been Lighting Designer there for most of the years since, also remembers:

> John would always pick one show a season and he didn't care if it did well. It was like a show for him. Some of those went beyond summer stock, into something else. *Dancing at Lughnasa* was one; another one I remember was *Driving Miss Daisy*, which was kind of an artistic triumph for me. Everyone agreed that it was done beautifully. But John freaked out. I came to his office thinking I was going to be praised, and he said, "I want it redone. I want it completely redone." He made me take all the subtlety out of it, all the delicateness, and I remember that nobody on the crew talked to him for a week.

Vivian Vance.

Following *The Little Foxes* in 1968, Vivian Vance, who for 14 years had played Ethel Mertz to Lucille Ball's Lucy on *I Love Lucy,* came to Ogunquit with a new comedy by John Patrick, *Everybody's Girl.* Patrick, a prolific author, had written *The Hasty Heart*, the play you remember in which John Lane made his most memorable appearance at Maude Hartwig's theatre in

1946. Vance had been in Ogunquit in 1966 in *Time of the Cuckoo*, and her co-star, Roy Scheider, was appearing for the first time in Ogunquit and the cast included his wife, Cynthia Bebout. At Ogunquit, the play was given in two acts, and the story goes that John Patrick found out about it, and insisted that they go back to three acts.

Craig Stevens and Alexis Smith, by this season well known to Ogunquit audiences, arrived next in *Cactus Flower*, by Abe Burrows. Stevens and Smith had co-starred seven years before in *Critic's Choice*. *Cactus Flower* was in its third year on Broadway that season, and was very well received at the Playhouse. Carole Lee, working as 'Lee Carroll, Set Designer,' was complimented on her "attractive and incredibly mobile sets."

The closing show that season was *Desk Set* with Shirley Booth and Paul McGrath. Elliot Norton wrote: "Shirley Booth's Just Great, But Oh, That Awful Play!"

> Shirley Booth is without question one of the great comediennes of the theatre today. *Desk Set* just as definitely is one of the most sadly inept plays of its time. Written by William Marchant and performed on Broadway in 1955, the play had been saved then, according to Norton, by the wonderful performance of Shirley Booth. [49]

As an aside, Harold Cail noted on August 19, 1968 that Bunny Hart, "press gal par excellence" was an off-stage voice for *Everybody's Girl* and that she and Bill Traber, John's business manager, were rehearsing for their roles in *Desk Set*. According to Bunny, she and Bill were part of a crowd scene and they were supposed to be "necking" when the lights came up. And on opening night, they got a standing ovation!

In 1969, as Mort Mather tells it, "I bought this place (their 100-acre farm in Wells) in June, fell in love with Barbara in July, and asked her to marry me in August. We got married in November. So you see, I owe a great deal of my happiness to John Lane."

Mort's account of how he proposed to Barbara makes John Lane the first one to know about it:

> We went out one night to the old Whistling Oyster, before it burned, and we were in the bar right down on the water, and that's where I asked her to marry me. She said, "Well, ask me again when you're sober." So the next day or the day after...." And Barbara interjects, "it was the same day actually, we went for drinks between shows, then we went over to Oarweed for lobster and we got back to the Playhouse late." Mort: "We pulled into the staff parking and John was right outside the stage door pacing around. Barbara just scurried on in. But John was furious with me. He said, "You've ruined a perfectly good property girl" I said, "Well, I'm sorry, but I just asked her to marry me." And he kind of spun around twice and went to the office.

The 1969 season brought Tom Ewell in *Don't Drink the Water,* a Woody Allen comedy with Jane Connell. Critics found the play lacking vitality and Tom Ewell less than wonderful.

The John Lane Years 115

Franklin Wright, *Portland Evening Express*, June 24, 1969 said "Woody Allen wrote some very funny stuff in *Don't Drink the Water* but in this production, too much of it has gone down the drain."

Other plays that season were *There's A Girl in My Soup*, by Terence Frisby, starring Laurance Hugo, a television actor known for his starring part in *The Edge of Night*; *The Prime of Miss Jean Brodie*, the award-winning play by Jay Allen which starred Betsy Palmer in her sixth appearance at the Ogunquit Playhouse since 1959; and *Sound of Murder*, by William Fairchild, starring Jeannie Carson, Hurd Hatfield and Biff McGuire. *The Chic Life* was a well-received pre-Broadway tryout starring James Whitmore and Audra Lindley. Likewise, the Ogunquit Playhouse production of *South Pacific*. Critics raved, audiences were delighted, the production sparkled.

James Whitmore.

The Glue That Held It Together

No enterprise as successful as the Ogunquit Playhouse became ever gets there without a cadre of people who work behind the scenes to hold it all together. For many of the years that John Lane ran the Playhouse, the group remained essentially the same. Henry Weller, who came the year after John and Helen bought the Playhouse and is there to this day, remembers:

> We had a nucleus of six people really who ran the theatre. There were Bill Traber, Bill Hoe, Joe Hill, Bunny Hart, me and John Lane. Somebody, one of the press persons who swarmed around the Playhouse every opening night, asked me what I did there? And I had to think. Well, I do everything that has to be done when nobody else is around to do it. And that pretty much was the truth. One of the secrets though, we started every day at 9. a.m. and Joe Hill was the one to turn the last light out at night. And it might be 1 a.m. in the morning. John had a thing about lights and if you left a light on where nobody was, there'd be hell to pay. So our electric bill was always under control. But you didn't come in late very often. Bill Traber (Business Manager from 1960 to 1980 and from 1990 to 1994) had an assistant that was often

late in the morning. So Bill took him aside and very tactfully said, "George, or whatever his name was, you know the fan starts turning at 9 o'clock here, and in case anything hits it, we want you to be here.

In addition to everything else he did, Joe Hill drove props, sets, casts and animals everywhere for years and years. He worked for John Lane in Palm Beach in the winter, and at the Ogunquit Playhouse in the summer.

When the magician was here during the seventies when we had gas shortages, I had to go get the lion. He was 120 pounds, a live lion in a cage. I picked him up in New Hampshire. And we set him up in the prop room with food and water. Then nobody wanted to take him to Long Island, so I did it. In a van. That was when you could only buy 10 gallons of gas at a time. So I got down to Connecticut and stopped for

Henry Weller, Bill Traber and Bunny Hart at the marquee in 1963.

gas. The garage attendant said, "Well, we can only put in 10 gallons." Just then the lion roared, and the man looked in the van and looked at me and said, "You want it filled up?" I said, "Well, I have to take him out for a walk." And the guy said, "Don't."

Joe Hill was the maintenance man for many, many years. He replaced Jim Ward who had been with the organization 12 years, and he grew up at the Ogunquit Playhouse and was with John Lane until Lane's death. Joe Hill and Henry Weller unveiled the plaque naming the Ogunquit Playhouse to the National Register of Historic Places in the State of Maine. The Playhouse received this designation on December 14, 1995, and the event was celebrated in June, 2001.

In 1966, Harold Cail observed that John had been producing for 15 of the 34 years the Playhouse had been in existence, that Henry Weller had been there 14 of those years, and that Francis Dixon, the tech director, had been there longer than either of them by about ten years. Francis came to work for Walter Hartwig in 1939. He also noted that Jim Ward, the maintenance man, had been with the organization 12 years, that two of the box office ladies, Pearl Hanson and Barbara Kemp, had been there ten years and Bill Traber, seven years.

Joe Hill and Henry Weller unveiling the plaque naming the Ogunquit Playhouse to the National Register of Historic Places in the State of Maine, 2001.

Bunny Hart came in 1963 as Publicity Director, although she knew John from working at the Cape Playhouse for a number of years (she was Stage Manager there in 1953).

> My father had been involved with the Cape Playhouse and so I went there as a child. I met John when he would come down to the Cape. We did a lot of the same shows. It was 1963 and I had spent many years working in public relations, political, product and personal – I worked with Eva Gabor trying to keep her out of the newspapers. I decided I wanted to go back to summer theatre.

Bill Hoe playing a patron at the box office for a story in Down East Magazine, *July 1974.*

Ogunquit and the Pocono Playhouse both needed a publicity person. I was told that Rowena Stevens liked to stay up all night and sleep half of the day and that I would have to adjust to that. Then I learned that John Lane got up in the morning and had working breakfasts. I decided I'd rather have breakfast with John Lane.

Bunny's recollections of how she was hired match those of Mort Mather. John wooed her, even talking about the distant future with her in the post. It seems John Lane had an almost paranoiac need to be certain of his staff, so much so that if he liked you and felt he could get along with you, you were hired for life, and he sort of fell in love with you. Until, as Mort mentioned, you stepped across the invisible line, and an iron curtain might fall down on you. In 1963, Bunny became one of the "nucleus" that Henry talked about.

Miss Paul at work at the York Press. Courtesy of Old York Historical society.

> John was packaging shows then, and we had ten in a row, which was exhausting. He would put them together in New York and the first year I arrived two weeks before the opening and was scrambling to get the preliminary work done.

In later seasons, Bunny would be able to start on publicity much earlier. She remembers working very closely with the York Press where all of the playbills were printed.

> The critic there was Miss Paul. She was a little lady who reviewed theatre for the *York Weekly*. That was where the program was printed and every week was a new show, so I spent my entire life down there (in York). Miss Paul would sit in the little office and she was probably about 80 years old, and she always wore a big hat. She would sit and type her stories. She was the social editor and also the critic. She would come on opening night and call me up the next morning to read me her review. "Now does that sound all right?" she would ask. And I would say, "That's wonderful, Miss Paul." She sat at a desk that was piled so high with old newspapers that you could hardly see her. And she always made sure that she hadn't hurt anyone's feelings.

Bunny considered Harold L. Cail of the *Portland Evening Express* a more genuine critic.

> He was very honest and he liked us. He was also very kind. Cail did interviews after each opening. On opening night, we would have three radio people doing interviews, along with the newspapers. It was a very busy night. I might have one star in the wardrobe room interviewing, and another actor would be in the prop room with someone else. Sibby Allen interviewed for WHEB in Portsmouth; and Alan Jasper was there for WIDE in Biddeford. On rare occasions we got Elliot Norton from Boston, whom I had known as a child. He was such a good reviewer, but he would say nothing rather than be unkind.

Bunny remained at the Playhouse as Publicity Director from 1963 for three years, went away in 1966 and came back in 1967 and '68. During that time, she got to know the staff and John Lane very well.

> He ran a very good theatre. Somehow, he was lucky because he had an awfully good staff. They were very loyal. And he had certain guarantees built in. He would guarantee that the backstage area and prop room were going to be nice. That Dunelawn would be part of it, that the rooms were going to be nice, that the Playhouse lawns were immaculate, the dressing rooms slick, etc. Everybody wanted to be part of that. Actors would come in and say "This is the most beautiful theatre we've ever been in." Because it was well run, and clean – to the point of obsession. The staff put up with a lot from John because they got so much praise from outside.

When describing the telephone system at the Playhouse during the 1960s, Bunny doesn't hold back. As funny as it seems now, it must have been a nightmare for the staff in those days.

> In the early and mid-'60s telephone communication between the two small Playhouse offices and the rest of the world consisted of two phone lines – one for incoming calls, the other for outgoing calls. The first line had three actual phones, one on John's desk, one in the outer office on Bill Traber's desk and a third one on my desk (also in the outer office). For all outgoing calls, there was one actual telephone. It sat between Bill's desk and mine. Obviously John was not going to come out and stand between Bill and me to make calls out. His calls were often lengthy ones to fellow producers on the circuit. So, he used his incoming phone for outgoing calls. Well, during those calls, no one could get through to us because the outgoing phone number could not be given to anyone (on pain of death). Realize, too, that except for Ogunquit and Wells local calls, all calls had to be placed through an operator! You can imagine the frustrations for everyone there trying to get their job done. Add to this, the outgoing number was supposed to be not merely for front office use but for the entire Playhouse staff. There were no other phones, probably because Henry convinced John that staff might abuse the system and make personal calls. So, the scenic and lighting designers, the tech director, prop person, stage manager and others would appear in the office door, often lining up into the lobby, to make business calls, place orders, etc. on that one solitary little telephone.

Somehow, America's Foremost Summer Theatre retained its status despite the antiquated phone system.

Bunny's experiences with summer theatre publicity at the Cape and at Ogunquit were different also.

> I knew people doing publicity at the Cape who had trouble getting posters around. People didn't really want to take the posters. In Ogunquit, I would get calls from little inns with four rooms asking why they didn't get a poster. The town adored the Playhouse, and John was very good with the town. He paid for my gas, and he knew to send me to the Gulf station while he was sending someone else to John Jacobs or Hutchins. He divided up the season's trade. He gave to the town and he would invite everybody to opening night. He was very savvy about how to deal with the town.

From 1970 until 1985 Bunny worked year round in other jobs, but she found herself missing the theatre and came back in 1985 and remained there through 1999. When she returned, she handled publicity, and for three years was the business manager. Having been at the Ogunquit Playhouse during the '60s and then again in the '80s and '90s, her observations about how Ogunquit had changed are quite relevant.

> The people who came to Ogunquit changed, and that changed how the Playhouse was received. When Rob [Townsend, Assistant to the Producer] asked, "Why can't we fill up the theatre?" I said, "Have you driven downtown on Shore Road and Main Street at 7 p.m. lately and seen what's down there. They're not going to go to the theatre. They're not going to get dressed up. They're going to buy pizza and rent a film."

Bunny's T-shirt Story

In the early '80s, John was persuaded, probably by Rob, to join the T-shirt craze which had even reached Ogunquit. To John, a T-shirt was underwear with writing on it and he wouldn't have been caught dead wearing one. But he bowed to the trend and allowed the whole season's schedule one year, taken from the flyer, to be printed on a T-shirt in "playhouse green." Just prior to the season's opening, large cartons arrived filled with four different sizes of the T-shirt. John, who was renowned for his tidiness, had cleared his desk of all playhouse business, and he proceeded to unpack the shirts and fold each one of them (300 or more), stacking them neatly on his shelves which had also been stripped bare. It must have been good therapy for him, because there he sat for one entire day, folding T-shirts. He would eventually distribute them to his staff and to incoming casts members free of charge. The leftovers were sold to the public.

By the time the '90s rolled around, Bunny remembers:

> We were having difficulty finding good material, and as the stars diminished, and the plays diminished, and we had just musicals, which everybody had already seen a couple of times, we did not sell out, and no amount of publicity was making the difference.

Rich Latta, who joined the Ogunquit Playhouse in 1985 and has remained there through three administrations after John Lane, has a similar theory about the '90s and what went on in the theatre.

> We were losing audiences through attrition, I think. A lot of it too was what plays were in the pipeline. We always joked about being here at our little Ogunquit, doing our rinky-dink shows and what would happen when the big musicals got onto the circuit. And now they have. And now we're getting them, and doing them, and we've gone through that growth process. We're completing the transition now into large scale technical theatre, which is what people want to see.

Rich Latta remembers:

> The way John had set it up, and the way he had run things, it was possible for him to sit there from 9 to 5 and have everything going on around him. But even when he started to fail a little bit, he always wanted to drive the "Billy Goat," the big vacuum cleaner that picked up all the cigarette butts outside. I think when you are a really successful producer, it's really true that if you are doing your job right, all that's left is to pick up the cigarette butts outside the theatre.

In the late '80s they reinvented stage lights and Rich Latta brought one to show John. He was thrilled because he said it was three times as bright as the old lights. But there were funny moments leading up to the changeover.

> When we did the upgrade, we started using more electricity. John was the only producer who ever chased me around waving the electric bill and shouting "Have you seen this?" He was also a bug about the electric bills so it took a while for him to get used to it.

Rich also ran into difficulties with John's "famous obsession about brightness."

> He would sit at the back of the auditorium during rehearsals and all you could hear was "Dark," "Dark," I was lighting *Desert Song*, and I was busy increasing the light for each scene as we went through it, when somebody came on stage, and John yelled, "Oh, look, it's the Prince of Darkness!" We put it on the wall in the shop. We called it the Prince of Darkness year. [See Color Plate XIX. It is a tradition of the Playhouse that each year's technical crew paints a staff list on the walls of the scene shop. In 1988, the list included the "Prince of Darkness," Rich Latta, to honor John Lane's remarks to Rich, who was then the Lighting Designer.]

The nucleus of people who ran the Playhouse were, of course, supported by many other people, some of them on John's staff, like Jim Ward who did the gardening with John for many years. Carole Lee remembers "When Jim Ward left, they had to replace him with several people. And then they named the high school gym after him."

Quentin Halstead, another longtime maintenance man at the Playhouse, died suddenly in October, 1982, and John Lane, devastated by his death, planted a red maple in his honor. Alden Shum was another friend and co-worker who contributed greatly to the lovely appearance of the Playhouse. Ed Hipple, was John's staff photographer for many years, and Ed's wife, Mary, was a good friend of the Playhouse. John was very proud of the Colony and fond of Francis and Betty Dixon who had been there for so long.

John counted on a lot of help from friends in Ogunquit as well. Harriet and George Smith who made Dunelawn available, and George's sister, Barbara Hilty, whose Lobster Bar fed many an actor, and who was happy to be a friend and dining companion to John during the years of his separation from Helen. Barbara remembers, "Maybe he was difficult around the Playhouse, but he also worked hard there himself."

> I remember John loved the riding mower and Henry said it was the best thing that ever happened to John because he could put those headphones on and nobody could get at him. He loved flowers. John was a big breakfast person, and often he would pick me up and off we would go. He was very good about bringing people to my restaurant. And he used to give parties at the restaurant. He gave a party for Helen Hayes and one for Joe E. Brown. I suspect he coerced his staff into lunching there. But because of that, Bunny Hart, Henry Weller, Bill Traber and Bill Hoe became very dear friends to me and my family. [See page 161 for a 1964 montage of photos at the Lobster Bar with Playhouse staff.]

Helen Horn shared her recollections of John popping in to the Pocket Watch Shop in the Cove when she and her friend Stretch were running the lunch and tea room there.

> John happened to be a devoted customer of the shop and everything stopped when he came in. He was quite special, a demanding customer and a tad imperious in his ways. He would demand perfection when he came in. We would send the best waitress or myself out of the kitchen because he would expect that if he wanted something off of the menu, that we would fix it for him. And we did.

Bunny also recalls that John loved to go to breakfast and lunch, and loved having company with him.

> I spent a couple of summers in one of the little attic rooms at Dunelawn, and John would appear at 7:30 for breakfast. He always wanted somebody to go to breakfast with him, or to lunch with him. That was fine with me, especially when I was at Dunelawn because I couldn't cook. But eventually, he really needed somebody who was not on the staff at the theatre. He was quite fond of Barbara and she enjoyed his company.

Barbara's experience of John was informed not by how he ran the Playhouse, but by the sort of man he was privately.

> John was a delightful gentleman to be with in my world, whether I was helping him with an after-theatre supper at Dunelawn, or he was leaping out of his old red pick-up to open my door for me in front of the General Store in Alfred where we used to go for wonderful fish chowder. He used to give me his apartment in New York, when I was working there during the summer. He introduced me to many actors, some of whom I got to know quite well in New York and Connecticut in the winter. These were fun and interesting people and I enjoyed being with them. John was a great story-teller – stories of all colors. In the fall, when everyone could relax and get together, he would have us in stitches with some of his tales. I think this was a side of him that he kept pretty much under cover. It was very difficult for him to relax.

Another non-staff friend, Ron Hayes, who would meet John through his weekly two-hour yoga sessions in the lobby of the theatre, became a very supportive friend and walking buddy. As John neared the end of his active career at the Playhouse, he often sought out the opinions of townspeople about the direction in which the Playhouse was headed. Hayes was one of those who came to sit under the shade trees on the side lawn and just chat. As he says, "Not that John ever took any of our advice." After John died, Ron painted a full-length portrait of him that was displayed in the lobby of the Playhouse during the first year of Roy Rogosin's tenure.

During the '70s, the Ogunquit Playhouse no longer had the very beneficial relationship with old time theatrical reviewer for the *Portland Evening Express*, Harold L. Cail. Cail, a prodigious reviewer and a good friend to the Ogunquit Playhouse, died in 1968, and afterward, there were no more gossipy columns called *Two on the Aisle*.

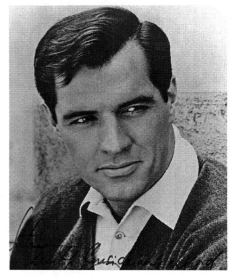

John Gavin.

In 1970, the thirty-eighth season, television's "Lonesome George," George Gobel, came back in *Play it Again Sam*. John Gavin appeared in *The Fantasticks!* William Shatner, the commanding officer of Star Ship Enterprise, appeared in *The Tender Trap*. Noel Harrison, son of Rex Harrison came to Ogunquit with a third revival of Noel Coward's *Blithe Spirit*. Other stars that season were Shirley Booth, Joan Fontaine, Van Johnson, Patrice Munsel, and Edward Mulhare – all of them back to Ogunquit for a second season, and Joan Fontaine and Shirley Booth were back for the third time.

Set of The Fantasticks! *Set design by Carole Lee Dixon, lighting by Marcia Madeira. Courtesy of Carole Lee Carroll.*

During the 1971 season, John Lane staged a period piece, *The Right Honourable Gentleman*, with Edward Mulhare, Beatrice Straight and Carolyn Lagerfelt. It was the story of a great scandal in Victorian England and it was well reviewed. Mulhare was then quite famous as the ghost in TV's *The Ghost and Mrs. Muir*.

1972 brought three musicals – *Man of La Mancha*, *The Merry Widow* for two weeks, and *Hello, Dolly!* Stars who appeared that year included Arlene Francis, Joan Fontaine, Robert Stack, Vivian Vance, Shirley Booth, and George Gobel.

In 1973, Art Carney returned in *The Prisoner of Second Avenue,* by Neil Simon. Barbara Carney, Art's second wife, appeared as his wife on stage. The critics gave the show excellent reviews. Gloria Hutchinson interviewed Carney for the *Coast Pilot*:

> (Carney) referred to the problem of losing his privacy, while other famous names thrive on making entrances, he'd rather sneak though the kitchen. He had gone down to the Ogunquit beach for a walk, but soon found himself running back to his room at the sedately private Dunelawn. "You know, you do like to go out and browse around, but you find you can't. So I go from this room to my dressing room and back." This Playhouse, he says, is his favorite among the New England summer theatres. "Well-managed, acoustically good, and an excellent crew." [50]

Sada Thompson starred in *Twigs*, four playlets written by George Furth. In New York, Sada had won the Tony Award for her performance. Even today Thompson says that she loved playing Ogunquit.

> John was always gracious and took me to late suppers. It was also the best run backstage on the circuit. Superb stage managers. And Harriet (Smith) always made her famous swordfish while I was there, and John could come.

Other plays and stars that year were Wilfred Hyde-White in *The Jockey Club Stakes,* Jerry Orbach in *6 Rms Riv Vu,* Jack Cassidy in *Suddenly At Home,* a new play being tested for Broadway that fall.

At the end of the 1973 season, Elliot Norton wrote in the *Boston Herald American* under the title, "Best Ogunquit Year; All Seats One Price"

Sada Thompson.

> The Ogunquit season, which ended last Saturday evening with the final performance of *Can-Can* was the best ever; most successful, most prosperous. Since the Playhouse has been running for 32 summers, this is a considerable record. Since one reason for the prosperity seems to be a change in pricing policy, it may be worth special attention.
>
> This year, for the second season, Lane followed an innovative ticket policy. Instead of offering seats for $5 in the front of the house and $3.50 farther back, he made them all one price: $5. To this raising of prices, paradoxically, he attributes the success of the season!
>
> Two years ago, he says, the box office people pointed out they were having trouble selling the cheaper seats. People who couldn't get $5 tickets refused to buy the others; they wanted the best or nothing. Or, in any case, if they couldn't get the best, they apparently wanted the most expensive tickets! Last summer's business was better than that of '71 at Ogunquit. This year, though many of the attractions seemed less likely to please than others which have played the theatre in previous

years, almost every seat was sold, every week. There were two weak Friday matinees, but no others. Because of higher prices? Apparently.

The Ogunquit season opened June 25 with Art Carney in *The Prisoner of Second Avenue* for two weeks. That was a likely hit: it is a Neil Simon play not yet shown in Boston and Art Carney is a summer favorite.

The popularity of some other Ogunquit shows might have been predicted in advance, but there were at least a few dubious ones: *Twigs,* for example, is three short plays dealing with some of the same characters: summer audiences don't ordinarily like short plays. Also, it stars Sada Thompson and although she is a fine actress, she is surely not a name. At Ogunquit, however, *Twigs* was a hit. So was *The Jockey Club Stakes* which is admittedly fun but which was by no means successful in New York; it had an abortive run on Broadway. *Can-Can* is twenty years old! But it was sold out in advance for the whole Ogunquit week. Of course, the price structure doesn't account for all of this successful season down Maine. But it may well be significant. It must have snob appeal.

Summer or winter, theatre managers have to have the attractions the public wants, and nobody can tell what these will be. The public makes up its own mind in its own mysterious ways. [51]

Rob Townsend who would replace a retiring John Lane in 1996, came to the Ogunquit Playhouse as a carpenter in 1972. He had come to Ogunquit the summer before to visit a friend, Bob Schenke, who was handling publicity for the Playhouse and had met John Lane and Henry Weller and in very short order, had been invited to come to work at the Playhouse.

> John Lane – who was Mr. Lane, of course, offered us both jobs for the following summer. I came, and that first summer was wonderful from the beginning. I stayed at the, then Governor King House, which became the Chapman house. I roomed with another guy, Dan Nelson, who was also from Freemont, Nebraska. It was a rigorous schedule. A typical week would be open the show on Monday night. Take Tuesday off, come back on Wednesday and start building and prepping for the next play, which would be mounted on Sunday after we tore down the standing set after the closing performance on Saturday night. We would "strike" the set into the wee hours, generally leaving by 5 a.m. on Sunday. It was mandated that we sleep five hours and then come back, so Sunday afternoon we would finish putting up the set, have a tech rehearsal with the incoming cast, tweak some more on Sunday night. Then on Monday, dress rehearsal in the afternoon and opening Monday night. It was pretty remarkable but it worked like clockwork.

Townsend worked as a "techie" for three summers and in the third summer (1974) he brought his new wife, Karen, to Ogunquit. She worked as a wardrobe mistress and he started the summer as a carpenter and wound up working with Darold Perkins, the set designer, as a painter. He says, "That was the summer that Nixon resigned, and there was a lot of stuff going on in the world, but our memories are all connected to Ogunquit."

The *Maine Sunday Telegram* on August 18, 1974, published a story called "Life Backstage Has Drama of its Own," by Elaine Killelea, in which she featured the new wardrobe mistress and other "techies" of that season. Karen Stein Townsend said of her job:

> It's a great way to learn the art of laundering and cleaning, says Karen Stein Townsend with amusement. Karen is spending her first summer in Maine…as a wardrobe mistress at the Ogunquit Playhouse. She wryly recalls that hot day during *No, No, Nanette* when she had more than fifty shirts to iron. "I took my ironing board outside on the back deck at the theatre, and just ironed all day long." "There's a certain aura of glamour and mystique that surrounds the theatre. But for all the glamour to the audience out front, work backstage means long hours, little recognition and lots of hassles," explains Paul Lambert, a young technician. But he adds proudly, "It's my way of life." Paul is in his fifth year at the Playhouse, a senior at Boston College. His sister, Suzy, is an usher, and his parents are longtime subscribers to the Playhouse. "When I was about 17, I guess, we were doing *Fiddler (On the Roof)* and one of the older kids in the show quit. They came backstage and asked who wanted a walk on? And I made my professional debut." [52] (Paul Lambert is today the Vice President of the Basketball Hall of Fame in Springfield, MA.)

The 1974 season carried *Sleuth*, with Patrick McNee; *No, No, Nanette*; *Born Yesterday*, starring Sandy Dennis; Steve Allen and Jayne Meadows in *Tonight at 8:30*; a two-week run of *The Unsinkable Molly Brown*, with Elaine Cancilla; Betsy Palmer and Fritz Weaver in *Life With Father*; Eileen Herlie and David McCallum starring in *Crown Matrimonial*; *Finishing Touches* with Barbara Bel Geddes; and *The Sunshine Boys* with Jack Guilford and Lou Jacobi. Starring in *Tonight at 8:30*, Steve Allen and Jayne Meadows received favorable notices and while in the area, Allen became a New Hampshire Volunteer to help promote public television throughout New Hampshire and southern Maine.

Finishing Touches was a new play by Jean Kerr, the author of *King of Hearts*, and *Please Don't Eat the Daisies*, which was turned into a television series and a movie. Barbara Bel Geddes returned to star with Laurence Hugo, who was also returning for a second season to Ogunquit.

With Betsy Palmer and Fritz Weaver starring in *Life With Father*, the Howard Lindsay/Russel Crouse award-winning comedy, Franklin Wright said "another huge success for John Lane and the Ogunquit Playhouse."[53]

That fall of 1974 Rob and Karen moved to New York so that he could pursue an acting career. But he never lost touch with John Lane. Rob remembers:

> I got a phone call from him one day asking if I would become a stage manager for one of the touring shows. Well, I had never stage managed, but I guess John saw

> something and thought I would be good at it. And actually, that decision, when I said yes, was a turning point for me. I stage managed *A Lion in Winter*, with Fritz Weaver and Beatrice Straight, and the young lady playing Alice in that production was Patty Lupone, who went on to great fame.

That opened a new door for Rob and he began a string of stage managing assignments. He was an advance stage manager.

> I did many shows and saw all of the New England theatres and how they operated. And I learned a great deal about the various means of production. What I learned basically was that Ogunquit did it right. That John Lane and Henry Weller had a system that worked. They were always treating actors who came in from out of town as guests, not simply as employees. They just made the system work very very well.

In 1975, the Ogunquit Playhouse produced the musical *Irene*; *The Two of Us* with Lynn Redgrave; *The Culture Caper*, a pre-Broadway Theatre Guild Production; Van Johnson starring in *Send Me No Flowers*; John Astin and Patty Duke Astin in *My Fat Friend*; Kitty Carlisle in *You Never Know*; Anne Russell in *The Boyfriend*; Sandy Dennis in *Cat on a Hot Tin Roof*; and Pat Carroll in *Something's Afoot*.

Robert Berkvist writing for the *New York Times* about the dearth of new material on the summer circuit, found a bright spot at the Ogunquit Playhouse

> Jerome Chodorov, whose credits include *My Sister Eileen,* and *Wonderful Town* has tackled John Updike's novel, *Bech* and the result is *The Culture Caper*, a comedy about a novelist whose horizons, sexual and otherwise, are considerably widened during a trip to Russia. [54]

But when Elliot Norton reviewed *The Culture Caper* for the *Boston Herald American,* he panned it.

> There is no plot in this story of a failed writer, so playwright Chodorov has had to invent one for his new play, which the Theatre Guild is touring on the summer circuit. ... Since it is still in the stages of reconstruction, under the direction of Jerome Chodorov's brother, Edward, no final judgement is possible ... As it looked at the Ogunquit Playhouse last Saturday, the principal problem was that newly invented plot.[55]

When Van Johnson opened in *Send Me No Flowers*, Franklin Wright wrote "Van Johnson has returned to the Ogunquit Playhouse, bringing with him something producer John Lane has been waiting for all summer – a non-musical hit." [56] Reviewers who saw Sandy Dennis in *Cat on a Hot Tin Roof* unanimously applauded Ronald Bishop as Big Daddy, and just as unanimously panned Dennis.

The Ogunquit Playhouse line-up for the 1976 centennial year included a two-week run of *Shenandoah* starring John Raitt; Victor Jory in *The Best Man*, by Gore Vidal, a political play for a summer with presidential primary conventions; Betsy Palmer and David Selby in *The Eccentricities of a Nightingale,* by Tennessee Williams; Eva Marie Saint with John McMartin in *The Fatal Weakness*, by George Kelly; two weeks of *Roberta* starring Ruth Warrick; David McCallum, Kurt Kasznar and Carole Shelley in Agatha Christie's *The Mouse Trap; Sabrina Fair,* the romantic comedy by Samuel Taylor, with a large cast of very notable actors; and *Godspell*, including two extra performances.

In 1976, the *Portland Press Herald* introduced a new column, *Thoughts and Things*, by Franklin Wright, and on June 9, 1976, he wrote:

> Operating a summer theatre is an enterprise well calculated to drive even the most even-tempered individuals to fits of fuming fury. … The challenge to summer theatre has grown in recent years. Costs have increased in all departments. Theatres have been forced to advance ticket prices. All seats, evening and matinee performances, will be $6.50 at the Ogunquit Playhouse this season. And while the cost problem plagues the producers, they are also finding it more difficult to come up with an acceptable schedule. The supply of quality contemporary plays has shriveled. I spoke of this with John Lane of the Ogunquit Playhouse last summer and I was reminded of it when I received his schedule for the coming season. Lane is not squeamish or prudish in his attitude toward plays and he does have what are possibly Maine's most sophisticated audiences. But he also has his standards. He won't do a play, however popular, which glorifies obscenity or which dwells on vulgarity merely for the sake of shock. That places further restraints upon a producer today. There used to be an adequate supply of "trickle down" plays. These were plays made available a year or two after their Broadway successes. That supply has almost dried up.[57]

Elliot Norton wrote in the *Boston Herald American:*

> *The Eccentricities of a Nightingale* by Tennessee Williams is a heroic revision of his *Summer and Smoke* and in its own right, a beautiful play. At the Ogunquit Playhouse now, with Betsy Palmer starred as Alma Winemiller, the Nightingale of the Delta, and David Selby as young Dr. Buchanan whom she loves, it is acted with honesty and insight.[58]

During the 1976 season, while Russell Nype appeared in *Sabrina Fair,* Ethel Merman was making a semi-annual visit to the Nype family in Kennebunkport and came to see the show. Franklin Wright wrote:

> The two of them together on stage again after all these years: Ethel Merman, one of the greatest stars the American musical theatre ever produced, and Russell Nype, longtime Kennebunkport resident who won national recognition when he appeared in *Call Me Madam.* They opened together on Broadway in October, 1950. [59]

In 1977, there were three musicals produced at the Playhouse, *Fiddler on the Roof, Oklahoma* and *I Do, I Do* starring John Raitt; *Seven Keys to Baldpate*; *Come Blow Your Horn*; *The Voice of the Turtle*; *The Royal Family*; and *An Almost Perfect Person*. The starring players, in addition to John Raitt, were David-James Carroll and Jane Rose in *Oklahoma,* Paul Lipson and Dolores Wilson in *Fiddler*, Doug McClure and Lou Jacobi in *Come Blow Your Horn*, Tony Perkins and wife, Berry Berenson, in *Voice of the Turtle*, Sandy Dennis and Gale Sondergaard (a last-minute replacement for Cathleen Nesbitt) in *The Royal Family* and Colleen Dewhurst, Rex Robbins and George Hearn in *An Almost Perfect Person*.

Billed as a zany comedy, *Seven Keys to Baldpate* by George M. Cohan rated a "short of standard" mark by Franklin Wright, who added:

> But however one may react to it, Ogunquit is the logical setting for it to be played. Cohan adapted it from a novel of that name written by Earl Derr Biggers while vacationing at Ogunquit's Cliff House in 1913. Biggers will be fondly remembered also as the creator of Charlie Chan, that Oriental Sherlock Holmes made famous in films.[60]

Sandy Dennis and Gale Sondergaarde in The Royal Family. *Photo courtesy of Dwight B. Shepard.*

Tony Perkins and his wife, Berry Berenson, starred in *The Voice of the Turtle*, and Berenson was featured in a *Boston Globe* story with her famous actress/model sister, Marisa Berenson. "The Berensons are the grand daughters of the late Paris couturier, Elsa Schiaparelli, who invented the term "shocking pink," and the daughters of diplomat Robert Berenson and the Marquesa Caciapuoli."[61] Berry made her first stage appearance that season. (Berenson was killed on flight 103 to Los Angeles on September 11, 2001.)

Fritzi Cohn reviewed *Come Blow Your Horn* for WCSH-TV, Portland. Though she gave the show a thumbs up, she said:

> Doug McClure, as the sophisticated playboy son, is handsome, tall, toothy and tow-headed...and completely miscast. At home in films, TV and on the range, he is hopelessly wrong as the New York Jewish Don Juan. Come on! Where would he park his horse on East 63rd Street?[62]

Young Richard Niles, in a non-starring role got rave reviews all around.

At the end of the 1977 season, Colleen Dewhurst starred in a Judith Ross play, *An Almost Perfect Person*. Kevin Kelly, reviewing for the *Boston Globe* wrote:

> *An Almost Perfect Person* is a menopausal romantic comedy in which Colleen Dewhurst plays a repressed New York widow who runs for Congress against a 72-year-old incumbent, gets defeated, and for reasons impossible to cram into this sentence, goes to bed with her campaign manager and her accountant in fairly rapid succession, all of which, I guess, comes under the heading: victory is sweet but defeat has its rewards. As written by Judith Ross, this slight, supposedly timely little comedy is padded, predictable and pathetically unfunny. If in fact it opens on Broadway, as it's scheduled to do…it's likely to have all the appeal of a rainy day at the polls.[63]

Elliot Norton said, "Although it has Colleen Dewhurst and two fine actors in support, An Almost Perfect Person is a notably imperfect comedy." [64]

The schedule for the 1978 season at the Ogunquit Playhouse included *Guys and Dolls*, with Julius LaRosa and Jo Sullivan; *The Play's the Thing*, with Patrice Munsel and Edward Mulhare; *Vanities* with a Broadway cast; *The Sound of Music*, by Rodgers and Hammerstein; Jean Marsh in Shakespeare's *Twelfth Night*; David McCallum and Carol Shelley in *Donkey's Years*; Maureen O'Sullivan in *No Sex, Please; We're British*; and Farley Granger as *Count Dracula*.

Nancy Grape, reviewing for the *Lewiston Evening Journal* said:

> If anybody had ever told me I'd drive well over 100 miles and stay up until after 1:00 in the morning to see one-time Arthur Godfrey crooner, Julius LaRosa, I'd have thought they were crazy. But that's exactly what we did last night, and – surprise! – it was worth it. [65]

At some point during those years, John asked Rob at the end of a summer to help him in the office during the winter. As Rob remembers:

> And so, again, that started a series of events for me. We would start about March 1 in an office at 111 West 57th Street, the Steinway building, and I never had a title, I just worked in the office with John and learned how the seasons were put together and how shows were put together. We worked from March until the season started and I became a sort of liaison for things needed in New York, while I pursued other stage managing jobs.

Sometime after 1974, Rob was invited to help John at the Royal Poinciana Playhouse in Palm Beach, where John ran a winter theatre season with Zev Buffman in Miami, an Atlanta theatre and some others. So eventually, Rob was working for John Lane on a year round basis: winter in Florida, spring and summer in Maine, and fall planning for the theatre in Palm Beach. He says:

> Then one day, John asked me if I would be the business manager at the Ogunquit Playhouse. That was a position that had gone through a series of people. Bill Traber had been, first and foremost, the business manager and what an act to follow!

So Rob came back to Ogunquit as the business manager in 1981. He learned long-hand accounting and how to do payroll, salary structures, and so forth, and do it with a pencil.

Rob Townsend and Henry Weller. Courtesy of Henry Weller.

Henry was a very patient teacher. So those years were about working in the office, getting the seasons ready in the spring and then going to Maine and operating them. By gum, those learning-on-the-job experiences – as a house manager, as a business manager, and a stage manager – I drank all that up and I learned from John Lane how theatres are run very effectively. Both of those theatres were run only on what we took in at the box office. That's no longer done, almost anywhere, except commercial theatre. Working in the front of the house in those days, we wore tuxes every night. The house management and John as producer, of course, wore a tuxedo.

During the 1980s, the Ogunquit Playhouse relied more heavily on musicals, and usually ran them for two weeks. For instance, Patrice Munsel appeared in *Mame* for two weeks at the beginning of the season. John Raitt came in *Carousel* for two weeks at the end.

And in between, Glynis Johns opened a new musical called *An April Song*, based on Jean Anouilh's romantic comedy, "which played New York and Boston in 1957 under the title of *Time Remembered*, with Richard Burton and Susan Strasberg," said Elliot Norton in a review on August 14, 1980. [66] He also said that *An April Song* "was a long way from Broadway." Midseason comedies included *Children*, with Sada Thompson, fresh from her appearances as Kate Lawrence on ABC's *Family*; and *The Gin Game*, by D.L.Coburn, starring Phyllis Thaxter and Larry Gates. Franklin Wright called their performance "peerless," and praised the Pulitzer-prize-winning play as well. [67]

In 1981, John Raitt returned for two weeks in *Pajama Game*, and Franklin Wright, [68] reminded readers that this was the musical that introduced Bob Fosse to Broadway and started Shirley MacLaine on her way to the top, when she was plucked out of the chorus line to fill in for Carol Haney one night. The third production of the 1981 season brought an alumna of Walter Hartwig's resident company, William Swetland, back on

John Lane in the front of the house.

The Gin Game, *Phyllis Thaxter and Larry Gates, 1980.*

An April Song, *Glynis Johns, 1980.*

Forever Plaid, *1994.*

Tracy Griswold and Lee Richardson in Arthur Miller's All My Sons, *1987.*

stage at the Ogunquit Playhouse. In *On Golden Pond*, with Janet Gaynor, he portrayed Norman Thayer, Jr. to her Ethel.

Townsend remained at the Playhouse as business manager through 1985 when an infant son called him back to New York to be a full-time dad. When he returned in 1994 as Assistant to the Producer, he brought the first computer into the Playhouse.

John really scoffed at that. He didn't want that new-fangled stuff. But that was the start of what happened ultimately in every business. We got computers in and got the box office on computers. And it was during that time that Henry and I began to realize that John was slowing down. I took more responsibility, in planning seasons, in negotiations and in executing contracts. As long as he was alive, John was the executive producer of the Playhouse, but the work shifted. In fact, if not in title, I took a lot of his work on, and Henry and I just maintained what had been before. There were some difficult days during that period. One year, during the 80s, John came down with shingles before the season opened and it affected him most of that year. That was really my first dip in the deep end because John really could not function. I would see him every day, visit with him and keep him abreast of what was going on. He had faith that things were going well, and I think Henry had good reports of what was going on, so we got through it.

Juliet Mills, Maxwell Caulfield, Tom Toner in Dial M For Murder *by Frederick Knott, 1998.*

Rob remembers:

Well then Mort (Mather) sort of got wind of what was going on. He'd been out at Laudholm and he understood nonprofit structures and I think it was probably Mort's idea, but between Henry and Mort, they came up with the idea to create the non-profit that could receive the Playhouse as a gift from John and therefore insure, not that the theatre would run as a theatre, but that the building and grounds would be maintained and not lost as a state property when John passed away.

Re-enter Mort Mather. Mather, who had been at the Playhouse as a stage manager for three seasons, 1966, 1968 and 1969, had gone on to organize the foundation that bought and preserved the 150-acre Laudholm Farm in Wells, turning it into a nonprofit institution under the direction of a board of directors and supported by fundraising. Mort remembers:

> I had saved Laudholm Farm and had that experience, and I had worked with people in Ogunquit for fundraising. I was an alumna of the Playhouse and Barbara and I were still friends with John – we had dinner with him a couple of times every summer for years, and he and Henry used to come out to the farm for breakfast. I was in a conversation with local businessman Steve Einstein and he asked something about the Playhouse, about after John what would happen to it. I said I didn't know, and he said the community would really be behind an effort to save the Playhouse. That kind of stuck in my mind, and I did something that I had never done before with John. I crossed the line. With John, if you crossed some line, it was like the iron curtain could come down on you. I don't know what gave me the courage to do it. But I remember it very well. I was sitting in my car outside the Playhouse and John was standing there. I said, "John, you know, you could do anything you wanted to perpetuate the Playhouse when you are no longer able or wanting to take care of it." And the iron curtain didn't come down, but what I saw in his face was that this was the first time that the thought of his not being there crossed his mind. We were both stunned. He was stunned at that first recognition of the future, and I was stunned that there was no plan in place. How can you have no heirs, and have this great big property and have cared for it so much year after year, and not have made any plan for the future.

John and Mort went their separate ways but sometime later, John called him to say that he wanted to talk to Mort about doing something for the Playhouse.

> I was told he had been to a lawyer who had told him that the first thing he had to do was get the Playhouse out of his estate. As long as it was there, everything would go to the IRS. Barbara and I talked. And I said I didn't want to do another fundraising campaign, and Barbara said, "Who else can do it? You've got to." So I drafted a letter for John to sign. It said if I could put together a 501-C3 organization, get tax-exempt status for this organization and raise $500,000 for an endowment by eighteen months after the date of the letter, John would gift the Playhouse to the town to be run by a foundation board of directors.

Mort recalls that, at the outset, he believed it would be very easy to raise the money.

> For me, that was a no-brainer. If I couldn't raise $500,000 in Ogunquit for the Playhouse, there was something wrong somewhere. I was not figuring on the lockboxes on the wallets in Ogunquit. It was amazingly difficult. I hadn't raised very much money in Ogunquit for Laudholm, but I thought, well, that's bad blood between Ogunquit and Wells and the farm is not in Ogunquit. Since this was the

Playhouse, the most visible property in Ogunquit, how could it possibly be difficult? But it was. But it was pulling hen's teeth all the way.

On August 11, 1996, the first board of directors of the Ogunquit Playhouse Foundation put on a magnificent fundraising tribute to John Lane, the *"Thank You, John Lane"* Gala.

Many of the actors who had populated the Playhouse over the years came to appear in the gala and offer their congratulations to the new Foundation. The show was staged by Evans Haile, a longtime associate of John's and now the producer at the Cape Playhouse. And Evans Haile shared MC honors with Betsy Palmer, who had appeared at the Playhouse 11 times. Betsy Palmer began by saying:

> I drove in that curving drive up to the front door of that beautiful place called Dunelawn. I walked into that door and looked through a hallway to another door that looked out on that lovely Atlantic Ocean. And in the center of that hall, was standing that man, that compact man, with delicious buns. With sparkling blue eyes and a face full of character.

Palmer went on to describe her first visit to John's studio in the Colony field:

> The first time I went into John's house, that little soft dove grey studio that he lived in. One thing I remember to this day. There was an oil canvas on the wall, a painting of a pair of hands. I thought it was beautiful and asked him whose hands they were, and he said, "Mine." Then he explained that Helen, his wife, had painted a portrait of him; that she hadn't been happy with it, so she cut out the hands. And those were the hands that helped me, that spanked me when I needed it, that applauded good work, that hammered sets, that planted and tended the grounds. (I remember you, John, working with Alden Shum always making things look more beautiful.) Those hands are the ones that built this wonderful Playhouse. And tonight, I am offering you my heart in my hands, for all that you have done. [See color plate II.]

Palmer amused the full-house audience of donors with this story:

> You know there is a shrub at the Playhouse – its part of the privet and near the stage door, and John shaped it into a heart and said, "Betsy, I'm giving this to you, here is your heart." And it's so funny because I work all around the country and I was just in Virginia doing *Blithe Spirit* and a man I was working with had been to Ogunquit and he said, "Oh, I saw your bush!" Well, it's known as my bush I guess, but it's really John's heart.

Kitty Carlisle, introduced by Evans Haile as "one of the best friends the arts can have in this country, a lovely tiger," was effusive in her praise for the Ogunquit Playhouse.

The John Lane Years 137

John Lane with John Raitt, Kitty Carlisle, Betsy Palmer, and Rob Townsend, at the 1996 Gala.

Betsy Palmer and John.

Cast of the "Thank You, John Lane" Gala, 1996.

> I am so pleased to be here tonight particularly because this is the night that belongs to you and to John Lane and to all of us who love him and love this theatre. This theatre has meant so much to so many people. It has trained so many people. I've seen so many young people here, and it has been arranged through the generosity of John that it is going to go on, and it is going to be a foundation and you here tonight are helping to do that. It is a wonderful institution that I really love.

Kitty Carlisle continued:

> You know, there are very few of these places left that can show the works of past playwrights to young people coming along, the generations behind us. And that is such an important part of our culture.

Midway through the evening's performance, Mort Mather and Rob Townsend announced that the full $500,000 endowment had just been raised [see color plate III]. Governor Angus King said:

> This state is like a big small town. We care about each other, and we care about our institutions. And the Ogunquit Playhouse is certainly one of our finest. I'm here to honor what you have achieved, and to honor John Lane.

On September 24, 1997, the *York County Coast Star* announced that the "deed is passed and a new day is dawning for the Ogunquit Playhouse." The article by Giselle Goodman said that approximately 825 people had donated money to the Foundation. And Mort Mather was quoted as saying, "I really feel good knowing that the Playhouse is going to be there in the future." Speaking for John Lane, Henry Weller said, "It was always John's goal to perpetuate the life of this theatre which was his life's work. With this gift of the theatre to the Foundation, he has been able to assure its continued existence."

The article went on to say:

> One certain change for the 1998 year, which opens on June 29, is a 10 percent discount on season subscriptions – which has never been offered before, Mather said. [69]

The Ogunquit Playhouse was about to begin its third act.

Henry Weller and Joe Hill at the Gala.

Governor King with Mort Mather and Rob Townsend.

Gathering for the transfer of deed of The Ogunquit Playhouse from John Lane to the Ogunquit Playhouse Foundation. From left, Ogunquit Foundation President Mort Mather, Vice President Karen Maxwell, attorney Brad Moulton, Henry Weller, representing John Lane, and Homer Waterhouse. Courtesy of the York County Coast Star.

Endnotes ~ Chapter 2

1. *Portsmouth Herald,* November 5, 2000, obituary John C. Lane.
2. *The Ogunquit Breeze*, mid-winter edition, December, 1950.
3. *Portland Evening Express,* July 8, 1952. Harold L. Cail, "Ogunquit Players' Presentation Welcome Relief from Glamour."
4. On October 28, 2006, an oral history on the subject of the Ogunquit Playhouse was hosted by the Ogunquit Heritage Museum, and a large group of people from town and away were invited to join Henry Weller and share recollections of their experiences at the Playhouse. Many of the people who attended are quoted in this book. Helen Horn was one of them.
5. *Wells-Ogunquit Compass,* July 2, 1959, by Paula Lawrence.
6. Ellie Asherman, a summer resident, who came to the October 28, 2006, oral history with her husband, Adrian Asherman. Ellie was a student at The Manhattan Theatre Colony in 1952 and 1953.
7. *Portland Press Herald,* June 25, 1956, Harold L. Cail, *Two on the Aisle.*
8. *Portland Press Herald,* July 4, 1956, Harold L. Cail, "*Bus Stop* Now at Ogunquit."
9. *Portland Evening Express,* July 24th, 1956
10. *Portland Evening Express*, July 27th, 1956, Harold L Cail, *Two on the Aisle.*
11. *Portland Evening Express,* July 27th, 1956, Harold L Cail, *Two on the Aisle.*
12. *Portland Evening Express,* July 31. 1956, Jeanette Pomeroy, "Excellent Cast at Ogunquit Offers Smart-Moving Comedy."
13. *New York Times,* July 23, 1956, Arthur Gelb, "Summer Try-outs for Three Shows."
14. *Portland Press Herald,* Harold Cail, August 11, 1956.
15. Recollections from Mike Horn, "Do You Remember, Part 5" recorded October 28, 2006, by the Ogunquit Heritage Museum.
16. *Boston Sunday Post*, Drama Page, pg 14, September 2, 1956.
17. *New York Post,* June, 1957, "Straw Hat," by Sylvia F. Porter.
18. *Boston Daily Record, Elliot Norton Writes,* "Christie's 'Witness' Doing Well on Road." August 13, 1957.
19. *Portland Evening Express,* August 20, 1957, Harold Cail, "Star of 'Inherit the Wind' Would Alternate Roles."
20. *Portland Evening Express,* August 22, 1957, Harold Cail, *Two on the Aisle.*
21. *Portland Evening Express,* Harold L. Cail, August 20, 1957.
22. *Boston Daily Record*, Elliot Norton, July 14, 1957, "Ogunquit's Tradition."
23. *Portland Evening Express,* May 16, 1958, Harold L. Cail, *Two on the Aisle.*
24. *Portland Evening Express,* August 15, 1958 Harold L. Cail, *Two on the Aisle,* "Budding Thespians."
25. *Portland Evening Express*, August 28, 1958, Harold L. Cail, *Two on the Aisle.*
26. *Boston Sunday Herald,* June 28, 1959, Elinor Hughes, "Summer Theater is Now Top Hat."
27. *Associated Press,* Portland, ME, July 16, 1959, wire story.
28. *Newsweek,* fall 1958, Betsy Palmer story.
29. *Portland Evening Express*, May 19, 1960, Harold L. Cail, *Two on the Aisle.*
30. *Boston Daily Record,* July 11, 1960, *Elliot Norton Writes.*
31. *Portland Evening Express*, July 11, 1960, Harold L. Cail, *Two on the Aisle.*
32. *Portland Press Herald,* August 31, 1960, Harold L. Cail.
33. *Show-Business*, 8/22/60, Ray Yates, "Maine Turning Back the Clock Toward More Resident Summer Stock

Companies."
34. *Portland Evening Express,* August 7, 1961.
35. *Boston Record American,* July 10, 1962, *Elliot Norton Writes.*
36. *Boston Record American,* July 17, 1962, *Elliot Norton Writes.*
37. *Boston Record American,* July 8, 1963, *Elliot Norton Writes,* "Art Carney at his Best in Stage 'Ginger' Play."
38. *Portland Evening Express,* July 31, 1963, "Prop Hat is Parisienne Treasure."
39. *Portland Evening Express,* July 2, 1964, Harold C. Cail, *Two on the Aisle.*
40. *Portland Evening Express,* June 3, 1964, Harold Cail, *Two on the Aisle.*
41. *Portland Evening Express,* June 29, 1964, "Barbara Bel Geddes Opens Season at Ogunquit Tonight."
42. *Boston Record American,* July 2, 1964, *Elliot Norton Writes.*
43. *Portland Sunday Telegram,* August 29, 1965, Harold Cail, *Two on the Aisle.*
44. *Portland Evening Express,* July 21, 1965.
45. *Boston Sunday Globe,* August 15, 1965.
46. *WCSH TV,* Portland, Fritzi Cohn, Drama Critic.
47. *Portland Press Herald,* July 17, 1968.
48. *Portland Evening Express,* July 30, 1968, Harold L. Cail.
49. *Boston Record American,* August 30, 1968, *Elliot Norton Writes.*
50. *Coast Pilot,* July 3, 1973, Art Carney.
51. *Boston Herald American,* September 7, 1973, "Best Ogunquit Year; All Seats One Price."
52. *Maine Sunday Telegram,* August 18, 1974.
53. *Portland Press Herald,* August 7, 1974, Franklin Wright, "Another huge success."
54. *New York Times,* July 18, 1975.
55. *Boston Herald American,* July 18, 1975, *Elliot Norton Writes.*
56. *Portland Press Herald,* July 23, 1975, Van Johnson.
57. *Portland Press Herald,* June 9, 1976, Franklin Wright on plays.
58. *Boston Herald American,* July 20, 1976, *Eccentricities.*
59. *Portland Press Herald,* August 26, 1976, Franklin Wright.
60. *Portland Press Herald,* July, 1977, Franklin Wright.
61. *Boston Globe,* July 15, 1977, Berensons.
62. *WCSH-TV* Portland, Fritzi Cohn, Drama Critic, July 19, 1977, McClure.
63. *Boston Globe,* August 16, 1977, "An Almost Perfect Person."
64. *The Boston Herald American,* August 31, 1977, Elliot Norton.
65. *Lewiston Evening Journal,* June 27, 1978, LaRosa.
66. *Boston Herald American,* August 14, 1980, Elliot Norton, *An April Song.*
67. *Portland Press Herald,* July 16, 1980, Franklin Wright, *The Gin Game.*
68. *Portland Press Herald,* July 2, 1981, Franklin Wright, *The Pajama Game.*
69. *York County Coast Star,* September 24, 1997. "Playhouse goes from founder to Foundation."

Gary Merrill and Bette Davis visit John Lane sometime during the 1950s, perhaps to see Dear Charles *in 1954.*

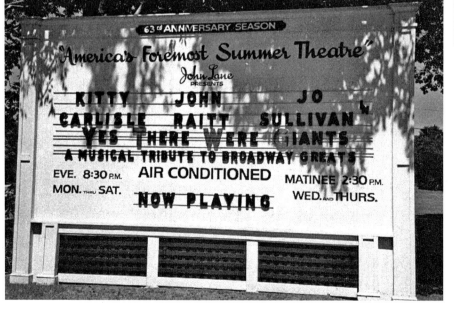

America's Foremost Summer Theatre

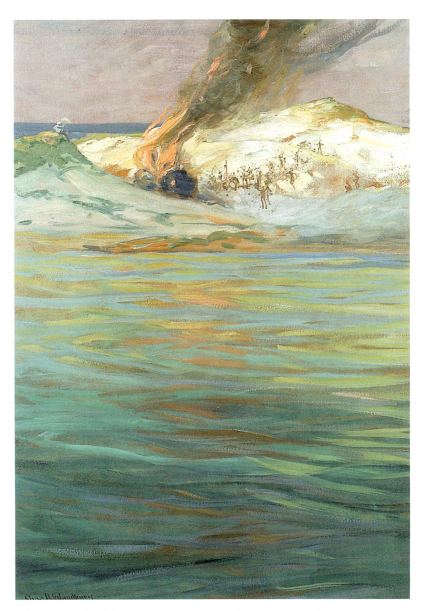

Plate I. "Bride of Ogunquit," oil on paper/board by Charles H. Woodbury.
Photo Courtesy of Skinner, Inc., Boston, MA

Plate II. John Lane's hands. Oil painting by Helen Lane. Courtesy of Henry Weller.

America's Foremost Summer Theatre

Plate III. Mort Mather and Karen Maxwell in front of the challenge board with $500,000 raised, 1996.

Plate IV. Cast of the "Thank You, John Lane" Gala, 1996. Courtesy of Ann Clark. All show images in this section by Stuart Nudelman.

Plate V. Grease, 2000.

Plate VI. Liz Sheridan and John Sloman in Something's Afoot, *a mystery musical based on* Ten Little Indians, *1998.*

America's Foremost Summer Theatre

Jana Robbins, Karen Black and Mike Burstyn in
The Tale of the Allergist's Wife, *2003.*

Plates VII. Felicia Finley and David Brummel in Evita, *2003.*

Plate IX. Annie, *2003.*

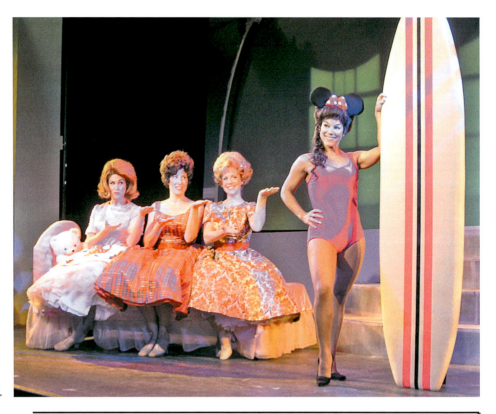

Plate X. Beehive, *2006.*

Plate XI. 42nd Street, *2001.*

Plate XII. Cinderella, *2006.*

Plate XIII. Leslie Uggams, Cinderella, *2006.*

Plate XIV. Ain't Misbehavin', *2003.*

Plate XVI. Hello Dolly!, *2006.*

Plate XV. Joseph and the Amazing Technicolor Dreamcoat, *2001.*

Plate XVII. Set design by Don Jensen, for Captain Brassbound's Conversion, *1961. Courtesy of Carole Lee Carroll.*

Plate XVIII. Darold Perkins' set design and notes for The Little Foxes, 1968. Courtesy of Barbara Mather.

Plate XIX. Crew list painted on scene shop wall, 1988.

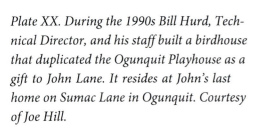

Plate XX. During the 1990s Bill Hurd, Technical Director, and his staff built a birdhouse that duplicated the Ogunquit Playhouse as a gift to John Lane. It resides at John's last home on Sumac Lane in Ogunquit. Courtesy of Joe Hill.

The Manhattan Theatre Colony

The resident company of the Manhattan Theatre Colony was originally and during all of the Hartwig years, a group of professional actors and actresses with many years of experience between them. They spent the season in Ogunquit, taking different parts each week in productions which either had a visiting starring actor or whose cast was entirely made up of the resident company members. From the beginning of the Manhattan Theatre Colony in 1927 in Peterborough, New Hampshire, the Hartwigs were always able to attract a very talented and widely accomplished resident company.

A *New York Times* article referred to Hartwig's second season at Bristol as a company of players with Broadway experience working without benefit of a visiting star system.

> A summer workshop and a smaller theatre for the production of comedies and old melodramas are additional features of this colony, which is advertised as "a training base for the arts of the theatre." [1]

In addition to the resident company, the Hartwigs offered a junior membership to younger, less experienced individuals who were interested in learning more about the theatre. These young people followed an elaborate schedule of classes, put on their own plays, and in Ogunquit, worked first in the Village Studio on Hoyt's Lane, and in 1936, moved to the Colony Club, a building that Hartwig had purchased for rehearsals and Colony shows. Later they moved into a tent in the field behind the Playhouse, and then into two pavilions built by Maude and later enclosed by John Lane. Rumor has it that the Colony Club building had been a speakeasy and dance hall during the '20s.

In the summer of 1927, The Manhattan Theatre Camp offered courses in acting, directing, playwriting, scenic and costume design and allied subjects for eight weeks. "The camp," declared Hartwig to the *New York Times*, "will not be a school in the ordinary sense, but rather a workshop of the theatre where practical training will be given by experts active in the commercial theatre." [2]

Mary-Leigh Smart remembers the years that the Hartwigs had a company in residence. She remembers A.J. Herbert ("Oh, I had an awful crush on him."), Carl Benton Reid, Daisy Atherton, Laurette Taylor, and Rhys Williams, who went on to become a prominent character actor in Hollywood.

Hartwig's vision of the Manhattan Theatre Repertory Company made the transition to Ogunquit without change. And in fact, in Ogunquit, the concept of a resident company and a junior company of students in training, flourished and grew. By 1935, the Manhattan Theatre Colony was a multi-faceted entity, the best description of which comes in the 1935 playbill under the title, "Our Apprentices."

> The Manhattan Theatre colony, of which the Ogunquit Playhouse is the most celebrated feature, comprises a good deal more than just the professional company at the Playhouse. Mr. Hartwig has established here in Ogunquit a colony of people whose interests are centered around the arts of the theatre. He has established an apprentice group which has grown each year until he has been forced to limit the number of members. The apprentices are young people who are studying the arts of the theatre-acting, directing, playwriting and the scenic arts. Mr. John Kirkpatrick is the director of the apprentice group, and has already presented at the Studio Theatre in Hoyt's Lane, two groups of one-act plays, laboratory productions for which the apprentices build their own sets, supervise their own lighting and devise their own costumes. The apprentices have two hours of dancing every morning, designed to develop poise and rhythm and to overcome defects in posture and body control. Apprentices work on props for the Playhouse productions and in some cases are chosen to play a small part with the company. This week two of the apprentices who have shown great promise, Sally Osmund and George Lloyd, are playing in Jane's Legacy. (Note: George Lloyd was associated with Orson Welles' Mercury Theatre, but later gained fame as a night club performer.)

Dance class at the Colony Theatre on School Street. Courtesy of the New York Public Library.

Bosley Crowther, in the *New York Times,* June, 1935, wrote:

> This season (Hartwig) will have on hand for his regularly distinguished permanent company such actors and actresses as Daisy Atherton, A.J. Herbert, Frank Roberts, Edward Emery, Stiano Braggiotti, John Drew Colt and others. These with his list of guest stars – Ethel Barrymore, Alexandra Carlisle, Fritzi Scheff, Mitzi Green and Libby Holman – should assure him of lively attendance. [3]

Of course, the playbill of July 20th proclaimed that "The air is still ringing with the praises accorded Mr. John Kirkpatrick and our apprentices for the splendid production of three one-act plays given at the Colony Club Theatre on School Street last week."

> **1936 Apprentice Plays**
>
> A bill of three one-act plays, the first presentation of our apprentice group, will be given at the Colony Club theatre of School Street, Ogunquit, under the direction of John Kirkpatrick, director of the apprentice group. The plays are *Number Ten,* by Sidney and Muriel Box; *The Great Dark,* by Don Tothero; and a satire by Audrey Ensor, six variations on an original theme, called *The Perfect Plot.* This production is a representation of how six famous dramatists would handle the same plot. The production will be entirely the work of the apprentice group, which is a separate entity from the professional company at the Playhouse. They are doing remarkable work under Mr. Kirkpatrick's supervision, and have designed and built the settings, and done the costuming themselves. The public is cordially invited to attend the performances, which will take place at 8:30 Friday evening and 4:30 Saturday afternoon. There will be a nominal admission of twenty-five cents, and tickets may be obtained at the Playhouse box office.

One innovation at the Colony Club Theatre in 1936 was the opening of the Colony Club, a café situated in the same building. It was a place where members of the Repertory Company could go for lunch and after the show to eat and talk. In the playbill it is described as:

> the place where the members of the company, the apprentices and staff and Big Chief W.H. and his charming missus and all friends of the colony get together for lunch and after-performance snacks. Miss Hillgas gives us delicious and too-tempting food, and there is gayety and theatre-talk galore.

Also in 1936, the apprentices staged the *Medea* by Euripides, under the direction of Ernita Lascelles. Costumes were designed based on the loan from Boston Public Library of a large number of plates illustrating authentic Greek costume. Sets were designed by one of a group of young artists who competed for the honor.

Ernita Lascelles and the apprentice group that appeared in The Medea. *Courtesy Carole Lee Carroll.*

John Kirkpatrick was practically a charter member of the Manhattan Theatre Colony, having started with Hartwig at Peterborough. He was the author of two successful Broadway plays, *Charm*, and *Ada Beats the Drum*, which was made into a motion picture. In 1937, following the successful revival of *The Lancashire Lass*, the playbill of week nine paid tribute to his successes with the apprentice group:

> For eight summers he has been in charge of the apprentice group of the Manhattan Theatre, and it is due in large measure to his splendid direction and sympathetic guidance that our apprentices have given the Colony such enthusiastic praise.

Jack Kirkpatrick would go on to run the Manhattan Theatre Colony until 1957. His tenure lasted for 25 years or more, and after he left, the Colony had several new directors and finally was closed after the 1965 season.

The Manhattan Theatre Colony – both the resident company and the junior members – thrived during the Hartwig years. During the war, Maude used the junior players and put on eight shows in 1942. By 1943, she was forced to close, but the theatre was open again in 1944. With this kind of strength, the Manhattan Theatre Colony of the Ogunquit Playhouse would continue under John Lane until 1965.

Colony instructors, 1953. Front row: Peter Poor, Design; George Fluharty, Voice and Diction. Back row: Alan Kass, Stage Movement; Daisy Atherton, Assistant Director; and Jack Kirkpatrick, Director. Courtesy of Carole Lee Carroll.

It continued as a theatre school but without the resident company of professionals also taking part in Playhouse productions. In fact, it became one of the premiere summer theatre schools in the country.

Maude Hartwig wrote about the junior players in the first playbill of the 1946 season:

> A junior membership in the Colony is designed for those who want training and experience in some particular department of the theatre. It is an opportunity for the potential actor to act, for the potential director to acquire the necessary technique, for the designer, the lighting technician, for all, in short, who plan a career in the theatrical world to broaden their knowledge and experience in their chosen fields. All the work of the Junior membership is practical; there is no abstract theory taught.

Members of the Manhattan Theatre Colony in 1942. Front row: Peggy Thedick, Rosalie Howell, Mary Keep, Rita Cardone. Back row: Laviah Lucking, Don Doherty, Kermit Kegley, Joe Emmet, Mahlon Ross. Behind: John Kirkpatrick.

Registration for the Colony players that year was the largest it had ever been, due in some measure to the return of G.I.s. (The Colony that year was accredited by the U.S. government, which allowed openings to be filled by veterans on the G.I. bill.) Mention is made that year of the fact that as soon as building restrictions are lifted, the new student theatre and snack bar will be constructed on the same property as the Playhouse occupies.

One tradition of the junior players that carried on into the '50s and '60s was the presence of offspring of celebrities in the theatre. Diana Barrymore, daughter of John Barrymore and Michael Strange, was there in 1939 and 1940. She starred with Phillip Faversham, the son of William Faversham, in *Romeo and Juliet* in 1939. Others had included Bill Hopper, son of Hedda and DeWolf Hopper; Russell Gleason, son of Lucille and James Gleason. In 1946, Barbara Brady, daughter of Katherine Alexander and grand-daughter of Grace George and William A. Brady, joined the junior players.

In the '50s and '60s, the Colony would be a proving ground for such actors as Linda Hope, daughter of Bob Hope; Brian Carney, son of Art Carney; Henry Hasso, son of Signe Hasso; Ted Nelson, son of Celeste Holm and Emmy award-winning director, Ralph Nelson; Judy Rice, daughter of Betty Field and playwright Elmer Rice; Susan Andrews, daughter of Dana Andrews; Barbara Grant, daughter of Bess Meyerson; Schuyler Aubrey, daughter of Phyllis Thaxter and her

Diana Barrymore and William Faversham in Romeo and Juliet.

ex-husband, CBS-TV president, James T. Aubrey; Penny Windust, daughter of the late theatre director, Bretaigne Windust; Julie Goldsmith, daughter of actress, Janet Fox; Ginger Brubeck, niece of Dave Brubeck, Susan Sawyer, daughter of Barbara Bel Geddes, Ian MacKenzie, Monty Compton, and Mary Fay Compton, the children of actor Francis Compton; Barbara Green, daughter of Betty Furness, and many others. Phyllis Thaxter would be the Colony student with the greatest longevity at the Ogunquit Playhouse. Thaxter began as a junior player and appeared in *At the Theatre*, with Laurette Taylor, and in the new Playhouse's first production, *Boy Meets Girl*, in 1937. She went on to appear many times at the Playhouse over the years, and her daughter, Skye Aubrey, was also a Colony student in the '60s. Thaxter's last role at the Playhouse was in *The Gin Game*, with Larry Gates in 1980.

During the '30s and '40s, under Maude Hartwig's direction, the Junior Players participated in productions almost every week. With Jack Kirkpatrick and others offering instruction each day, the students certainly learned and also had a wonderful time.

Carol Collery, Colony student, 1952 and 1953. Courtesy of Carole Lee Carroll.

By the '50s, the Manhattan Theatre Colony of the Ogunquit Playhouse had become the place for young aspiring actors to be. Carol Collery Shuttleworth, who arrived in 1952, came because Bramwell Fletcher, the president of Actors' Equity Association at the time, met up with her at another summer theatre and said:

> "This place is a dump, the place to go is Ogunquit." He sent me a one-cent postcard telling me to contact John Lane, which I did. We met at the Town Hall Club in New York. And I came to the Colony in 1952. It was the most wonderful experience. I didn't follow up in acting, but I learned a lot. I learned poise. I learned to talk in front of people. I feel that it's true, it was the best school in the country. There was George Fluharty, who taught us diction; there was Jack Kirkpatrick, who was our director, and Francis Dixon, who was our tech director. On opening night, we got dressed up. John had said bring dressy clothes because people get dressed up here. We went to elegant parties at Channing Hare's (a well-known portrait painter in Ogunquit). It was social, it was educational, it was a wonderful experience. I look back on it as such a happy time. Ogunquit was such a pretty little village. The theatre, the art colony. Everything contributed to making it a very rich experience.

* In October, 2006, a large group of people from town and away were invited to join Henry Weller and share recollections of their experiences with the Playhouse. Many of these people have been quoted here and elsewhere in the text. Carol Shuttleworth and Ellie Asherman, who had been Colony students in 1952 and 1953, were there. Their recollections and others were captured and used in this book.

Luncheon at "Act IV," the cottage that Carol Shuttleworth and Ellie Asherman shared in 1952. Left to right: Jane Seiden, Carol Collery, Lilia Skala (a featured actress in Here's Mama). Seated on Miss Skala's right is Jo Taub, on her left are Ellie Treble and Judy Alexander, and in front is Doris Davis. Courtesy of Carol Shuttleworth.

Three Men on a Horse, Colony production 1952. Courtesy of Carol Shuttleworth.

Peg O My Heart, Colony production 1952. Left to right: Donal Cardwell, Judy Alexander, Dick Dow, Jo Taub, Hank Gillen and Carol Collery. Courtesy of Carol Shuttleworth.

The Manhattan Theatre Colony students not only staged their own shows, with the help of Jack Kirkpatrick, Daisy Atherton and George Fluharty, and others, they also were called upon from time to time to appear in lesser parts at the "big" Playhouse. Ellie Asherman recalls that her first appearance at the Playhouse was as the ghost in *Gramercy Ghost* at the Playhouse, a non-speaking part, but it was her first.

Carol Shuttleworth remembers:

> Daisy Atherton was the acting coach and she was absolutely superb. She was here as part of the resident company before I came. By the time I came in the '50s, they didn't have a resident company. But from what I heard, she could upstage anybody. She was so charming. She often played with Monty's father (Francis Compton), they were both character actors. As she aged, she couldn't remember her lines so that after a while, I heard she put little post-its around the set to remind herself. But she could upstage anyone.

Ellie Asherman told the group (at the oral history in 2006):

Colony students Judy Alexander, Ellie Treble and Doris Davis with Daisy Atherton in New York. Courtesy of Carol Shuttleworth.

> I got this idea when I was 16 years old that I wanted to go into the theatre, so I told my father that I wanted to be in the Manhattan Theatre Colony. But I didn't tell him that I was going into the theatre. I think he smelled a rat, and felt like he had to investigate it. So I think that he went to Helen Lane and had tea with her in her apartment in Manhattan, and from then on he knew that everything was going to be wonderful. And it was absolutely thrilling. I think part of that was that we were doing something that we believed so strongly in, that our hearts and souls were in it. We worked so hard for Daisy Atherton and George Fluharty. He used to tell me that I had a lisp. I never had a lisp. But he would make me say "peaches" over and over again. I remember looking out over the audience in *I Remember Mama*. I had a very dramatic scene and I looked out over the audience and there really is a marriage between you and the audience. I think also that John Lane and Henry and Daisy and George, they were all so sincere in what they were teaching us. And I don't remember that there was ever any jealousy. Carol would get a part, or I would get a part. And I don't think anybody was jealous. It was such a thrilling time.

In 1953, Carol Collery and Ellie Asherman returned. On the next page are the casts of some of the plays that the Colony put on that year.

Goodbye My Fancy. *All photos this page courtesy of Carol Collery Shuttleworth.*

Charm.

The Women, *in which Mary Fay Compton, daughter of Francis Compton, appeared (standing, first on the right).*

During these years, the Colony students were often invited to meet with the stars and sometimes that even led to a lecture or even just an opportunity to ask questions.

Students learn how to execute "stage business," demonstrated by Joan Blondell. Courtesy of Carol Shuttleworth.

Students who supported Lillian Gish in Miss Mabel, *1951. Courtesy of Carol Shuttleworth.*

Colony students in class, 1953. Courtesy of Carol Shuttleworth.

Colony students working on the script of Glad Tidings *with Melvyn Douglas, 1952.*

Basil Rathbone discusses voice and diction with the students. Courtesy of Carol Shuttleworth.

Hume Cronyn and Jessica Tandy give an acting class for Colony and staff, 1958.

Colony students with Francis Compton, 1951. Courtesy of Carole Lee Carroll.

Colony students rehearse curtain calls. Courtesy of Carol Shuttleworth.

Colony students in those days even got recognized in public because they were acting in new plays every week, and the performances were often sold out. Ellie remembers:

> Once I was in Tower's Drugstore where they had a soda fountain, and a little kid asked me for my autograph. I couldn't tell him how totally thrilled I was, but that was a wonderful memory. I have memories from the Colony that have lasted all my life. And I have to say that Henry was the man. He was about 30 years old, so handsome and so wise. And he was looking out after us all.

Henry Weller recalled at this point, "We very often had breakfast in the drugstore because they had a counter. And there was a little lady who made all the muffins. That was Flo!" (He was referring to the Flo who later became quite famous for her hot dogs and now has numerous hot dog stands, even in Freeport, ME.)

Ellie Asherman continued:

> Betty Furness was really a show woman. And didn't she tell a story about how she always had to open the refrigerator door, and one time the refrigerator door wouldn't open? I remember Lillian Gish once went with us on an evening picnic in the dunes. She was quite old at the time, so I really thought that was super of her to do.

During the 1960s, the Manhattan Theatre Colony attracted many off-spring of theatre folk. But in the early years, that dynamic was just getting started. Ian MacKenzie, youngest son of Francis Compton, a longstanding resident company member under the Hartwigs and a very successful actor with a long and distinguished career, remembers growing up in Ogunquit:

> When I grew up in Ogunquit in the early '50s, we lived at the entrance of Perkins Cove, and the street was a dirt road. I started out delivering posters for the Colony Theatre. I was Jack Kirkpatrick's godson and also John Lane's godson. I was very lucky. When you were a student there, you'd be in a show at the Colony, and you'd be in a bit part at the Playhouse, you were always busy.

Monty Compton, the second son of Francis Compton, was also very much a part of the Ogunquit Playhouse in the '50s. "I was very young and I had a few walk-on parts." Later he worked as an usher and concession manager in the Playhouse.

> I worked in the concession and nowadays most people use calculators; but I remember on a hot day at a matinee, everybody wanted a cold drink. So it was like a ballet. I just remember how tight the ship was. Everyday the deposits went in, both for the bar and for the

Colony students work light crew with Francis Dixon, and build sets for the main stage.

At the oral history in October, 2006: 1. Betty Dixon. 2. Carole Lee Carroll. 3. Helen Horn. 4. Henry Weller. 5. Adrian Asherman and Mike Horn. 6. Brad Kenney. 7. Ellie Asherman. 8. Ian MacKenzie and Henry Weller. 9. Carol Collery Shuttleworth. 10. Monty Compton. 11. Sylvia Rubin. 12. Barb Woodbury, Henry Weller and Ellie Asherman. 13. Barbara Hilty.

Celeste Holm joined Colony students Monty Compton, Sandra Kulcson, John Handy, Penny Armstrong, Barbara Keith, Ken Vitulli, Helen Gulley, David Knapp and Jackie Munsol, while appearing in Invitation to a March, *1961.*

Gale Dixon, left, dressed for the role of Little Willie in the Colony production of East Lynn, *1948, and taking a fencing lesson, in 1951, right. Both photos courtesy of Carole Lee Carroll.*

theatre. I also remember the excitement of the opening nights, and one actually got dressed up in those days. I regret that that has changed today. In those days, we used to raid the costume closet and wear some weird things. I have to say, it was the only endeavor that I've been involved with where everybody was absolutely selfless. And I remember those wonderful black & white photographs of actors. There was one in a black and white t-shirt that inspired me especially. (For many years, there was a large sepia print of Tonio Selwart in a black and white striped shirt hanging in the lobby.) And John Lane set the tone. He would walk out of the office, always looking elegant. I can tell you this. John stayed with me for a long time. He went to the Royal Academy of Dramatic Arts and he had a suit made at the Savoy and he gave it to my dad who wore it for many years, and then I wore it for many years. The only bad thing I remember is when Henry made the mistake of asking me to do some gardening. I totally failed at that job.

Monty moved into the Colony in the sixties, and was among the students who posed with Celeste Holm in front of the stage door in 1961.

In 1959, Harold Cail wrote about Gale Dixon, an apprentice at the Manhattan Theatre Colony who had captured the role of Gloria Swanson's daughter.[4]

That "lucky break" which thespians dream of, especially fledglings, has come to Gale Dixon, 17-year-old apprentice at the Manhattan Theatre Colony. Gale got the chance to appear as Gloria Swanson's daughter in *Red Letter Day*, coming to the Ogunquit Playhouse next Monday. Two years ago another Manhattan Colony apprentice was the happy victim of "the lightning," going on at brief notice in *Inherit the Wind*, with Ed Begley. So good was Julie Strong she continued with the show for several weeks. Gale Dixon hales from Scranton, Pa., where she was graduated from high school last June. She enters Syracuse University's School of Theater Arts this fall to pursue her desire of becoming an actress. Miss Dixon, has a good background for it. Her father, Francis Dixon, is general director of the Colony. She too was in *Inherit the Wind*. Gale played Little Willie at the Colony when she was only six years old, and had to learn her lines by rote. She's been a student at the Colony for three years.

Several newspapers did features during the season of 1963 on Colony students Linda Hope, daughter of Bob Hope, Judy Williams, daughter of Rev. & Mrs. J. L. B.Williams (John Lane's pastor in Palm Beach, Florida.), and Sylvia Thorndike, daughter of Mr. & Mrs. Richard K. Thorndike of Beverly Farms, Massachusetts. [5]

On July 8, 1964, the *Portland Evening Express* did a feature story on the Manhattan Theatre Colony and some of the children of celebrities there: Bess Myerson's daughter, Barbara Grant; Art Carney's son, Brian; Phyllis Thaxter's daughter, Schuyler Aubrey; Francis Compton's son, Ian; Bretaigne Windust's daughter, Penny; and Julie Goldsmith, who was the

Left, John Lane helps to get the Lobster Bar Sign into the shot, as Linda Hope, Sylvia Thorndike and Judy Williams pose for the Portland Evening Express, July, 1963. Below, the picture that wound up in the paper. Courtesy of Barbara Hilty.

daughter of TV actress, Janet Fox, and the great-niece of novelist Edna Ferber. "They are among the 33 students at the Colony, one of the most unique theatrical workshops in the U.S., an adjunct to the Ogunquit Playhouse, where many of their parents have played."[6]

Another Colony student who was successful in the theatre in later years, returned with Hermione Gingold's play, *Oh Dad, Poor Dad, Mama's Hung You in the Closet and I'm Feeling So Sad*. In 1964, young Portland actor, John Handy, came back to Ogunquit where he had spent several summers previously as a student in the Colony.

In 1965, the Colony Theatre School got a new director, Dr. Frank G. Davidson, who said it had taken him three applications to get the job. He was a resident professor of speech and drama at City College of New York. That year, the Manhattan Theatre Colony drew fewer students, but one of them was Susan Andrews, the daughter of Dana Andrews. And Harold Cail rushed to interview her.

> Susan wants very much to be an actress. But success – or lack of same – this summer will have a strong bearing on her future. "It's a weeding-out time," she said "a time of determining if I've got what it takes to go on."

Brian Carney and Schuyler Aubrey, Portland Evening Express, *July 8, 1964.*

Portland Evening Express, *July 8, 1964,* "Chips off the Old Block," *clockwise from left: Schuyler Aubrey, daughter of Phyllis Thaxter and CBS-TV president, James T. Aubrey; Penny Windust, daughter of late theatrical director, Betaigne Windust; Julie Goldsmith, daughter of actress Janet Fox; Ian Compton, son of actor Francis Compton; Barbara Grant, daughter of Bess Myerson; and Brian Carney, son of Art Carney.*

The Darien [CT] *Review,* August 17, 1961. Ray Yates, "Along the Lobster Trail in Maine." This busy and highly successful producer also runs the Colony Players summer theater workshop in Ogunquit where young people including the niece of Dave Brubeck and the daughter of Barbara Bel Geddes try their wings at acting in the smaller barn type theater which has William F. Cope and Francis Dixon directing and managing a very talented and earnest group of potential theater stars. We enjoyed their performance of *Come Rain or Shine* and think Ginger Brubeck, Susan Sawyer (Barbara Bel Geddes' daughter) and several other drama students who made the audience chuckle and roar all evening have the talent to make their way up the Broadway ladder, with the excellent training of the Colony Theater School giving them a fine boost on their careers.

Portland Evening Express, *July 8, 1964, Ian Compton and Barbara Grant.*

She went on to describe the rigors of working as a Colony student.

> Speech classes every morning at 8:30, then rehearse in the afternoon, have dinner and rehearse some more. Rehearsals last until 10:30 p.m. Plays are performed the last three nights of the week. What might jokingly be called free time is from when work is done striking the sets on Sunday morning until 1:30 p.m. Sunday, when the cycle begins again. [7]

The Manhattan Theatre Colony closed after the 1965 season. Henry Weller has said that it became harder and harder to get instructors for the Colony, and that kids seemed to be younger and harder to manage.

In 2003, when heavy snow demolished these buildings, Roy Rogosin, then Producing Artistic Director, and the Ogunquit Playhouse Foundation built a new Colony. As Roy Rogosin says:

> When the snows caused the historic Colony Theatre to come tumbling down, we had an extraordinary challenge to rebuild it and make it a venue not only for our new theatre classes but for on-site rehearsals for the main stage productions. This enabled us to put everything under one roof and not have to explore outside opportunities for venues in which we could rehearse. Over a period of a year, we were able to restore the history of the Colony Theatre by literally rebuilding it from the ground up. Today it stands as a monument to the history and past of the Ogunquit Playhouse in addition to providing class space and rehearsal space for productions and classes now and in the future.

Colony students Barbara Keith, Penny Armstrong and John Handy.

Bradford Kenney, current Executive Artistic Director at the Ogunquit Playhouse, is grateful that Rogosin accomplished what he did with the Children's Theatre and rebuilt the Colony building, and claims, "Roy struggled with the collapse of the Colony building, but foresaw that it could be a rehearsal studio."

Since then it has significantly grown. In 2005, the Ogunquit Playhouse Children's Theatre received a generous grant from Nelson Checkoway and his wife, Paula Morgan, in remembrance of their daughter, Chloë. The Chloë Checkoway Pavilion, as the Colony is now named, was dedicated in 2006.

Kenney explains the evolution of the Colony this way:

> The old stage portion still exists and this year, for the first time, we'll start having productions back at the Colony. Roy and Eileen created the children's theatre camp, for people who were summering here or who lived in the region, to have their children learn theatre craft, for one week only and then put on a show that was attractive to their own age group. We've expanded that to include teens and a

Edna Roberts, Mary Hipple, Barbara Hilty.

John Lane.

Marguerite Waak, Harriet Smith, Susan and Paul Day.

Walter Dolan, Penny & Henry Weller.

Bill Traber

Bill Traber, George Rondo and Bunny Hart.

Julia Meade, John Lane and Warsham Rudd.

The Playhouse staff and friends celebrate the closing of The Lobster Bar in 1964. Photos courtesy of Barbara Hilty.

younger demographic – kindergarten to grade two. We are going to revive the Colony as a public assembly and a place where people can come and see theatre. We've restored the dressing rooms and the original stage area has become two different things: a wardrobe workshop for the Playhouse, but also at night, those things roll off and it becomes the backstage area as it was in its history for these teen and "shining star" groups to perform.

As for long range plans for the Colony, Kenney thinks it could wind up being a venue for smaller works, dramas, or something new, that can't play a 700-seat house when there are only 10 or 20 weeks to pay for the entire year.

So maybe Shakespeare, or something cutting edge. There are some fairly well-known playwrights that are starting to swirl around us and say, "Well, you know you need a smaller black-box space." Well, now we have it, thanks to the special talents of Eileen Rogosin, and a wonderful grant from the Checkoway family.

Also for the main stage, in 2007, the Junior Player Workshops will produce some Disney titles for which the Playhouse charges admission and usually fills 700 seats.

In 2007, a full eighty years after Walter and Maude Hartwig created the Manhattan Theatre Colony (then called the Manhattan Theatre Repertory Company) in 1927, the institution has seen many changes and has had closures of one sort and another, but it too is entering a third act as the Ogunquit Playhouse Children's Theatre, and may one day compete with the Ogunquit Playhouse, offering theatrical productions and training young people, even as it did in its earliest days.

The Chloë Checkoway Pavilion, opened in 2006.

Endnotes Chapter 3

1. *New York Times*, July 12, 1931.
2. *New York Times*, July, 1927.
3. *New York Times*, June 23, 1935, Bosley Crowther, "As Maine Goes…"
4. *Portland Evening Express*, August 6, 1959, Harold L. Cail, *Two on the Aisle*, "First Break."
5. *Portland Evening Express*, August 15, 1963, "Youth + Talent + Ogunquit, Maine."
6. *Portland Evening Express*, July 8, 1964, "Chips off the Old Block."
7. *Portland Evening Express*, July 2, 1965, Harold L. Cail.

The Manhattan Theatre Colony during the John Lane years.

The Foundation

In September, 1997, John Lane gave the Playhouse as a gift to the local community, to be overseen by a foundation with a board of directors. In 1998 and 1999, the Ogunquit Playhouse was run by Rob Townsend, long-time heir apparent to John Lane. Then, Rob's wife changed jobs and was sent to St. Louis, and naturally, Rob moved to the midwest with his family.

Enter Roy and Eileen Rogosin. Roy came from Seacoast Repertory Theatre and eagerly accepted the challenge and opportunity at the Ogunquit Playhouse under the guidance of the Foundation. The challenge was "to live up to the famed reputation of the Playhouse's then 68-year history and the opportunity was to move the Playhouse forward into the millennium and beyond, establishing new levels of creativity, education and performance."[1]

In 2000, the Ogunquit Playhouse staged *The Compleat Wrks of Wllm Shkspr (Abridged)*, by Adam Long, David Singer and Jess Winfield, directed by Scott Schwartz. Stephanie Zimbalist and Richard Kind from TV's *Spin City* starred in the second production, *Accomplice*, by Rupert Holmes. This was a comedy-thriller co-produced by Ogunquit and the Cape Playhouse. Then Rogosin moved into a big musical, *The Will Rogers Follies*, another joint venture with the Cape Playhouse. At the same time, Eileen Rogosin introduced to the community her children's theatre programs which she had originated at the Seacoast Repertory Theatre and at the Portsmouth Performing Arts Academy. The playbill announced: "The premiere edition of the Ogunquit Playhouse Children's Theatre will run from August 7 through August 12 and will culminate in a production of *Snow White*."

Rogosin's production of *Art*, directed by Judd Hirsch, who had starred in both the Broadway and London productions of the play, was well received by the critics and generated some good press for the Playhouse. Starring William Atherton, David Dukes and Jack Willis, the production prompted Dana Pearson at the

Jack Willis, William Atherton and David Dukes in Art, *2000. Photo: Stuart Nudelman.*

~ 165 ~

York County Coast Star to exclaim "First, this: *Art* is the best play I have ever seen." He went on to say:

> I've seen scores of plays, from tragedies and dramas to farce and mystery, of varying degrees of production value and acting; however, none of them have matched the power and sheer brilliance of *Art*, which made its New England debut Monday night at the Ogunquit Playhouse.[2]

Interviewed by Ray Routhier at the *Maine Sunday Telegram* (July 30, 2000), Judd Hirsch talked about why he was directing a play in a tiny Maine town for a fraction of the money he could get elsewhere: [3]

> You never forget your beginnings. I started in a theatre like this one, in Woodstock, NY. I never learned anything else. You don't learn to be a TV star; you learn to act on stage in front of an audience. There's no other place where you can reproduce the feeling you get in a theatre.

Ray Routhier went on to say:

> When the Playhouse gets stars today, they are usually people who know the theatre and are coming back to visit – John Raitt falls into that category.

And then he quoted Rogosin:

> This house was built on stars, people like Bette Davis and Anthony Quinn, but there are no stars of that magnitude any more. The money is so huge in Hollywood, people can get $100,000 an episode to do TV, and then we ask them to come to Ogunquit for 3 to 5 percent of that. [4]

Routhier comments:

> Rogosin and the Playhouse's board of directors try to keep the 750-seat theatre going by providing the best entertainment they can. That usually means five shows a summer, with a mix of musicals, familiar plays and newer, critically acclaimed works, such as *Art*.

Art was followed that season by *Grease*, the famous musical by Jim Jacobs and Warren Casey, made more famous by the 1979 motion picture starring Olivia Newton-John and John

Rehearsing Grease *at the Dunaway Center, 2000.*

Travolta. Set in the 1950s, the musical opened on Broadway in 1970. Ogunquit audiences and regional critics loved it. [For production photo, see color plate V.]

The 2001 season played *42nd Street*, the 1980 Tony-Award-winning musical that had just won a 2001 Tony for Best Broadway Revival. [See color plate XI.] The Ogunquit production was directed by Lee Roy Reams, an actor, singer, dancer and director who had been nominated for a Tony Award when he originated the part of Billy Lawlor in the original Broadway production. *I Love You, You're Perfect, Now Change*, the 1996 musical review about the battle of the sexes, opened with Marie Pressman as Woman #2, who had returned to the stage after spending four years in Harpswell, Maine, being a new mother.

The 2002 season led off with *George M*, a musical retrospective of the life and music of George M. Cohan, starring Cleve Asbury as George M. Cohan, followed by *Buddy: The Buddy Holly Story*, a co-production with the Helen Hayes Theatre in Nyack, New York, directed and choreographed by Richard Sabellico. *Buddy* had local critics cheering. The third production that season was *Chicago*, the Bob Fosse musical based on the play by Maurine Dallas Watkins.

Cleve Asbury rehearsing "I'm a Yankee Doodle Dandy" in George M! *Photo: Stuart Nudelman.*

Cast on set of George M! *Set by Richard Ellis. Photo by Stuart Nudelman.*

Oldest Subscribers to the Ogunquit Playhouse

In 2005, the first opening night audience at the Playhouse was asked who had been subscribers the longest. Two subscribers won: Barbara Hilty, who had been brought by her parents at age 14 to see plays at the old Ogunquit Playhouse, and who had even before that participated in Mrs. Hoyt's productions. Betty Dixon was the second oldest, having begun her subscription at the Playhouse in 1940 a year after her husband had gone to work for Walter Hartwig. There should also have been a third longest, Charlotte Chapman, but unfortunately, she had passed away only that year. Chapman was not only a subscriber going back to the days at the old Playhouse, she was also an usher at the Ogunquit Square, and later a box-office stalwart for a number of years, being a help to Maude Hartwig, during her hardest years of the early 1940s.

Barbara Hilty, left, and Betty Dixon, center, at the October, 2006, oral history of the Ogunquit Playhouse. Both photos from the Ogunquit Heritage Museum archives. Early photograph of Charlotte Chapman, courtesy of Steve Twombly.

Nunsense, the fourth production of the 2002 season was directed by its creator, Dan Goggin. It was also the first authorized version to cast a male, David Titus, who appeared as the Mother Superior.

The final show of the season was *Footloose,* a musical taken from the 1984 hit movie starring Kevin Bacon and Lori Singer, and featuring the music from the 1984 multi-platinum soundtrack of *Footloose,* the movie.

Nunsense, *2002. The cast of the first authorized mixed-gender production of Dan Goggin's play.*

2002 opening night: Kim Starling, Box Office Manager; Jean Benda, Assistant to the Director; Roy Rogosin, Artistic Director.

The Ogunquit Playhouse Children's Theatre

The Ogunquit Playhouse Children's Theatre shows in 2002 included *Stuart Little, Jack and the Bean Stalk, James and the Giant Peach,* and *Madeline.* There were also four concerts performed on Sunday nights throughout the summer.

According to a playbill history written in 2005:

> 2004 ushered in a new era for the Playhouse as Producing Artistic Director Roy Rogosin put together a dazzling array of musicals, including the regional premieres of two highly acclaimed Broadway hits, *Cats* and Disney's *Beauty and the Beast.* With the high-quality productions worthy of the Great White Way itself, along with appearances by national stars such as Sally Struthers and Lucie Arnez, the Playhouse continues its role as America's Foremost Summer Theatre.

The 2005 season included *Forever Plaid,* written by Stuart Ross; *Aida,* by Elton John and Tim Rice; *The Best Little Whorehouse in Texas,* starring Sally Struthers; *Swing;* and *Nunsensations! The Nunsense Vegas Revue.* The Ogunquit Playhouse Children's Theatre Program, under the

Beehive, 2006. All photos this page by Stuart Nudelman.

Right, Andrea McCardle as Sally Bowles, and, above, dancers at the Kit Kat Club, in the 2006 production of Cabaret.

Sally Struthers, in Hello, Dolly!, 2006.

Characters in Menopause, The Musical. *Photos: Stuart Nudelman.*

Paolo Montalban and Jessica Rush in Cinderella. *Photo: Stuart Nudelman.*

direction of Eileen Rogosin, featured performances of *The Lion, The Witch and The Wardrobe*, *The Little Mermaid*, *Charlotte's Web*, and *Peter and the Wolf*.

At the end of the season in 2005, Roy and Eileen Rogosin retired to Sante Fe, New Mexico, and Bradford T. Kenney joined the Playhouse as Executive Artistic Director.

Brad Kenney says:

> Roy (Rogosin) came in and laid the groundwork for the creation of a regional theatre, where the plays were developed for the most part on site. It was probably a difficult time period then because I'm sure he tried to honor the desires of the community, and in those days, the community wanted what they had had with John Lane. I've had people walk up to me and say, "People should wear blazers to the Ogunquit Playhouse," and "I want my parking space that John Lane gave me," or even, "You should be doing one musical a year and the dramas that John Lane did." Well, our culture has changed and that schedule may not fill as many seats as it used to any more. Roy, I think, had to struggle with a lot of those changes. I came on board and had the luxury of a board of directors saying this is what we want, we want you to do all musicals. Well, that's an easy way to be a hero. Musicals sell. Roy probably didn't have that luxury – he was still trying to honor the artistic traditions

of the past. He only switched to all musicals the year before I got here. And that was one of the most successful years, financially.

Brad told of his own experiences at Foothills Theatre in Worcester, Massachusetts:

> I produced *Art* also, and I know that I did one-third of the box office that I had done when we did *Miss Saigon*. So if the board of directors said we still want an Agatha Christie murder mystery each year, I would have to budget that and know in my head that it's going to do about half what *Hairspray* will do.

The 2006 season under the new leadership of Brad Kenney, offered five musicals beginning with *Beehive*, the '60s Musical Sensation created by Larry Gallagher. *Beehive* was followed by Andrea McCardle starring in *Cabaret*; Sally Struthers starring in the David Merrick production of *Hello, Dolly!*; Leslie Uggams in Rodgers & Hammerstein's *Cinderella*; and the season ended with *Menopause, the Musical*, with book and lyrics by Jeanie Linders. The success of that show led to an extension of the season, first from September 16 to September 23, and finally to Columbus Day weekend. The show had the distinction of being the first production that the Ogunquit Playhouse ever ran for six weeks!

Kenney says the Ogunquit Playhouse is on its way to being a full regional theatre, by which he means a theatre where every production is built from the ground up, a theatre that uses the resources of the region, but also can call on its Broadway connections to produce full-scale Broadway shows that go beyond traditional summer stock, and a theatre that gives back to its community.

Ogunquit Playhouse's current Executive Artistic Director, Bradford T. Kenney.

> The Ogunquit Playhouse is presenting all musicals of a Broadway scale. We have other colleagues like Maine State Music Theater nearby who are doing musicals with a repertory company, but Ogunquit is unique in that we are producing five to seven huge Broadway shows, building each from the ground up, handpicking the actors, designers, directors, to best suit that show. It's much more costly.

In only his second season at Ogunquit, Kenney believes that one of his contributions so far has been in the area of:

...bringing to the theatre a sense of responsibility toward the community and social service agencies. We're bringing in boys and girls clubs, we're reaching everywhere from Portland to Portsmouth, and writing grants to bus kids in, at-risk youth who would never get a chance to see the shows here. They get to meet actors, they have a special orientation out in the gazebo garden. Another strong point about regional theatre, you need to be accessible, so Maine Arts and the Tramuto Foundation wrote a grant and funded it at 100% for assisted-listening devices. It needs to be here for everybody. There's youth literacy programs that we brought in last year to see *Cinderella*. That is what regional theatre does, it reaches back into the curriculum of the schools and into the community.

About that community, Kenney has only great things to say:

We are blessed that we're here. I think one of the reasons that the Playhouse is so strong is that it's in this magnificent community that still cares about and is attached to its heritage, yet it is hip, eclectic, cutting-edge. Hotel rooms go for $200-$300 a night, a martini is $10 downtown, and that's where Broadway stars can still walk in and be treated hugely, magnificently. And they go home and say, "My God, you have got to go to Ogunquit."

About the lodge, a motel that the Foundation bought during the Rogosin years, Kenney is thrilled to say:

We have a wonderful asset there. The lodge is now worth definitely three times what we paid for it. We haven't taken full advantage of it yet, but we will. Housing is a significant part of the budget. It is the largest, most volatile number next to actors in the budget. Tens of thousands of dollars are now spent to house actors in this community. And as we go into a longer season, it gets more expensive. The town has become more affluent, the rooms are more expensive, and we don't have Dunelawn, we don't have these luxuries of getting the stars ocean front.

And this season, the Foundation will lease rooms at Joe Young's Village Lodge, on the southbound field where Kenney points out, "Maude used to house company members."

Kenney recalled the responses he got from people when he told them he would be coming to the Ogunquit Playhouse.

They immediately went back to the heritage of the Hartwig years, and John's early years, even up to the '70s and early '80s. But they were curious about where the theatre was now. It's as if they hadn't heard of it lately.

That led him to return to the Foundation saying, "You have something in your stewardship that is of national significance. And it needs to be treated that way."

Ogunquit Playhouse - "La Cage aux Folles" - Overture - Designed by Richard Ellis 5-07

Ogunquit Playhouse - "La Cage aux Folles" - Chez Jacqueline - Designed by Richard Ellis - 5-07

The Foundation 175

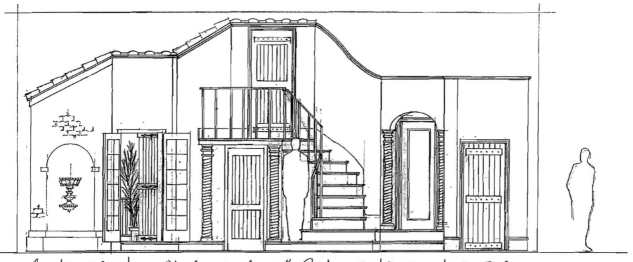

Richard Ellis set designs for La Cage Aux Folles, *2007.*

Hopefully under his leadership, the Ogunquit Playhouse will be returned to its former glories, even as summer stock becomes more and more a thing of the past. As the Foundation and Kenney move into the 75th anniversary year of the Ogunquit Playhouse, they will try again to expand the season. Kenney says, "We're trying to do it smartly."

Menopause The Musical, *2006*.

We own the scenery of *Menopause*, so we're going to start with it, only earlier than usual, on May 23rd. Then we'll open with *The Full Monty*, with Sally Struthers, a familiar and popular star. She's our season opener. We'll do huge shows with Broadway sets, Broadway costumes and Tony-award-winning designers up until the end of August. Then we'll bring back Struthers and *The Full Monty* because we own the sets and costumes, the cast is already rehearsed, so we'll try to make more of a profit there. While we are learning to stretch these dates, we're doing it with a show that has a higher profit margin for us. One of the huge shows will be *La Cage aux Folles,* for which Richard Ellis will design the sets.

Kenney has said, "We are going to revive the Colony as a public assembly and a place where people can come and see theatre." He believes that the Ogunquit Playhouse could once again be a two-theatre operation, with smaller works, dramas, or anything that can't command the full 700-seat main stage, being put on in the Checkoway Pavilion, along with the expanded children's theatre productions. Kenney points out:

> The Children's Theatre Program continues to grow as well. On the main stage, the Junior Player Workshops this season will produce some Disney titles for which the Playhouse will charge admission and these productions easily fill 700 seats.

And the play goes on…

The Foundation 177

Endnotes Chapter 4

1. Roy Rogosin recollections.
2. *York County Coast Star,* August 3. 2000. Dana Pearson, "A Brilliant Work of *"Art."*
3. *Maine Sunday Telegram*, July 30, 2000, Ray Routhier, "Judd Hirsch in the House."

Photo by James B. Russell. Courtesy of the Russell family.

1933

Blanche Ring
in
Stepping Sisters
by Howard Warren Comstock

Faye Marbe
in
Candle Light
by Siegfried Geyer
Adapted by P.G. Wodehouse

Carl Benton Reid
in
The Late Christopher Bean
by Sidney Howard

Mary Nash
in
The Second Mrs. Tanqueray
by Sir Arthur Wing Pinero

The Manhattan Theatre
Repertory Company
in
Adam The Creator
by Karel & Josef Capek

Ruth St. Denis
in
Monna Vanna
by Maurice Maeterlinck

The Manhattan Theatre
Repertory Company
in
Philip Goes Forth
by George Kelly

The Manhattan Theatre
Repertory Company
in
Tomorrow and Tomorrow
by Philip Barry

Mabel Taliaferro
in
The Cradle Song
by Gregorio Martinez Sierra
& Maria Martinez Sierra

Fay Marbe   A.J. Herbert
& Roland Drew
in
Trio
by Leo Lenz
Adapted by Walter Hartwig

1934

The Manhattan Repertory
Theatre Company
in
The Curtain Rises
by B.M. Kaye

Florence Britton
in
The Sacred Flame
by W. Somerset Maugham

Maude Adams
in
Twelfth Night
by William Shakespeare
Directed by Miss Adams

Peggy Wood
in
The Closed Room
by Patterson Greene

Daisy Atherton & A.J. Herbert
in
Her Master's Voice
by Clare Kummer

Russell Gleason & Florence Britton
in
Loose Moments
by Courtenay Savage
& Bertram Hobbs

Laurette Taylor & Tullio Carminati
in
At Marian's
by Laurette Taylor

The Manhattan Theatre
Repertory Company
in
Obsession
by Martin Berkely

The Manhattan Theatre
Repertory Company
in
Yellow Sands
by Eden & Adelaide Phillpotts

Faye Marbe
in
His Favorite Wife
by George James Hopkins

1935

Libby Holman
in
Accent on Youth
by Samson Raphaelson

Fritzi Scheff
in
Tonight or Never
by Lili Hatvany

Ethel Barrymore
in
The Silver Box
by John Galsworthy
Directed by Miss Barrymore

Mitzi Green & Libby Holman
in
The Farmer's Wife
by Eden Phillpotts

Florence Reed
in
Murder With Pen and Ink
by Frederick Jackson

Alexandra Carlisle
in
Oliver Oliver
by Paul Osborn

Mollie Pearson   A.J. Herbert
Daisy Atherton   Frank Roberts
& Lygia Bernard
in
Jane's Legacy
by Eden Phillpotts

Mitzi Green
in
Service for Two
by Laurence and Alice Eyre

Libby Holman
in
Gypsy
by Maxwell Anderson

Violet Heming
in
There's Always Juliet
by John Van Druten

1936

Rosemary Ames, Thomas W. Ross
& Edward Emery
in
Three Wise Fools
by Austin Strong

Ruth Gordon
in
Saturday's Children
by Maxwell Anderson

Frances Starr
in
Kind Lady
by Edward Chodorov

Morgan Farley   Charlotte Walker
Thomas W. Ross   Rosemary Ames
in
Russet Mantle
by Lynn Riggs

Morgan Farley   Anne Seymour
& Rosemary Ames
in
The Wind and the Rain
by Merton Hodge

Lillian Foster   Joanna Roos
Wilfred Seagram   Thomas W. Ross
in
Erstwhile Susan
by Marian de Forest

Florence Reed
in
Mademoiselle
by Jacques Deval & Grace George

Margalo Gillmore
in
The Night of January 16th
by Ayn Rand

Margaret Anglin
in
Fresh Fields
by Ivor Novello

The Ballet Caravan
with
twelve dancers from the
American Ballet Company

1937

J. Augustus Keogh   Grace O' Malley
Wilfred Seagram   Violet Besson
in
The White Headed Boy
by Lennox Robinson

Lillian Foster
in
Hay Fever
by Noël Coward

The Manhattan Theatre
Repertory Company
in
Libel
by Edward Wooll

The Manhattan Theatre
Repertory Company
in
Boy Meets Girl
by Bella & Samuel Spewack

Sally Rand
in
They Knew What They Wanted
by Sidney Howard

Estelle Winwood
in
At Mrs. Beam's
by C.K. Munro

Laurette Taylor
in
At The Theatre
by Laurette Taylor

Nance O'Neil & Morgan Farley
in
Criminal at Large
by Edgar Wallace

Frances Starr
in
The Queen Was in the Parlour
by Noël Coward

Carl Benton Reid
in
The Lancashire Lass
by Henry J. Byron

Morgan Farley   John Williams
Carl Benton Reid   Wilfred Seagram
in
Journey's End
by R.C. Sherriff

Jean Muir & Donald Cook
in
Dearly Beloved
by Charles Beahan & Robert Buckner

1938

Florence Reed
in
Yes, My Darling Daughter
by Mark Reed

The Manhattan Theatre
Repertory Company
in
Room Service
by John Murray & Allan Boretz

Dorathe Burgess
in
The Lady from Broadway
by Fred Ballard

Elena Miramova
in
Fata Morgana
by Ernest Vajda

Tonio Selwart
in
Liliom
by Ferenc Molnár

Frances Starr
in
Susan and God
by Rachel Crothers

Cornelia Otis Skinner
& Donald Cook
in
Romance
by Edward Sheldon

Nance O'Neil & John Williams
in
Time and The Conways
by J.B. Priestley

Else Argal & Donald Cook
in
Soubrette
by Jacques Deval

Donald Cook & Dorathe Burgess
in
Snow Train
by Edward Childs Carpenter

Lanny Ross
in
Petticoat Fever
by Mark Reed

1939

The Manhattan Theatre
Repertory Company
in
You Can't Take It with You
by Moss Hart & George S. Kaufman

Clifton Webb & Libby Holman
in
Burlesque
by George Manker Watters & Arthur Hopkins

Frances Starr
in
End of Summer
by S.N. Behrman

Douglass Montgomery
in
The Firebrand
by Edwin Justus Mayer

Madge Evans
in
Brief Moment
by S.N. Behrman

Grace George
in
The Circle
by W. Somerset Maugham

Sinclair Lewis
in
Our Town
by Thornton Wilder

Cornelia Otis Skinner
in
Madame San Gene
by Victorien Sardou & Emile Moreau

Edward Everett Horton
in
Springtime for Henry
by Benn W. Levy

Glenda Farrell
in
With All My Heart
by Austin Parker

The Manhattan Theatre
Repertory Company
in
Payment Deferred
by Jeffrey E. F. Dell
Adapted from the novel by C.S. Forester

1940

Jimmy Savo
in
Mum's the Word
by Jimmy Savo

Bramwell Fletcher & Doris Dalton
in
The Guardsman
by Ferenc Molnár

Laurette Taylor
in
Outward Bound
by Sutton Vane

Cornelia Otis Skinner
in
Biography
by S.N. Behrman

Madge Evans
in
The Greeks Had a Word for It
by Zoe Akins

Frances Starr
in
No Time for Comedy
by S.N. Behrman

Michael Strange & John Lodge
In
Amphitryon 38
by Jean Giraudoux, adapted by S.N. Behrman

Violet Heming
in
Design for Living
by Noël Coward

Arthur Treacher
in
The Hottentot
by Victor Mapes & William Collier

Buddy Ebsen
in
Elmer the Great
by Ring Lardner

Sinclair Lewis
in
Ah, Wilderness!
by Eugene O'Neil

1941

Betty Furness
in
Something Gay
by Adelaide Heilbron

Dorothy Sands
in
By Your Leave
by Gladys Hurlbut & Emma Wells

Fay Wray
in
One Sunday Afternoon
by James Hagan

Anna Sten
in
Nancy's Private Affair
by Myron Fagan

Fritzi Scheff & Estelle Winwood
in
Ladies in Retirement
by Edward Percy & Reginald Denham

Conrad Nagel
in
The Male Animal
by James Thurber & Elliott Nugent

Buddy Ebsen
in
The Poor Nut
by J.C. & Elliott Nugent

Tallulah Bankhead
in
Her Cardboard Lover
by Jacques Deval & P.J. Wodehouse

Elsa Maxwell
in
Our Betters
by W. Somerset Maugham

Anita Louise
in
Kiss the Boys Good-bye
by Clare Boothe

1942

The Junior Members
of
The Manhattan Theatre
Repertory Company
in
What a Life
by Clifford Goldsmith

A Murder Has Been Arranged
by Emlyn Williams

Incognito
by N. Richard Nusbaum

Quiet Wedding
by Esther McCracken

Nothing but the Truth
by James Montgomery

Post Road
by Wilbur Steele & Norma Mitchell

Out of the Frying Pan
by Francis Swann

Letters to Lucerne
by Fritz Rotter & Allen Vincent

Douglas Fairbanks

1944

Eugenia Rawls
in
Having Wonderful Time
by Arthur Kober

James Ganon   Eugenia Rawls
& Augusta French
in
The Luck
by Reginald Denham & Edward Percy

Daisy Atherton & Arthur Jarrett
in
Arsenic and Old Lace
by Joseph Kesselring

Daisy Atherton
in
The Late Christopher Bean
by Sidney Howard

Francis Compton
in
French Without Tears
by Terence Rattigan

Eugenia Rawls   Francis Compton
& Maxine Stuart
in
Pursuit of Happiness
by
Lawrence Langer & Armina Marshall

Daisy Atherton   Ernita Lascelles
John McQuade   Lew Sisk
in
The Bat
by Mary Roberts Rhinehart
& Avery Hopwood

Eugenia Rawls
in
Three-Cornered Moon
by Gertrude Tonkonogy

1945

The Manhattan Theatre
Repertory Company
in
George and Margaret
by Gerald Savory

Katherine Alexander & Doro Merande
in
Three's a Family
by Phoebe and Henry Ephron

Lilian Harvey & Anton Dolin
in
Blithe Spirit
by Noël Coward

Leila Ernst & Suzanne Caubaye
in
The Doughgirls
by Joseph Fields

Whitford Kane   Frederick Bradlee III
Millicent Brower & "Pansey"
in
White Wings
by Philip Barry

Katherine Alexander
in
Kiss and Tell
by F. Hugh Herbert

Mary Morris & Curtis Cooksey
in
Roseanne
by Nan Bagby Stephens

Neil Hamilton
in
Dear Brutus
by James M. Barrie

The Manhattan Theatre
Repertory Company
in
Snafu
by Louis Soloman
& Harold Buchman

1946	1947	1948

1946

Erik Rhodes
in
That's Gratitude
by Frank Craven

Tonio Selwart
in
Autumn Crocus
by C.L Anthony

Leo G. Carroll
in
The Late George Apley
by John P. Marquand
& George S. Kaufman

Lilian Harvey
in
Tonight at 8:30
*Ways and Means   Family Album
& We Were Dancing*
by Noël Coward

Leo G. Carroll
in
Angel Street
by Patrick Hamilton

John Lane
in
The Hasty Heart
by
John Patrick

Nicholas Joy
in
Ten Little Indians
by
Agatha Christie

McKay Morris
in
Michael Myerberg's production of
Balloon
by Padraic Colum

Katherine Alexander & Daisy Atherton
in
Mr. Pim Passes By
by A.A. Milne

Daisy Atherton
in
Cradle Snatchers
by Russell Medcraft & Norma Mitchell

1947

Daisy Atherton & Francis Compton
in
Years Ago
by Ruth Gordon

Ruth Chatterton
in
The Little Foxes
by Lillian Hellman

Zazu Pitts
in
The Late Christopher Bean
by Sidney Howard

Faye Emerson
in
State of the Union
by Howard Lindsay & Russel Crouse

Edith Fellows   Harold Lang   Alice Pearce
Hugh Martin   Michael Hall   Beverly Janis
in
Best Foot Forward
Book by John Cecil Holm
Music & Lyrics by Hugh Martin & Ralph Blane

Judith Evelyn & Richard Widmark
in
Joan of Lorraine
by Maxwell Anderson

The Michael Myerberg Production
of
Dear Judas
Adapted from the poem by Robinson Jeffers
by Michael Myerberg

Jane Cowl
in
The First Mrs. Fraser
by St. John Ervine

Ruth Chatterton
in
Caprice
by Sil-Vara

Lillian Gish
in
The Marquise
by Noël Coward

Peggy Wood
in
The Fatal Weakness
by George Kelly

1948

Robert Burton
in
Apple of His Eye
by Kenyon Nicholson
& Charles Robinson

Oliver Thorndike
in
John Loves Mary
by Norman Krasna

Frances Starr
in
The Corn Is Green
by Emlyn Williams

Frank McHugh
in
Is Zat So?
by James Gleason & Richard Taber

Carl Benton Reid
in
Excursion
by Victor Wolfson

Lois Hunt & Frank Rogier
in
Ting-Ling
Music by Ignatz Waghalter
Book & Lyrics by Richard Diamond

Eugenie Leontovich
in
And So to Bed
by J.B. Fagan

Anthony Quinn
in
The Gentleman from Athens
by Emmet Lavery

Lillian Gish
in
The Legend of Leonora
by James M. Barrie

Anton Dolin
in
For Love or Money
by F. Hugh Herbert

Sara Allgood
in
Juno and the Paycock
by Sean O'Casey

1949

Edward Everett Horton
in
Present Laughter
by Noël Coward

Daisy Atherton
in
Charm
by John Kirkpatrick

Eddie Dowling
in
The Time of Your Life
by William Saroyan

Richard Arlen
in
Made in Heaven
by Hagar Wilde

Carl Benton Reid
in
The Inspector Calls
by J.B. Priestley

Donald Cook
in
Strange Bedfellows
by Florence Ryerson & Colin Clements

A New Musical Revue
Of All Things
by Ken Welch

Marcia Walter   Boyd Crawford
Helen Harrelson
in
The Voice of The Turtle
by John Van Druten

Paul Lucas
in
Accent on Youth
by Samson Raphaelson

Francis Compton   Noel Leslie   John McQuade
in
A Highland Fling
by Margaret Curtis

Helmut Dantine   Signe Hasso   John Newland
in
Love From a Stranger
by Agatha Christie

1950

Stuart Erwin
in
Harvey
by Mary Chase

Anna Lee
in
Miranda
by Peter Blackmore

Jack Hartley & Dodie Bauer
in
Born Yesterday
by Garson Kanin

Michael Todd
Presents
The Live Wire
by Garson Kanin

Just Around the Corner
Book by Abby Mann & Bernard Drew
Music by Joe Sherman
Lyrics by Langston Hughes
Additional lyrics by George Jaffe

William Eythe
in
The Silver Whistle
by Robert E. McEnroe

Leo G. Carroll
in
Once An Actor
by Rosemary Casey

Imogene Coca
in
Happy Birthday
by Anita Loos

Jean Parker & Robert Lowery
in
Light Up the Sky
by Moss Hart

Edward Everett Horton
in
His French Wife
by Charles Deane & Richard Doscher

1951

Edward Everett Horton
in
Springtime for Henry
by Benn Levy

Doro Merande
in
See How They Run
by Philip King

The Chocolate Soldier
Based on *Arms and the Man*
by George Bernard Shaw
Music by Oscar Strauss

Ruth Chatterton
in
O Mistress Mine
by Terence Rattigan

Lillian Gish
in
Miss Mabel
by R.C. Sherriff

Doro Merande
in
This is My Valley
by Dorothy Rood Stewart

Melvyn Douglas & Signe Hasso
in
Glad Tidings
by Edward Mabley

Arthur Treacher
in
Clutterbuck
by Benn Levy

Brigadoon
Book & Lyrics by
Alan Jay Lerner
Music by Frederick Loewe

Basil Rathbone
in
The Gioconda Smile
by Aldous Huxley

Joan Blondell
in
Come Back, Little Sheba
by William Inge

1952

Melvyn Douglas
in
Season With Ginger
by Ronald Alexander

On Your Toes
Book by Richard Rodgers,
George Abbott & Lorenz Hart
Music by Richard Rodgers
Lyrics by Lorenz Hart

June Dayton & Dean Harens
in
Gramercy Ghost
by John Cecil Holm

Peggy Wood
in
Here's Mama
by Frank Gabrielson

Ruth Chatterton
in
Old Acquaintance
by John Van Druten

Kiss Me Kate
Book by Bella & Sam Spewack
Music & Lyrics by Cole Porter

Beatrice Lillie
in
An Evening with Beatrice Lillie
with Reginald Gardiner

Mia Slavenska   Frederic Franklin
Alexandria Danilova Nicholas Orloff
in
Ballet Variante

Kay Francis
in
Theatre
by Guy Bolton &
W. Somerset Maugham

Dorothy Gish
in
The Man
by Mel Dinelli

Edward Everet Horton
in
Nina
by André Roussin, adapted by Samuel Taylor

1953

Alexis Smith
in
Bell, Book and Candle
by John Van Druten

Cedric Hardwicke & Lili Darvas
in
Island Visit
by Andrew Rosenthal

Betty Furness
in
Affairs of State
by Louise Verneuil

Zachary Scott
June Dayton & Dean Harens
in
The Moon is Blue
by F. Hugh Herbert

Carousel
Book & Lyrics by Oscar Hammerstein, 2nd
Music by Richard Rodgers

Wally Cox
in
Three Men on a Horse
by John Cecil Holm & George Abbott

Anthony Ross   Hiram Sherman
Valerie Bettis   Barbara Baxley
in
The Frogs of Spring
by Nathaniel Benchley

The original California Strawhatters
in a musical revue
One Thing After Another:

Richard Arlen
in
Mister Roberts
by Thomas Heggen & Joshua Logan

Enzio Pinza
in
The Play's the Thing
by Ferenc Molnár

Gentlemen Prefer Blondes
Book by Joseph Fields & Anita Loos
Adapted from the novel by Anita Loos
Music by Jule Styne   Lyrics by Leo Robin

Billie Burke
in
Life with Mother
by Howard Lindsay & Russel Crouse

1954

Margaret Truman
& George Voskovec
in
Autumn Crocus
By C.L. Anthony

Rudy Vallee
in
Jenny Kissed Me
by Jean Kerr

Mary Astor
in
Late Love
by Rosemary Casey

Steve Cochran
in
Heaven Can Wait
by Harry Segall

Song of Norway
Based on the Life and Music
of Edvard Grieg
Book by Milton Lazarus
Musical adaption & lyrics by
George Forrest & Robert Wright

Stalag 17
by Donald Bevan
& Edmund Trzcinski

Dennis King
in
My Three Angels
by Sam & Bella Spewack

The Boys from Syracuse
Book by George Abbott
Music by Richard Rodgers
Lyrics by Lorenz Hart

Tallulah Bankhead
in
Dear Charles
by Alan Melville

Joe E. Brown
in
The Show Off
by George Kelly

1955

Donald Cook John Dall & Monica Lovett
in
Champagne Complex
by Leslie Stevens

Eva Marie Saint
in
The Rainmaker
by N. Richard Nash

Wonderful Town
Book by Joseph Fields & Jerome Chodorov
Music by Leonard Bernstein
Lyrics by Betty Comden & Adolph Green

Jeffrey Lynn
in
The Caine Mutiny Court-Martial
by Herman Wouk

John Baragrey & Georgiann Johnson
in
Sabrina Fair
by Samuel Taylor

The Great Waltz
Book by Moss Hart
Music by Johann Strauss (I & II)
Lyrics by Desmond Carter

Gary Merrill
in
Two Fingers of Pride
by Vincent J. Longhi

Billie Burke
In
Mother Was a Bachelor
by Irving Phillips

Robert Webber & Sandra Church
in
Picnic
by William Inge

Ethel Waters
in
The Member of the Wedding
by Carson McCullers

Claudette Colbert
in
A Mighty Man Is He
by Arthur Kober & George Oppenheimer

1956

Billie Burke
in
The Solid Gold Cadillac
by Howard Teichmann & George S. Kaufman

Barbara Baxley & Elaine Stritch
in
Bus Stop
by William Inge

Bert Parks
in
You Never Know
by Rowland Leigh
Based on the play *Candle Light*
Music & lyrics by Cole Porter

Ballet Theatre
Starring Nora Kaye & John Kriza

Dolores Del Rio & Lili Darvas
in
Anastasia
by Marcel Maurette
English adaptation by Guy Bolton

Carol Bruce & Edmund Ryan
in
Anniversary Waltz
by Jerome Chodorov & Joseph Fields

Donald Cook
in
The Golden Egg
by Philip King

Art Carney
in
The Seven Year Itch
by George Axelrod

Celeste Holm
in
A Sudden Spring
by Halstead Welles

Plain and Fancy
Book by Joseph Stein & Will Glickman
Music by Albert Hague
Lyrics by Arnold Horwitt

Beatrice Lillie
in
Beasops Fables

1957

Donald Cook & Joan Bennett
in
Janus
by Carolyn Green

Jessica Tandy & Hume Cronyn
in
The Man in the Dog Suit
by William Wright & Albert Belch

Brigadoon
Book & Lyrics by Alan Jay Lerner
Music by Frederick Loewe

Nancy Walker
in
The Desk Set
by William Marchant

Dennis King
in
The Reluctant Debutante
by William Douglas Home

Basil Rathbone
in
Witness for the Prosecution
by Agatha Christie

The Boy Friend
Book, Music & Lyrics
by
Sandy Wilson

Ed Begley
in
Inherit the Wind
by Jerome Lawrence & Robert E. Lee

Vivica Lindfors & Cathleen Nesbitt
in
The Chalk Garden
by Enid Bagnold

The Pajama Game
Book by George Abbott
& Richard Bissell
Music & Lyrics by Richard Adler
& Jerry Ross

Peggy Wood
in
Jane
by S.N. Behrman

1958

Dody Goodman
in
Dulcy
by George S. Kaufman & Marc Connelly

Jessica Tandy & Hume Cronyn
in
Triple Play
Bedtime Story by Sean O'Casey
The Island of Cipango by Benn Levy
A Pound on Demand by Sean O'Casey

Claude Dauphin & Lili Darvas
in
The Waltz of the Toreadors
by Jean Anouilh

Ella Logan
in
Maggie
Based on J.M. Barrie's play
What Every Woman Knows
Book by Hugh Thomas
Music & Lyrics by William Roy

Burgess Meredith
in
The Remarkable Mr Pennypacker
by Liam O'Brien

Celeste Holm
in
The Third Best Sport
by Eleanor & Leo Bayer

Victor Jory
in
The Happiest Millionaire
by Kyle Crichton

Don Ameche
in
Holiday for Lovers
by Ronald Alexander

Ann Harding & Gig Young
in
September Tide
by Daphne du Maurier

Wendell Corey
in
Goodbye Again
by Allan Scott & George Haight

Hermione Gingold & Carol Bruce
in
Fallen Angels
by Noël Coward

1959

Shirley Booth
in
Nina
by André Roussin
Adapted by Samuel Taylor

Li'l Abner
Book by Norman Panama & Melvin Frank
Based on cartoon characters by Al Capp
Music by Gene de Paul
Lyrics by Johnny Mercer

Faye Emerson
in
Biography
by S.N. Behrman

Betsy Palmer & Kurt Kasznar
in
Once More, With Feeling
by Harry Kurnitz

Fay Bainter & Ann B. Davis
in
The Girls in 509
by Howard Teichmann

Celeste Holm
in
What a Day
Music by Claire Richardson
Lyrics by Paul Rosner
Sketches by Max Wilk & Manya Starr
Conceived by Manya Starr

Gloria Swanson
in
Red Letter Day
by Andrew Rosenthal

Bells Are Ringing
Book & Lyrics
by Betty Comden & Adolph Green
Music by Jule Styne

Ben Gazzara
in
Epitaph for George Dillon
by John Osborne & Anthony Creighton

Jenny Lou Law
in
Lend an Ear
Book, Music & Lyrics by Charles Gaynor

1960

John Vivyan
in
The Second Man
by S.N. Behrman

Dana Andrews & Jerry Jedd
in
Two for the Seesaw
by William Gibson

Betsy Palmer
in
Roar Like a Dove
by Lesley Storm

West Side Story
Book by Arthur Laurents
Music by Leonard Bernstein
Lyrics by Stephen Sondheim

Edward Mulhare
in
Memo for a Green Thumb
by Charles Robinson

Ballet Espanol
Starring
Roberto Ximenez & Manolo Vargas
& the Ballet Espanol Dancers

Howard Keel
in
Sunrise at Campobello
by Dore Schary

Shirley Booth
in
The Late Christopher Bean
by Sidney Howard

Hans Conried
in
Not in the Book
by Arthur Watkyn

Joan Fontaine
in
Susan and God
by Rachel Crothers

Bette Davis & Leif Erickson
in
The World of Carl Sandburg
Adapted from Carl Sandburg's works
by Norman Corwin

1961

Siobhán McKenna & Zachary Scott
in
Captain Brassbound's Conversion
by George Bernard Shaw

Celeste Holm
in
Invitation to a March
by Arthur Laurents

Myrna Loy & Claude Dauphin
in
The Marriage-Go-Round
by Leslie Stephens

Susan Oliver & Scott McKay
in
Under the Yum-Yum Tree
by Lawrence Roman

Herbert Marshall
& Zamah Cunningham
in
A Majority of One
by Leonard Spigelgass

Jane Wyatt & Tom Helmore
in
O Mistress Mine
by Terence Rattigan

Faye Emerson & Reginald Gardiner
in
The Pleasure of His Company
by Samuel Taylor
& Cornelia Otis Skinner

Julia Meade & Orson Bean
in
Send Me No Flowers
by Norman Barasch & Carroll Moore

Martha Scott & Donald Woods
in
Future Perfect
by Whitfield Cook

Craig Stevens & Alexis Smith
in
Critic's Choice
by Ira Levin

1962

Bye Bye Birdie
Book by Michael Stewart
Music by Charles Strouse
Lyrics by Lee Adams

Mark Richman Peggy Ann Garner
& Ethel Griffies
in
Write Me a Murder
by Frederick Knott

Tallulah Bankhead
in
Here Today
by George Oppenheimer

Myrna Loy
in
There Must Be a Pony
by James Kirkwood

The Music Man
Book, Music & Lyrics by
Meredith Willson

Paul Ford & Maureen O'Sullivan
in
Cradle and All
by Sumner Arthur Long

Walter Pidgeon & Martha Scott
in
The Complaisant Lover
by Graham Green

Eileen Brennan
in
The Miracle Worker
by William Gibson

Nancy Walker
in
Everybody Loves Opal
by John Patrick

Betsy Palmer
in
Maggie
Based on the play
What Every Woman Knows
by James M. Barrie
Book by Hugh Thomas
Music & Lyrics by William Roy

1963

Spring Byington
in
The Curious Savage
by John Patrick

Art Carney & Phyllis Thaxter
in
Time Out for Ginger
by Ronald Alexander

John Forsythe & Patricia Barry
in
Kind Sir
by Norman Krasna

The Unsinkable Molly Brown
Book by Richard Morris
Music & Lyrics by
Meredith Willson

Walter Slezak
in
Romanoff and Juliet
by Peter Ustinov

Joan Caulfield & Peggy Cass
in
She Didn't Say Yes
by Lonnie Coleman

Cesar Romero
in
Strictly Dishonorable
by Preston Sturges

Hans Conried
in
Take Her, She's Mine
by Phoebe & Henry Ephron

Julia Meade
in
You Never Know
by Rowland Leigh
Based on the play *Candle Light*
Music & Lyrics by Cole Porter

1964

Barbara Bel Geddes
in
The Constant Wife
by W. Somerset Maugham

Merv Griffin
in
Broadway
by Philip Dunning & George Abbott

Van Johnson
in
A Thousand Clowns
by Herb Gardner

Lloyd Bridges
in
Anniversary Waltz
by Jerome Chodorov & Joseph Fields

My Fair Lady
Book by Alan Jay Lerner
Music by Frederick Loewe
Lyrics by Alan Jay Lerner

Cyril Ritchard & Cornelia Otis Skinner
in
The Irregular Verb to Love
by Hugh & Margaret Williams

The Sound of Music
Book by
Howard Lindsay & Russel Crouse
Music by Richard Rodgers
Lyrics by Oscar Hammerstein, 2nd

Hermione Gingold
in
**Oh Dad, Poor Dad,
Mama's Hung You in the Closet
and I'm Feeling So Sad**
by Arthur Kopit

Helen Hayes & James Daly
in
The White House
by A.E. Hotchner

1965

Eve Arden
in
Beekman Place
by Samuel Taylor

Hans Conried
in
Absence of a Cello
by Ira Wallach

Walter Pidgeon
in
The Happiest Millionaire
by Kyle Crichton

Camelot
Book by Alan Jay Lerner
Music by Frederick Loewe
Lyrics by Alan Jay Lerner

Mindy Carson, Rita Gam
& Betsy von Furstenberg
in
The Frog Pond
by Georgette Scott

Anne Baxter & Gene Raymond
in
Diplomatic Relations
by Alfred Allan Lewis

Darren McGavin & Will Hutchins
in
Here Lies Jeremy Troy
by Jack Sharkey

Arlene Francis & Ralph Meeker
in
Mrs. Dally Has a Lover
by William Hanley

Leslie Caron

1966

**How to Succeed in Business
Without Really Trying**
Book by Abe Burrows, Jack Weinstock
& Willie Gilbert
Music & Lyrics by Frank Loesser

Gertrude Berg
in
Dear Me, The Sky is Falling
by Leonard Spigelgass

Dennis Weaver
in
Catch Me if You Can
by Jack Weinstock & Willie Gilbert

Oliver! Book, Music & Lyrics by
Lionel Bart

Vivian Vance
in
The Time of the Cuckoo
by Arthur Laurents

Julia Meade & Scott McKay
in
Mary, Mary
by Jean Kerr

Betsy Palmer & Donald Madden
in
Jack Be Nimble
by Pamela Herbert Chais

Riverwind
Book, Music & Lyrics by
John Jennings

Alexis Smith & Gabriel Dell
in
The Coffee Lover
by Stefan Kanfer & Jess Korman

1967

Don Porter & Rosemary Prinz
in
Any Wednesday
by Muriel Resnik

Gary Moore & Dorothy Loudon
in
The Male Animal
by James Thurber & Elliott Nugent

Tab Hunter
in
Barefoot in the Park
by Neil Simon

Barbara Bel Geddes
in
Wait Until Dark
by Frederick Knott

Linda Gerard
In
Funny Girl
Book by Isobel Lennart
Music by Jule Styne
Lyrics by Bob Merrill

Betsy Palmer
in
Luv
by Murray Schisgal

Tom Ewell
in
The Impossible Years
by Bob Fisher & Arthur Marx

Half a Sixpence
Book by Beverley Cross
Music & Lyrics by David Heneker

Shirley Booth
in
The Torch-Bearers
by George Kelly

Alan Young & Mike Kellin
in
The Odd Couple
by Neil Simon

1968

Allen Ludden & Betty White
in
Once More, With Feeling
by Harry Kurnitz

Rosemary Prinz
in
A Girl Could Get Lucky
by Don Appell

Joan Fontaine
in
Private Lives
by Noël Coward

April Shawhan
in
Sweet Charity
Book by Neil Simon
Music by Cy Coleman
Lyrics by Dorothy Fields

Geraldine Page   Richard Dysart
Betty Field & John Beal
in
The Little Foxes
by Lillian Hellman

Show Boat
Book & Lyrics by
Oscar Hammerstein, 2nd
Music by Jerome Kern

Vivian Vance
in
Everybody's Girl
by John Patrick

Craig Stevens & Alexis Smith
in
Cactus Flower
by Abe Burrows

Shirley Booth
in
The Desk Set
by William Marchant

1969

Tom Ewell
in
Don't Drink the Water
by Woody Allen

Laurence Hugo
in
There's a Girl in My Soup
by Terence Frisby

Betsy Palmer
in
The Prime of Miss Jean Brodie
by Jay Allen

Jeannie Carson, Hurd Hatfield
& Biff McGuire
in
The Sound of Murder
by William Fairfield

James Whitmore & Audra Lindley
in
The Chic Life
by Arthur Marx & Robert Fisher

Sandra Deel & Paul Ukena
in
South Pacific
Book by Oscar Hammerstein, 2nd
& Joshua Logan
Music by Richard Rodgers
Lyrics by Oscar Hammerstein, 2nd

Arlene Francis & Joe Masiell
in
Pal Joey
Book by John O'Hara
Music by Richard Rodgers
Lyrics by Lorenz Hart

Eddie Bracken
in
**You Know I Can't Hear You
When the Water's Running**
by Robert Anderson

The Most Happy Fella
Book, Music & Lyrics by
Frank Loesser

1970

George Gobel
in
Play It Again Sam
by Woody Allen

John Gavin
in
The Fantasticks
Book by Tom Jones
Music by Harvey Schmidt
Lyrics by Tom Jones

William Shatner
in
The Tender Trap
by Max Shulman
& Robert Paul Smith

Noel Harrison
in
Blithe Spirit
by Noël Coward

Carousel
Book & Lyrics by
Oscar Hammerstein, 2nd
Music by Richard Rodgers

Shirley Booth
in
The Best of Friends
by James Elward

Edward Mulhare & Inga Swenson
in
The Secretary Bird
by William Douglas Home

Joan Fontaine
in
Relatively Speaking
by Ian Martin

Van Johnson
in
Boeing-Boeing
by Marc Camoletti

Patrice Munsel
in
I Do! I Do!
Book by Tom Jones
Music by Harvey Schmidt
Lyrics by Tom Jones

1971

Vivian Vance & Dody Goodman
in
My Daughter, Your Son
by Phoebe & Henry Ephron

Sandy Dennis
in
And Miss Reardon Drinks a Little
by Paul Zindel

Vivian Blaine Kitty Carlisle
Sam Levene Ruth McDevitt
in
Light Up the Sky
by Moss Hart

Douglas Fairbanks, Jr.
in
The Pleasure of His Company
by Samuel Taylor
& Cornelia Otis Skinner

Mike Kellin
in
Fiddler on the Roof
based on stories by Sholom Aleichem
Book by Joseph Stein
Music by Jerry Bock
Lyrics by Sheldon Harnick

Edward Mulhare & Beatrice Straight
in
The Right Honourable Gentleman
by Michael Dyre

Barbara Britton
in
Forty Carats
From a play by Barillet & Gredy
Adapted by Jay Allen

Eve Arden
in
Natural Ingredients
by Lee Thuna

Don Porter & Sheila MacRae
in
Plaza Suite
by Neil Simon

1972

Allan Jones
in
Man of La Mancha
Book by Dale Wasserman
Music by Mitch Lee
Lyrics by Joe Darion

Arlene Francis
in
Who Killed Santa Claus
by Terence Feely

George Gobel
in
Last of the Red Hot Lovers
by Neil Simon

Shirley Booth
in
Mourning in a Funny Hat
by Dody Goodman

The Merry Widow
Book revised by Milton Lazarus
Music by Franz Lehar
Lyrics by Forman Brown

Robert Stack, Eileen Heckart
& Marion Seldes
in
Remember Me
by Ronald Alexander

Joan Fontaine
in
Dial M for Murder
by Frederick Knott

Anne Russell
in
Hello, Dolly!
Book by Michael Stewart
Based on *The Matchmaker* by
Thornton Wilder
Music & Lyrics by Jerry Herman

Vivian Vance & George S. Irving
in
Clark & Myrna
by Elliot Baker

1973

Art Carney
in
The Prisoner of Second Avenue
by Neil Simon

Vivian Vance
in
Butterflies Are Free
by Leonard Gershe

Sada Thompson
in
Twigs
by George Furth

Mame
Book by Jerome Lawrence & Robert E. Lee
Music & Lyrics by Jerry Herman

Wilfrid Hyde-White
in
The Jockey Club Stakes
by William Douglas Home

Jerry Orbach & Marcia Rodd
in
6 Rms Riv Vu
by Bob Randall

Jack Cassidy
in
Suddenly at Home
by Francis Durbridge

Elaine Cancilla
in
Can-Can
Book by Abe Burrows
Music & Lyrics by Cole Porter

Jayne Meadows & Steve Allen

1974

Patrick MacNee & Jordan Christopher
in
Sleuth
by Anthony Shaffer

Helen Gallagher
in
No, No, Nanette
Book by Otto Harbach & Frank Mandel
Music by Vincent Youmans
Lyrics by Irving Caesar & Otto Harbach

Sandy Dennis & Gary Merrill
in
Born Yesterday
by Garson Kanin

Steve Allen & Jayne Meadows
in
Tonight at 8:30
Hands Across the Sea
Still Life   Fumed Oak
by Noël Coward

The Unsinkable Molly Brown
Book by Richard Morris
Music & Lyrics by Meredith Willson

Betsy Palmer & Fritz Weaver
in
Life With Father
by Howard Lindsay & Russel Crouse

Eileen Herlie & David McCallum
in
Crown Matrimonial
by Royce Ryton

Barbara Bel Geddes
in
Finishing Touches
by Jean Kerr

Jack Gilford & Lou Jacobi
in
The Sunshine Boys
by Neil Simon

1975

Irene
Book by Hugh Wheeler & Joseph Stein
Based on the play by James Montgomery
Music by Harry Tierney
Lyrics by Joseph McCarthy

Lynn Redgrave
in
The Two of Us
by Michael Frayn

Gabriel Dell & Jill O'Hara
in
Culture Caper
by Jerome Chodorov

Van Johnson
in
Send Me No Flowers
by Norman Barasch & Carroll Moore

John Astin & Patty Duke Astin
in
My Fat Friend
by Charles Lawrence

Kitty Carlisle
in
You Never Know
Based on the play *Candle Light*
Book adapted by Bruce Blain
Music & Lyrics by Cole Porter

Anne Russell
in
The Boy Friend
Book, Music & Lyrics by
Sandy Wilson

Sandy Dennis
in
Cat on a Hot Tin Roof
by Tennessee Williams

Pat Carroll
in
Something's Afoot
Book, Music & Lyrics
by James MacDonald,
David Vos and Robert Gerlach

1976

John Raitt
in
Shenandoah
Book by James Lee Barrett, Peter Udell
& Phillip Rose
Music by Gary Geld
Lyrics by Peter Udell

Victor Jory, Don Porter
& Scott McKay
in
The Best Man
by Gore Vidal

Betsy Palmer & David Selby
in
The Eccentricities of a Nightingale
by Tennessee Williams

Eva Marie Saint & John McMartin
in
The Fatal Weakness
by George Kelly

Ruth Warrick
in
Roberta
Book & Lyrics by Otto Harbach
Music by Jerome Kern

David McCallum, Carole Shelley
& Kurt Kasznar
in
The Mousetrap
by Agatha Christie

Anita Gillette   Russell Nype
David O'Brien   Maureen O'Sullivan
in
Sabrina Fair
by Samuel Taylor

Godspell
Based on the gospel according to
St. Matthew
Book by John Michael Tebelak
Music & Lyrics by Stephen Schwartz

1977

Christine Andreas & David Carroll
in
Oklahoma!
Book & Lyrics by Oscar Hammerstein, 2nd
Music by Richard Rodgers

Tony Tanner
in
Seven Keys to Baldpate
by George M. Cohan

Doug McClure & Lou Jacobi
in
Come Blow Your Horn
by Neil Simon

Paul Lipson
in
Fiddler on the Roof
based on stories by Sholom Aleichem
Book by Joseph Stein
Music by Jerry Bock
Lyrics by Sheldon Harnick

Tony Perkins & Berry Berenson
in
The Voice of the Turtle
by John Van Druten

Sandy Dennis & Gale Sondergaard
in
The Royal Family
by George S. Kaufman & Edna Ferber

John Raitt & Gaylea Byrne
in
I Do! I Do!
Book & Lyrics by Tom Jones
Music by Harvey Schmidt

Colleen Dewhurst & George Hearn
in
An Almost Perfect Person
by Judith Ross

1978

The Sound of Music
Book by Howard Lindsay & Russel Crouse
Music by Richard Rodgers
Lyrics by Oscar Hammerstein, 2nd

Jean Marsh
in
Twelfth Night
by William Shakespeare

David McCallum & Carole Shelley
in
Donkey's Years
by Michael Frayn

Maureen O'Sullivan
in
No Sex Please, We're British
by Anthony Marriott & Alistair Foot

Farley Granger
in
Count Dracula
Based on Bram Stoker's novel *Dracula*
by Ted Tiller

Patrice Munsel & Edward Mulhare
in
The Play's the Thing
by Ferenc Molnár

Kathy Garver
in
Vanities
by Jack Heifner

Julius La Rosa & Jo Sullivan
in
Guys and Dolls
Book by Jo Swerling & Abe Burrows
Based on a story by Damon Runyon
Music by Frank Loesser

1979

Camelot
Book & Lyrics by Alan Jay Lerner
Music by Frederick Loewe

Betsy Palmer
in
Wait Until Dark
by Frederick Knott

Geraldine Page   Anne Jackson
Kevin McCarthy Michael Higgins
in
Slightly Delayed
by James Prideaux

Joseph Abaldo
in
The Magic Show
Book by Bob Randall
Songs by Stephen Schwartz
Magic created for Broadway
by Doug Henning

John Raitt
in
Man of La Mancha
Book by Dale Wasserman
Music by Mitch Leigh
Lyrics by Joe Darion

George Grizzard
in
Deathtrap
by Ira Levin

Dorothy Collins
in
Ballroom
Book by Jerome Kass
Music by Billy Goldenberg
Lyrics by Alan & Marilyn Bergman

Sandy Dennis & Charles Kimbrough
in
Same Time, Next Year
by Bernard Slade

1980

Patrice Munsel
in
Mame
Book by Jerome Lawrence
& Robert E. Lee
Music & Lyrics by Jerry Herman

Anita Gillette   David Hedison
Susan Browning   Sal Viscuso
in
Chapter Two
by Neil Simon

Phyllis Thaxter & Larry Gates
in
The Gin Game
by D.L. Coburn

The Student Prince
Book & Lyrics by Dorothy Donnelly
Music by Sigmund Romberg

Sada Thompson
in
Children
by A.R. Gurney, Jr.

Van Johnson
in
Tribute
by Bernard Slade

Glynis Johns
in
An April Song
Based on Jean Anouilh's Leocadia
Adapted by Albert Marre

John Raitt
in
Carousel
Book & Lyrics by
Oscar Hammerstein, 2nd
Music by Richard Rodgers

1981

John Raitt
in
The Pajama Game
Book by George Abbott & Richard Bissell
Music & Lyrics by Richard Adler & Jerry Ross

Lawrence Pressman
in
I Ought to Be in Pictures
by Neil Simon

Janet Gaynor & William Swetland
in
On Golden Pond
by Ernest Thompson

The Merry Widow
Book by Victor Leon & Leo Stein
Music by Franz Lehar
Lyrics by Adrian Ross

Jane Powell & David Hedison
in
The Marriage-Go-Round
by Leslie Stevens

David McCallum & Dawn Wells
in
Romantic Comedy
by Bernard Slade

Marcia King & Stephen Pender
in
West Side Story
Book by Arthur Laurents
Music by Leonard Bernstein
Lyrics by Stephen Sondheim

Phyllis Newman

1982

Dolores Gray
in
Gypsy
Book by Arthur Laurents
Music by Jule Styne
Lyrics by Stephen Sondheim

Arlene Francis   Anita Gillette
Jeffrey Lynn   Donny Most
in
The Inkwell
by Harold J. Kennedy

John Raitt
in
South Pacific
Book by Oscar Hammerstein, 2nd
& Joshua Logan
Music by Richard Rodgers
Lyrics by Oscar Hammerstein, 2nd

James MacArthur
& Cybill Shepherd
in
Lunch Hour
by Jean Kerr

Shaun Cassidy   Betsy Palmer
& John McMartin
in
The Subject Was Roses
by Frank D. Gilroy

Sandy Dennis & Barbara Rush
in
The Supporting Cast
by George Furth

John Reardon
in
Kismet
Music from Alexander Borodin
Book by Charles Lederer
& Luther Davis
Musical adaption & lyrics
by Robert Wright & George Forrest

1983

John Hillner & Lauren Mitchell
in
They're Playing Our Song
Book by Neil Simon
Music by Marvin Hamlisch
Lyrics by Carole Bayer Sager

Jean Stapleton
in
Clara's Play
by John Olive

Shelley Winters & Donal Donnelly
in
84 Charing Cross Road
From the novel by Helene Hanff
Adapted by James Roose-Evans

Richard Kiley
in
Mass Appeal
by Bill C. Davis

Keir Dullea   Tammy Grimes
John Ireland   David McCallum
& Maureen O'Sullivan
in
Outward Bound
by Sutton Vane

Edie Adams
in
**The Best Little Whorehouse
in Texas**
Book by Larry L. King
& Peter Masterson
Music & Lyrics by Carol Hall

Bernie Kopell
in
The Dining Room
by A.R. Gurney, Jr.

Annie
Book by Thomas Meehan
Music by Charles Strouse
Lyrics by Martin Charnin

1984

John Raitt
in
Kiss Me Kate
Book by Bella & Samuel Spewack
Music & Lyrics by Cole Porter

Joseph Bottoms   Maeve McGuire
Valerie Mahaffey   Laurence Hugo
in
The Middle Ages
by A.R. Gurney, Jr.

Betsy Palmer
in
Breakfast with Les and Bess
by Lee Kalcheim

Linda Purl
in
Snacks
by Leonard Gersche

The American Dance Machine
Under the Supervision & Direction
of Lee Theodore

Fannie Flagg, Larry Linville
& David Doyle
in
Murder at the Howard Johnson's
by Ron Clark & Sam Bobrick

Pump Boys and Dinettes
Music, Book & Lyrics Created by
Pump Boys & Dinettes

Show Boat
Book & Lyrics by
Oscar Hammerstein, 2nd
Music by Jerome Kern

1985

Anne Russell
in
Hello, Dolly!
Book by Michael Stuart
Based on *The Matchmaker* by
Thornton Wilder
Music & Lyrics by Jerry Herman

Nanette Fabray
in
Upper Broadway
by James Prideaux

Leslie Caron
in
One for the Tango
From a comedy by Maria Pacome
Adapted by Mawby Green
& Ed Feilbert

Evita
Book & Lyrics by Tim Rice
Music by Andrew Lloyd Webber

Bob Denver
in
The Foreigner
By Larry Shue

David McCallum
in
Run For Your Wife
by Ray Cooney

Larry Kert
in
The Music Man
Book, Music & Lyrics
by Meredith Willson

Sally Struthers

1986

Jesus Christ Superstar
Music by Andrew Lloyd Webber
Lyrics by Tim Rice

Rosemary Prinz & Fannie Flagg
in
The Odd Couple
by Neil Simon

Conrad Bain
in
Country Cops
by Robert Lord

A Chorus Line
Book James Kirkwood & Nicholas Dante
Music Marvin Hamlisch
Lyrics Edward Kleban

Robert Sean Leonard
in
Brighton Beach Memoirs
by Neil Simon

Michael Learned & Eileen Heckart
in
Pack of Lies
by Hugh Whitemore

William Chapman & Jo Sullivan
The King and I
Book & Lyrics by
Oscar Hammersteirn, 2nd
Music by Richard Rodgers

1987

Sugar Babies
Conceived by Ralph G. Allen & Harry Rigby
Music by Jimmy McHugh
Lyrics by Dorothy Fields & Al Dubin

John Monteith & Suzanne Rand
in
Monteith & Rand

Lee Richardson & Frances Sternhagen
in
All My Sons
by Arthur Miller

1776
Book by Peter Stone
Music & Lyrics by Sherman Edwards

Nunsense
Book, Music & Lyrics by
Don Goggin

Robert Sean Leonard
in
Biloxi Blues
by Neil Simon

42nd Street
Book by Michael Stewart & Mark Bramble
Music by Harry Warren
Lyrics by Al Dubin

Noel Harrison

1988	1989	1990
My One and Only Book by Peter Stone & Timothy S. Mayer Music by George Gershwin Lyrics by Ira Gershwin	**Anything Goes** Book by Guy Bolton, P.G. Wodehouse, Howard Lindsay & Russel Crouse Music & Lyrics by Cole Porter	**Seven Brides for Seven Brothers** Book by Lawrence Kasha & David Landay Music by Gene de Paul Lyrics by Johnny Mercer
Return Engagements by Bernard Slade	Elizabeth Ashley in **All the Queen's Men** by John Nassivera	Anita Gillette, Margo Martindale & Marilyn Cooper in **Steel Magnolias** by Robert Harling
Beehive Created by Larry Gallagher	Jaston Williams, Joe Sears & Ed Howard in **Greater Tuna** by Jaston Williams, Joe Sears & Ed Howard	**Me and My Girl** Book & Lyrics by L. Arthur Rose & Douglas Furber Music by Noel Gay
La Cage Aux Folles Based on the play by Jean Poiret Book by Harvey Fierstein Music & Lyrics by Jerry Herman	**Broadway Bound** by Neil Simon	Rosemary Prinz & Ellis E. Williams in **Driving Miss Daisy** by Alfred Uhry
Paul Soles & Samuel E. Wright in **I'm Not Rappaport** by Herb Gardner	**Ain't Misbehavin'** Music by Thomas *Fats* Waller Conceived & Directed by Richard Maltby, Jr.	**Fiddler on the Roof** based on stories by Sholom Aleichem Book by Joseph Stein Music by Jerry Bock Lyrics by Sheldon Harnick
Michael Constantine & Lawrence Pressman in **A Walk in the Woods** by Lee Blessing	**The Sound of Music** Book by Howard Lindsay & Russel Crouse Music by Richard Rodgers Lyrics by Oscar Hammerstein, 2nd	
The Desert Song Book & Lyrics by Otto Harbach, Oscar Hammerstein, 2nd & Frank Mandel Music by Sigmund Romberg		

Arlene Francis

Frances Sternhagen

1991

Where's Charlie?
Book by George Abbott
Music & Lyrics by
Frank Loesser

George Grizzard, Jack Gilpin
& Jane Connell
in
Lend Me a Tenor
by Ken Ludwig

John Raitt
in
Man of La Mancha
Written by Dale Wasserman
Music by Mitch Lee
Lyrics by Joe Darion

Rumors
by Neil Simon

Annie Get Your Gun
Book by
Herbert & Dorothy Fields
Music & Lyrics by Irving Berlin

1992

Funny Girl
Book by Isobel Lennart
Music by Jule Styne
Lyrics by Bob Merrill

Carole Shelley & Doris Belack
in
Lettice and Lovage
by Peter Shaffer

Jamie Farr
in
Damn Yankees
Book by
George Abbott & Douglass Wallop
Music & Lyrics by
Richard Adler & Jerry Ross

Gary Sandy
in
Breaking Legs
by Tom Dulack

Pat Carroll
in
Nunsense
Book, Music & Lyrics by
Dan Goggin

1993

Phantom
Book by Arthur Kopit
Music & Lyrics by
Maury Yeston

Millicent Martin
in
Noises Off
by Michael Frayn

Pat Carroll
in
Nunsense II
Book, Music & Lyrics by
Dan Goggin

Dancing at Lughnasa
by Brian Friel

Oil City Symhony
by Mike Craver, Mark Hardwick
Debra Monk & Mary Murfitt

Lloyd Bridges

Jane Wyman

Tab Hunter

1994

Karen Valentine & Anita Gillette
in
How the Other Half Loves
by Alan Ayckbourn

Loretta Swit
in
Song of Singapore
Book by Alan Katz, Erik Frandsen
Michael Garin, Robert Hipkens
& Paula Lockheart
Music & Lyrics by Erik Frandsen,
Michael Garin, Robert Hipkens
& Paula Lockheart

The Most Happy Fella
Book, Music & Lyrics
by Frank Loesser

Maureen Anderman,
Frank Converse
& Carole Shelley
in
Later Life
by A.R. Gurney, Jr.

Forever Plaid
Written & originally directed by
Stuart Ross

1995

A Chorus Line
Book by James Kirkwood
& Nicholas Dante
Music by Marvin Hamlisch
Lyrics by Edward Kleban

The Supporting Cast
by George Furth

Frank Converse, Robert Hogan
& David Huddleston
in
Camping With Henry and Tom
by Mark St. Germain

Kitty Carlisle, John Raitt
& Jo Sullivan
in
Yes, There Were Giants
Conceived by Evans Haile

Gavin MacLeod
in
Last of the Red Hot Lovers
by Neil Simon

1996

David McCallum & Jean LeClerc
in
Angel Street
by Patrick Hamilton

George Dvorsky & Edwardyne Cowan
in
Brigadoon
Book & Lyrics by Alan Jay Lerner
Music by Frederick Loewe

Stephanie Zimbalist   Edward Genest
Mary Beth Peil   Tim Donoghue
in
Sylvia
by A. R. Gurney, Jr.

Five Guys Named Moe
Book by Clarke Peters
Music & Lyrics by Louis Jordon

"Thank You, John Lane"
Sunday Aug. 11th, 1996
Starring
Maureen Brennan   Kitty Carlisle
George Dvorsky   Russell Nype
Betsy Palmer   John Raitt
Lee Roy Reams   Jo Sullivan
Karen Ziemba
& The Company of
Five Guys Named Moe

Bonnie Franklin, Dody Goodman
& David Hedison
in
Social Security
by Andrew Bergman

Eva Marie Saint

1997

Carousel
Book & Lyrics by
Oscar Hammerstein, 2nd
Music by Richard Rodgers

Pat Carroll & Bonnie Franklin
in
Grace & Glorie
by Tim Ziegler

Spider's Web
by Agatha Christie

Lee Roy Reams & Florence Lacy
with Jerry Herman
in
An Evening With Jerry Herman
Music by Jerry Herman

Gavin MacLeod & Millicent Martin
in
Moon Over Buffalo
by Ken Ludwig

1998

La Cage Aux Folles
Based oon the play by Jean Poiret
Book by Harvey Fierstein
Music & Lyrics by Jerry Herman

Anita Gillette & David Hedison
in
Alone Together
by Lawrence Roman

Dodie Goodman & Mary Fogarty
in
Expectations
by Susan Barsky

Juliet Mills & Maxwell Caulfield
in
Dial M for Murder
by Frederick Knott

Liz Sheridan
in
Something's Afoot
Book, Music & Lyrics
by James MacDonald, David Vos
& Robert Gerlach

1999

**A Funny Thing Happened
on the Way to the Forum**
Book by Burt Shevelove
& Larry Gelbart
Music & Lyrics by
Stephen Sondheim

Kier Dullea, Mia Dillon
& Elizabeth Parrish
in
Deathtrap
by Ira Levin

Phyllis Newman
& Randall Duk Kim
in
A Majority of One
by Leonard Spigelgass

Carolyn Michel, Sharon Spelman
& Bradford Wallace
in
The Last Night of Ballyhoo
by Alfred Uhry

Light Up the Sky
by Moss Hart

Broadway's Best Sing Gershwin
Conceived by Evans Haile
Music by George Gershwin

Patrick Macnee

Fanny Flagg

2000

Joey Kern, Nick Paonessa
& Steven Rosen
in
**The Compleat Wrks
of Wllm Shkspr**
Based on the works of
William Shakespeare

Stephanie Zimbalist & Richard Kind
in
Accomplice
by Rupert Homes

The Will Rogers Follies
Book by Peter Stone
Music by Cy Coleman
Lyrics by Betty Comden
& Adolph Green

William Atherton, David Dukes
& Jack Willis
in
Art
by Yasmina Reza
Translated by Christopher Hampton

Grease
Book, Music & Lyrics
by Jim Jacobs & Warren Casey

2001

Eva Marie Saint & Jeffrey Hayden
in
Love Letters
by A. R. Gurney, Jr.

Jean LeClerc
in
Dracula
Based on the novel by Bram Stoker
by Hamilton Deane
& John L. Balderston

42nd Street
Book by Michael Stewart
& Mark Bramble
Music by Harry Warren
Lyrics by Al Dubin

**I Love You, You're Perfect,
Now Change**
Book & Lyrics by Joe DiPietro
Music by Jimmy Roberts

**Joseph and the Amazing
Technicolor Dreamcoat**
Book & Lyrics by Tim Rice
Music by Andrew Lloyd Webber

2002

George M!
Book by Michael Stewart, John Pascal
& Francine Pascal
Music & Lyrics by George M. Cohan

Buddy
Book by Alan Janes
Music & Lyrics by Buddy Holly

Chicago
Book by Fred Ebb & Bob Fosse
Music by John Kander
Lyrics by Fred Ebb

Nunsense
Book, Music & Lyrics by
Dan Goggin

Footloose
Book by Dean Pitchford
& Walter Bobbie
Based on the original screenplay by
Dean Pitchford
Music by Tom Snow
Lyrics by Dean Pitchford

Cesar Romero

2003

Ain't Misbehavin'
Music by Thomas *Fats* Waller
Conceived & originally directed by
Richard Maltby, Jr

Karen Black, Mike Burstyn
& Jana Robbins
in
The Tale of the Allergist's Wife
by Charles Busch

Felicia Finley
in
Evita
Book & Lyrics by Tim Rice
Music by
Andrew Lloyd Webber

Sally Struthers & Christa Jackson
in
Always…Patsy Cline
Written & originally directed by
Ted Swindley

Annie
Book by Thomas Meehan
Music by Charles Strouse
Lyrics by Martin Charnin

2004

Sally Struthers & Christa Jackson
in
Always…Patsy Cline
Written & originally directed by
Ted Swindley

Charles Busch
in
Auntie Mame
Written by Jerome Lawrence
& Robert E. Lee

Smokey Joe's Café
Music & Lyrics by
Jerry Leiber & Mike Stoller

Cats
Music by Andrew Lloyd Webber
Lyrics by T.S. Eliot

Barbara Hunt
in
Late Night Catechism
by
Maripat Donovan & Vickie Quade

Beauty and the Beast
Book by Linda Woolverton
Music by Alan Menken
Lyrics by Howard Ashman & Tim Rice

2005

Forever Plaid
Written & originally directed by
Stuart Ross

Aida
Book by Linda Woolverton
Robert Falls & David Henry Hwang
Music by Elton John
Lyrics by Tim Rice

Sally Struthers
in
**The Best Little Whorehouse
in Texas**
Book by Larry L. King
& Peter Masterson
Music & Lyrics by Carol Hall

Swing
A Dance Review
Original concept by Paul Kelly
Original direction & choreography by
Lynne Taylor-Corbett

Nunsensations
The Nunsense Vegas Revue
Book, Music & Lyrics by
Dan Goggin

Lynn Redgrave

2006

Beehive
Created by Larry Gallagher

Andrea McArdle
in
Cabaret
Book by Joe Masteroff
Based on *I Am a Camera*
by John Van Druten
Based on Christopher Isherwoods's
Berlin Stories
Music by John Kander
Lyrics by Fred Ebb

Sally Struthers
in
Hello, Dolly!
Book by Michael Stewart
Based on *The Matchmaker* by
Thornton Wilder
Music & Lyrics by Jerry Herman

Leslie Uggams
Jessica Rush, Paolo Montalban
& Ryan Landry
in
Cinderella
Book & Lyrics by
Oscar Hammerstein, 2nd
Music by Richard Rodgers

Menopause, The Musical
Book & Lyrics by Jeanie Linders

2007

Menopause, The Musical
Book & Lyrics by Jeanie Linders

Sally Struthers & Hunter Foster
in
The Full Monty
Book by Terrence McNally
Based on the original screenplay by
Simon Beaufoy
Music and lyrics by David Yazbek
(reprised at the end of the season)

Rue McClanahan
Jeffrey Denman & Beverly Ward
in
Crazy for You
Book by Ken Ludwig
Music by George Gershwin
Lyrics by Ira Gershwin

Maxwell Caulfield & James Beaman
in
La Cage aux Folles
Based on the play by Jean Poiret
Book by Harvey Fierstein
Music and lyrics by Jerry Herman

Lorenzo Lamas
in
The King and I
Book & Lyrics by Oscar Hammerstein 2nd
Music by Richard Rodgers

Ryan Landry & Eddie Mekka
in
Hairspray
Book by Mark O'Donnell & Thomas Meehan
Music by Marc Shaiman
Lyrics by Scott Wittman & Marc Shaiman

Ezio Pinza

Leslie Uggams

The Staff

THE MANHATTAN THEATRE REPERTORY COMPANY
Mrs. Maude Hartwig Producer 1941-1949
George Abbott Producer & Robert Fryer Managing Director 1947
Mrs. Maude Hartwig with John Lane 1950

ny Albert	Arthur Gerwick	Pat Meikle
rold Anderson	Edmund Gibb	Alice Menendez
n Andrews	Edwin Gifford	James Miller
rence Ardery	Lenore Goodkin	Estele Morrison
uglas Baker	Vincent Gookin	Howard Muller
bert Barry	Ray Graham	Culbertson Myers
gia Bernard	Paul Heller	Larry Parker
nes Biondo	Melvin Helstien	Elizabeth Parrish
bert Boak	Mary E. Hervey	Peter Preses
rothy Bourne	Charles Hill	Jock Purinton
n Bower	Erborn Hilton	Jack Ragan
rothy Bragdon	Stephen Hindrich	Carl A. Reed
te Brown	Ralph Holmes	Sally Jane Rohm
ricia Blomfield Brown	F. Richard Hopkins	Victor Salmone
bert Bullock	Tom Jewett	Rudolph Sauerhering
wrence Carr	John Kirkpatrick	Charles Schon
arlotte Chapman	Hilary Knight	Alexander Segal
rroll Clark, Jr.	Naomi Kramer	Leonard Sheldon
elyn Cohen	Jane Leech	Garrison P. Sherwood
l Cooper	Noel Leslie	Emma B. Smith
n Cosgrove	John Robert Lloyd	Herman Smith
rothy Davies	Eugene Loring	Pamela Stiles
ward Colin Dawson	Robert Lowen	Charles Suggs
ncis Dixon	Laviah Lucking	James Thrasher
ester Doherty	Charles MacArthur	Joseph Trovato
n Doherty	Robert MacKichan	Kenneth Trueman
arles Elson	Richard Mansur	Ann Van Dyke
n T. Evans	Helen Marcus	Philip Van Dyke
bert Evans	Carolyn Marshall	James Walworth
orge Fluharty	Olive Matthews	Prescott Wellman, Jr.
nifred Forwood	John McDivit	Lorraine Wheeler
nee Franklyn	John H. McDowell	Wade Williams
hard Franklyn	S. Wesley McKee	Esther Wilson
orge Fuller	Frances McKeeman	Alexander Wycoff

Often when we pay tribute to plays and their stars, we forget that it takes many people and many hours to achieve the results which are seen onstage. In recognition of those who have applied their varied s endeavor, we have compiled a list of staff members spanning the 75-plus years of Playhouse history. So for only a week, and others were there for many years. Some had more important positions than other worked for many hours to make this theatrical history happen. We apologize for those who were n Because of a shortage of records and a sizeable number of employees, some may have been neglected gratitude and admiration, we present the following list of names and congratulate them on their achieve

THE MANHATTAN THEATRE REPERTORY COMPANY
Walter Hartwig, Producer and Director 1933-1940

Richmond Adams
John Alexander
Albert Allen
Paul Anglim
Gibbons Ash
Aldon Asherman
David Asherman
Edward Asherman
Charles Babcock, 3rd
Frederick Banker
Nelson Barclifft
Ernest Carriere
Raymond Chamberlain
Alvin Cohen, 2nd
Evelyn Cohen
Belmont Corn, Jr.
Maria Coxe
Henry Darbee
Arthur Davidson
Edward Colin Dawson
Dedie Dickinson
Francis Dixon
Charles Elson
Charles Eschmeyer
Bernard Fabrizi
Harry Forwood
Nannie Foster
Robert Foulk
David S. Gaither

Beata Gray
Justin Gray
Robert Gundlach
John Winchester Gunnell
Stephen Harriman
Maude Hartwig
Carl Z. Heller
Mary E. Hervey
Cay Hillegas
Chester Hilton
Erborn Hilton
Richard Hopkins
Russell J. Kenty
James Kirkpatrick
John Kirkpatrick
Paul Kunasz
Johannes Larson
Ernita Lascelles
Paul Laurent
Eugene Loring
Kyra Markham
John M. McDowell
Kenneth Michael
Anne Minor
Howard Muller
Ruth Adele Mysel
Hubert Osbourne
Douglas G. Pannier
Paul Parker

Howard Patch, Jr.
Sam Pearce
Henry Pickering
D. Cameron Pond
Alexander Redcow
Sidney Redish
Carl A. Reed
Michael Robinson
Betty Rosoff
Rudolph Sauerhering
Stephen Searles
Eloise Sheldon
John Simonds
Peter Sprague
Jean Stephenson
George Stonehill
Mary Stonehill
Mary X. Sullivan
James Thrasher
Arthur B. Tourtellot
Prescott Wellman, Jr.
Edna Westervelt
Bolton Wilder
Thomas Wilfred
Giles Wilson
David Woodbury
Alexander Wycoff
Charles Kendall Yeaton
Asa Zatz

Manhattan Trio Members

Harold Bogin
Frank Brieff
Bernard Greenhouse

Eugene Kusmiak
Jacques Larner
Morris Lawner

Geoge Ockner
Sascha Rubenstein
Alice Wachtel

John Lane, Producer
1951-1997

Thomas Ahart
Carmen Albanese
Milton Aldrich
David Alexander
Jack L. Alexander
Carol Amorosi
Michael Anania
Joan Apter
Annamarie Arcery
Chris Armen
Breck Armstrong
Virginia Armstrong
Daisy Atherton
Howard Atlee
Ross Bachelder
David S. Baird
Fred Baker
S. Neill Baker
Thomas Baldwin
John Ballenger
Kathleen Ballo
Bill Ballou
Jennifer Banta
Lise Baratta
John Barna
William E. Barnes
Bob Barnett
Lucy Barry
Thomas M. Beall
Carroll Beals
Donald Beckman
Carol Behr
Ursula Beldon
Robert Bennett
Rick Berger
Robert Berkley
Louis Berman
Lygia Bernard
Laurie Berry

Paul Bertelsen
Rolf Beyer
James Bierman
Gerald Bihm
Alan Billings
Robert Birmingham
Randi Bishop
Scott Blaufuss
Joseph Bly
Susan M. Boodey
Christopher Bos
Robert C. Boston, Jr.
T. L. Boston
Richard Bradley
Evelyn Breitenbach
Cornelia S. Brewer
William Briggs
Tom Brittingham
Harry Brodsky
Larry Brodsky
Mitch Bronfman
Sean Brosnahan
Bette Brown
Walter Brownsword
Jane M. Bruskiewitz
Hannah Burnham
Nick Burns
Don Buschmann
W. Scott Bussey
Isabelle Calais
Matthew Calardo
Ian Calderon
Stephen Caldwell
Reagan Campbell
Donal Cardwell
John Carlson
Carole Lee D. Carroll
Robert Carrow
Stanley H. Carter

Betty Jane Casey
Thomas Casker
Joseph G. Casper
Ray Caton
Greg Chabay
Richard Chambers
Susan Chamblee
Paul Charette
Stanley Chase
John Christopher
Nicholas Chrumka
Mathew Clancy
Ann C. Clark
Nancy Clark
Scott E. Clement
Janice A. Clermont
Charles Cohen
Tamar Cohn
Matthew Colt
Roderick Cook
D.R. Cooke
Graham Cookson
Helen Coonley
William Cope
Aaron Copp
Claire Cousineau
Deborah M. Coutts
Stephen Cowles
David Crabtree
John Craig
Darcey Crandall
Jan Cream
Deborah A. Cross
Neil Curtis
Mark Cytron
Eileen Dahill
Laurel A. Dahill
Kate Dale
James D'Asaro

John Lane, Producer (cont'd)

- Frank Davidson
- Charles Davisson
- Paul Day
- Kenneth Decker
- Michael Deegan
- Elizabeth May Degitz
- Michael Degitz
- John E. DelCarlino, Jr.
- Christine DelVecchio
- Paul DePass
- Paul Deschenes
- Jacques Desnoyers
- Patricia Dillon
- Mary Ellen DiMartino
- Steven Diroif
- Francis Dixon
- Gale Dixon
- Miles Doane
- Walter Dolan
- Mary Jo Dondlinger
- Jonathan M. Doyle
- Stephen Drueke
- Brenda Duncan
- William B Duncan
- Cathy Dunham
- Norma Echroate
- Simon Eckles
- Julian Edwards
- Terrence Edwards
- Brian Elmer
- Steve Enderes
- James Engstrand
- Amy S. Evans
- Bob Evans
- Cassandra J. Ewing
- Kenneth R. Farley
- Paul Farrell
- J. Reid Farrington
- Martha Fay
- Thomas Fellows
- Vanessa Fenton
- Kristin Feret
- Colin Ferguson
- Audrey Field
- Thomas Field
- Charles Fields
- Stephen Filipiak
- Barry R. Finch
- Nancy T. Finn
- Suzann Fischer
- Deborah M. Fisher
- Abigail Fitzgibbons
- Donnie Fleming
- David Fletcher
- Deanna Fleysher
- George Fluharty
- Kevin W. Flynn
- William J. Flynn
- Mrs. Paul Foley
- Paul Foley
- Jim Foote
- John S. Fore
- Charles Forman
- Edward Forys
- Donald Foss
- Paul Foster
- David T. Fowle
- Renee Franklyn
- Richard Franklyn
- Stephanie Fretwell
- Deidre Friebely
- John Friebely
- Sheree H. Friesen
- John Fusco
- Michael Gall
- Victor A. Gelb
- Dawn Genstil
- Susan Gervais
- S. Michael Getz
- Christina Giannini
- Stephen Glassman
- Aaron Glazier
- Marci A. Glotzer
- Jeffrey M. Glovsky
- Andrew L. Goldberg
- Kevin Golden
- Jess Goldstein
- Charlotte Gooch
- George Gooch
- Bill Goodwin
- Vincent Gookin
- Joseph Goshert
- Lance Goss
- Susan A. Goulet
- Carol A. Graebner
- Steve Graham
- Jennifer R. Graves
- Jennifer A. Gray
- Robert Gray
- Sebastian Grouard
- Wade B. Gum
- Mark Haack
- David Habercom
- Carolyn Hagood
- David Halstead
- Elizabeth Halstead
- Quentin Halstead
- David Hale Hand
- Joseph Hanley
- Timothy J. Hanlon
- Pearl Hanson
- Gillian Harker
- David Harper
- Maureen Harrington
- Frederica D. Hart
- William Haviland
- Helen Hayes
- Joshua Hayes
- Ron Hayes
- Derek Healy

John Lane, Producer (cont'd)

- Patrick J. Healy
- Jeffery W. Heath
- Karen A. Heath
- Alex Helfenbein
- Tina Henry
- Kathleen Herald
- John Hiemstra
- Elaine V. Hildago
- Robert Hileman
- Joseph C. Hill
- H. N. Hinkle
- Mark A. Hoch
- William Stryker Hoe
- Barry Hoffman
- Carol Holbrook
- John Holden
- Diane Holly
- Neil A. Holmes
- Roni Holtzberg
- William Horehlad
- William G. Horton
- Sean Houle
- David Hudnall
- David W. Hughes
- Rene Hulitar
- William T. Hurd
- Betty Hutchins
- David Hutchins
- Cynthia Hyde
- Carolyn Irons
- Paul J. Israel
- Heath Jackson
- Susan Jackson
- William Jackson
- Theresa Jacques
- Daniel Jaffee
- Ana Janssen
- Seth Jason
- Jennifer Jebejian
- Connie Jennings
- Donald Jensen
- Doris Joaquin
- Juanita Johnson
- Sabrina Jones
- Bruce Kagel
- Alan Kass
- Scott W. Kearney
- Susan Kearns
- Anne Elizabeth Kelley
- Barbara Kelly
- Barbara Kemp
- Craig Kennedy
- Ralph E. Kerr
- Breck Ketchum
- Tamara Kirkman
- John Kirkpatrick
- Regina Knight
- Ruth E. Kramer
- Margo Kuhne
- Jimm Kunkle
- John LaCourse
- Michael LaCourse
- Charles LaFehr
- Laura Lambert
- Paul Lambert
- Pearl Lambert
- Tim Lambert
- Maura Landis
- Margaret D. Landry
- Michael D. Landry
- Steven J. Landry
- Joe Lane
- Donald LaPlant
- Catherine A. Lass
- Richard Latta
- T.W. Laughner
- Alan Leach
- Patricia Frey Leach
- Joan Leary
- Gloria M. LeBlanc
- Robert LeBlanc
- Jim Leger
- Michael Leitschuh
- Ralph Levinson
- Bradford Lewis
- Cheryll Lewis
- Andrew M. Liliskis
- James Lissenden
- Charles Littlefield
- John Locke
- Douglas P. Loftus
- Paul Lombardo
- Sheila Lombardo
- G. A. Longo
- Jack Lovett
- Harry E. Lowell
- Catherine Case Lutes
- Christine Lynam
- Michael Maddux
- Carol Madeira
- Marcia Madeira
- Rosalind K. Magnuson
- Gail Eve Malatesta
- David Mann
- Melissa Margolies
- Arthur Marlowe
- Greg Marriner
- Esther Martin
- Lynda Martin
- R. Bruce Martin
- John Martin-Cotton
- Barbara Jones Mather
- Joshua Mather
- Mort Mather
- Mark McCullough
- Tennent McDaniel
- Dr. Charles McGaw
- John McGee
- Brian McMahon
- Mary McNelis

John Lane, Producer (cont'd)

- Caroline Meade
- David Meltzer
- Michael Meyer
- M. Ross Michaels
- Gordon Micunis
- John Drew Miglietta
- Andrew Mihok
- Michael Miles
- James H. Miller
- Nathan W. Miller
- Nelson Miller
- David Millman
- David Mockler
- Karin S. Moller
- Bruce Monroe
- Steve Monsey
- Marian Mooney
- Leavitt E. Moulton
- Lynn M. Moulton
- Sherrill Ann Moyer
- Peter B. Mumford
- Brian Murphy
- William J. Nacy
- Cliff Nancarrow
- Joseph Nederlander
- Dean Nelson
- Jan A. Nelson
- Blair Nesbitt
- Willard R. Neuert
- Kathleen Norman
- David Nowakowski
- Scott Nutter
- Madeline M. O'Connell
- Erin Oestreich
- Deborah Olney
- Laura A. O'Neill
- Don Padgett
- King Page
- Stephen Page
- Dale Parry
- Cary Parsons
- John Patterson
- Michael Patterson
- John Paul
- Vickie Paul
- Kitty Pearson
- Lynn Pecktal
- Darold Perkins
- Ralph J. Perrone
- William Lee Perry
- Joseph Peters
- Richard Peterson
- Norma Petisi
- Kathleen Siobhan Phelan
- Roger D. Pippin
- Gerarda Pizzarello
- Charles Platt, 4th
- Amanda Plummer
- Jose Polansky
- Peter Politanoff
- Peter Poor
- Abe Pounds
- Ann Powderly
- Jock Purinton
- Harold Radochia
- Joan Ragusa
- William Ralph
- Alison Ramsey
- F.D. Rawlinson
- Timothy Rayel
- Patrick Reaves
- Richard Reece
- Renee Reed
- Sean W. Reese
- Stuart Reese
- Leigh Resnik
- Suzanne Ress
- Edith Reveley
- Michael Reznicek
- Joshua Rich
- Bradley Richard
- Barbara Richter
- Della Ridley
- Amanda Riemer
- Nicholas Riotto
- Michael Rizzo
- Guy M. Roberge
- Janet Roberts
- Linda Roberts
- Laura Rockefeller
- George Rondo
- Rim Rose
- William P. Ross
- Shawn M. Rouillard
- Joe Roulier
- Sandra Rowe
- William J. Ryan
- Michele E. Sammarco
- Enrique Sanchez
- Adam P. Sanford
- Marilyn Sarelas
- Robert A. Schanke
- Ruth Schanke
- Charles Scheitler
- Lauren Schneider
- Roland Scott
- James R. Seely
- David Sell
- Charley Shafor
- Allen Shapiro
- Stephen Shapiro
- Harold Shaw
- Joanne L. Shaw
- Harriet L. Sheets
- Michael Sheridan
- Robert J. Sheridan
- Ray Sherman
- Virginia Shields
- Jamie Shows
- Alden Shum

John Lane, Producer (cont'd)

Sally Sieber
Daniel Siegelson
James Singlar
Richard L. Sirois
Mathew Skinner
Herman Smith
Neil B. Smith
Patrick M. Smith
Tim Smith
Deborah A. Snyder
Maria A. Somma
Edward Sostek
John P. Spears
William Stackhouse
Robert Stanton
Julia Palin Staples
Russell A. Staples
Hilda Stark
Sally Starkey
James St. Clair
Paul St. Pierre
Hope Stearns
Richard Stern
Bradford Sterl
Jeffrey Stevens
Charles B. Stockton
Michael Stone
Ben Strobach
Julie Strong
Benjamin Strout
Carolyn Suder
Greg Sullivan
Vickie Sussman
Jack Douglas Sutton
Sherwood J. Tarlow
Gary Tenenbaum

David Thalenberg
Patrice Thomas
Robert Thomas
Dorothy A. Thompson
Julie Thurlow
Cynthia Tillotson
Michael Toner
Jason Townley
Karen Townsend
Robert Townsend
Edwin Toy
William A. Traber
Louise Tragard
Mathew Tragert
Victoria Traube
Laura Trezza
William Tucker
Michael Tushaus
Sara Valentine
Charles Van Metre
Celeste Varricchio
John Vaul
Hannah Vesenka
Suzie Vincent
George J. Viney
Bernard Voichysonk
Olthje Von Erpecom
Martha Wadsworth
Richard Waite
Alan Walker
Daniel Walker
Jessie Walker
Kathy Walker
Frederick Walsh
Katie Walsh
Misty J. Warburton
Clara E. Ward

David Ward
James Ward
J. Paul Wargo
Sam Warner
Kimberly Weatherill
Paul Webber
Ronald Weirick
Henry J. Weller
Parmalee Welles
Christopher S. Wells
Michael Werman
Douglas Werts
Christopher White
Derek Whitehead
Carol Whittier
Kaye Wild
Jennie Willink
Barbara Wilson
John Wilson
Molly Windover
Nancy Winters
Jeffrey Wonders
Elizabeth A. Wood
Steven Wood
James Woolley
Vance Wormwood
Wayne Wormwood
Joyce Worsley
John G. Wright
Liz Wright
Eric Young
Neil W. W. Young
Scott A. Young
Gary Zieff
Daniel Zittel
Mark Zola

OGUNQUIT PLAYHOUSE FOUNDATION
Robert Townsend, Producer 1998-1999
Roy Rogosin, Producing Artistic Director 2000-2005
Bradford T. Kenney, Executive Artistic Director 2006-present
*Former Board Members

Shari Arlin
Antonio Arosemena
Matt Ballinger
Byron Batista
Thomas M. Beall
Meghann M.G. Beauchamp
Jean Benda
Sean Berdick
Lea Bergford
Kim Beringer
Josh Bey
Laura Bice
Ani Blackburn
Beth Bloomfield
Jim Boyle
Thomas Bresnahan*
Robert G. Brown*
Timothy Bruneau
Danielle Buccino
Electra Buhalis
Sean Burdick
Jim Burkholder
Hannah Burnham
Derek Buschman
Michelle J. Bussiere
Heather Cammarn
Reagan E. Campbell
Margaret Canning
Carrie Capizzano
Tammy Carter
Greg Carville
Vince Cirivello
Ann C. Clark
Fran Clark
Janice Clermont
Kim S. Codner

Mathew F. Colt
Gina Brannagan Connolly
Scott Cooke
Phillip Cope
Ryan Cope
Matt Cost
Sarah Cost
James E. Crochet
Charlie Dahill
Eileen Dahill
Wendy Davidson
Jewel Davis
James Dell'Erba
Michelle DeMello
Ed Desper
Rene DesRoberts
Philip DeVaul
Amber Dickerson
Huguette P. Doherty
Geof Dolan
Emily S. Doyle
Stephen Drueke
Sarah Duclos
Becca Dunhaime
Eric Dwyer
Susan Boyle Dziura
Benjamin James Edwards
Meg Edwards
Richard Ellis
Bonnie Evans
Mary Fagen
Cheryl Farley
Craig Faulkner
Brandon Fischer
Alexander Fisher
Alison Ford

Ericka Foss
Alan Fox
Kat Friedman
Jeff Fritz
Jason Gagnon
Colin Garstka
John Giles
Carl Girard
Marci A. Glotzer
Crystal Gomes
Kimani Gordon
Travis Grant
Jennifer Grassi
Joan Griffith
Jill Hallen
Amy Handy
Ian Hannan
Heidi Hanson
Dewitt Hardy
Frederica D. Hart
Madelaine Hartman
Jesse Havea
Leslie Hawkins
Ron Hayes*
Andrea Hayward
Jason Helias
Tammy J. Heon
Christine Hevelone
Emma Higham
Joseph C. Hill
H.N. Hinkle
William M. Hobbs*
Teresa Hoffman
Greg Hofmann
Valeda L. Hood
Lisa Horowitz

OGUNQUIT PLAYHOUSE FOUNDATION (cont'd)
Former Board Members

Gail Huhtamäki*
Rob James
Dawn M. Jenks
Joshua Jock
Denise Johnson
Jaclynn Jones
Karen Kaizer
Robby Kenney
Lecea A. Ketzler
Nathan Keyes
Maureen King
Rachel Klaes
James Knipple
Paul Kochman
Daniel Lane
Vince Laropoli
Richard Latta
Elizabeth Lauber
Corey Lauro
Elizabeth Layman
Gloria LeBlanc
Melissa Heath Lee
Irene E. Lemay
Patricia Levenson*
Toby Levine
Robert Levinstein
Cheryll A. Lewis
Gordon Lewis*
Colin Liander
Dawn Lipinski
Wally Lugo
Katherine MacDonald
Marie MacDonald
Brian MacLean
Brenda Mannino
Cory Marhn
Emilia Martin
Michael Martineau
Mort Mather*

Tielor McBride
Sean R. McCarthy
Elizabeth McClosky
Kelly McDowell
Sharon McEneaney
Havilah J. Meinel
Amanda Michaels
Stephen Michalek
Larry Miller*
Travis Milliken
Ashley W. Mills
Michael Minahan
Nancy Moeur
Jennifer Moody
Michael Moriarty
Sergei Morosan
John Mosele
Brad Moulton*
William Munette, Jr.
Erik A. Nelson
Gary Thomas Ng
Susan E. Norris
Stuart Nudelman
Kimberly O'Brien
Patrick O'Brien
Kelly G. O'Donnoghue
Kevan K. Oliver
Hannah O'Neill
Jurg E. Oppliger
Paul O'Toole
Elizabeth Otto
Neil Patel
Kristen Peters
Cyndle Plaisted
Barbara M. Potter*
Cathy Nelson Price
Katie Raben
Jenn L. Ralston
Sarah Ramspott

Keith Reilly
Ann Reynolds*
Clare Richard
Ellen Richardson
Alexandra Rickoff
Adam Rigby
Ebony Riley
Mark D. Rinis
Meg Robbins
Jason Roberts
Taylor Rodgers
Eileen Rogosin
Benjamin C. Roney
Torin Rozzelle
Fred Rubino
Jonathan Rustebakke
Vince Ryan
Sarah J. Schetter
Nathaniel Seekins
Timothy Sheetz
Adam Smith
Joel Smith
Kristy D. Smith
Lauren Smith
Nicole Smith
Patrick M. Smith
Deborah Snyder
Cory M. Spinney
Joe Stanganelli
Kimberly A. Starling
Joel Stevens*
Andrea Stewart
Quentin S. Stockwell
Josh Sturman
Maura Suter
O. Palmer Swecker*
Tony Tambasco
Jill Tarantino
Kyler Taustin

OGUNQUIT PLAYHOUSE FOUNDATION (cont'd)
Former Board Members

Linda M. Taylor	Andrea Weeks	Asha Wilkus-Stone
Mark Thomas	Henry J. Weller	Miranda Wilson
Lisa Thompson	Asa Wember	Frida Wirick
Ed Thurber	Jonathan West*	Marni Woloszyn
Sandra Trullinger	Lauren Wetherell	Jeffrey Wonders
Elisabeth Tung	Deborah Wiley	Lisa Wondolowski
Ashley Walsh	Christina Wilhelms	Crys Worden
Misty J. Warburton	Erin Williams	Thea Yatras
Mariah L. Weaver	Krista Williams	Adam Zorn

OGUNQUIT PLAYHOUSE FOUNDATION
2007 Board of Directors

Karen M. Maxwell – President
Donna L. Lewis – First Vice President   Elizabeth M. Hirshom – Second Vice President
Cathy J. Brown – Secretary
Jeffrey Troiano – Treasurer   Henry J. Weller – Assistant Treasurer
Ronald W. Schneider, Jr., Esq. – Clerk
Kristine Cuzzi – Guild President

Gina Brannagan Connolly	Noel R. Leary	William Manfull
Glenn Deletetsky	Peter Lewis	Larry A. Smith
Stephen R. Eberle		Donato J. Tramuto

OGUNQUIT PLAYHOUSE THEATRE GUILD

The mission of the Ogunquit Playhouse Theatre Guild is to support activities which will benefit and promote the Playhouse, foster a broader appreciation of the performing arts in the community, develop the interest of children, increase their exposure to theatre and the arts, and preserve the heritage of the Ogunquit Playhouse.

THEATRE GUILD
2007 Board of Directors

Kristine Cuzzi – President

Margaret Miller-Weeks – Vice President	Karen Theriault – Kiosk Coordinator
Joanne Tomao – Treasurer	Patti Levenson – Publicity
Pam Sawyer – Recording Secretary	Joseph Acquaviva – Special Events
Blanche Feinberg – Corresponding Secretary	Mark Thomas – Special Events
Mimi Roll – Volunteers	Diane Schneider – Hospitality
Jan Shaw – Volunteers	Jeanne Ashworth – Hospitality

THEATRE GUILD MEMBERSHIP

Joseph Acquaviva
Barbara and Robert Adams
Jeanne Ashworth
Robert and Martha Banfield
Marianne Bauman
Jean and Christian Benda
Joyce Boughner
Robb Brigham
Cathy Brown
Jerome Brown
Dean Bushey
Diane Carpenter
Marilyn Cate
Beverly Cerini
Janet Cibulas
Thomas Clarie
Polly Coletti
Arlene Connor
Gloria Coon
Joy Cronin
LouAnn Cusa
Kristine Cuzzi
Charles and Eileen Dahill
Elizabeth Duffy
Janette Dunlap
Steve Eberle
Sally Feeney
Yale and Blanche Feinberg
Angela Festa
Antoinette Ford
Ann Gallup
Geraldine Gibbons
Bob Glidden
Constance Griffin

Kay and Raymond Hamlin
Tammy Heon
Elizabeth Hirshom
Jaclynn Jones
Ed and Marcia Katz
Betty Kehoe
Margaret Kelly
Jane Kelley
Brad Kenney
Ray and Joyce Kenney
Jeanne Kerrigan
lyman Krohn
Alan and Leila Kupper
Jackie Langlois
Anita Lauten Schein
Noel and Carol Leary
Patti Levenson
Norman and Barbara Levey
Carol Levine
Donna and Gordon Lewis
David and Rebecca Linney
Ryna Lipkind
Michael Lynch
Debra L. MacNeill
Eileen and Bob Maerz
Rosalind and Chris Magnuson
Paula Mamone
Brenda Mannino
Debora Manzi
Andrienne Markham
Lesley Mathews
Karen Maxwell
Kathleen Moseley

Amy Dutton Murphy
James and Anne Murphy
Phyllis Norton
Judi and Jack O'Donnell
Ann Mary Paccia
Linda Perrault
Virginia Poe
Jim Ready
Wanda Richard
Kristin and Dean Rinaldi
Margaret Rioux
Mimi Roll
Fred Rubino
Vince Ryan
Ruth and Paul Sampson
Pamela Sawyer
Diane and Charles Schneider
Dana and Jeanette Shaw
Anthony Spina Jr.
Dolores Strauss
Betsy Swartz
Andrew and Karen Theriault
Mark Thomas
Denise Thorne
Joanne Tomao
Leslie Ware
Margaret Weeks
Henry Weller
Jeri Wells
Claire and Harold White
Norman and Dorothy Wilkinson
Marcia Williams
Julie Woods
Cheryl Yarckin

About the Authors

Susan Day Meffert

Susan grew up at Dunelawn in Ogunquit, Maine, working in the kitchen, the dining room and finally, in reservations, all during the heyday of the straw hat summer circuit, and the first two decades of the Ogunquit Playhouse under John Lane. She met her first husband backstage at the Playhouse, and married him when she graduated from Bennington College four years later.

A writer and publicist, she worked for many years in fashion publishing at Conde Nast in New York, then moved into journalism as she relocated around the country and abroad with a second husband who was a corporate executive.

Carole Lee Carroll

Carole Lee spent her entire young life in and around the Ogunquit Playhouse where her father was Technical Director in the years of Maude Hartwig and General Manager of the Manhattan Theatre Colony under John Lane. With theatre in her blood, she graduated from Boston University with a Masters in Set Design, began work as a Scenic Artist for John Lane in 1963 and wound up as Set Designer at the Ogunquit Playhouse for six years during the 1960s.

She was active as a set designer and scenic artist in New York for many years, finally landing the post of Designer for *Today* at NBC where she remained for 18 years. Carole Lee is also an avid theatre history buff and collector.

Bunny Hart

Bunny came to the Ogunquit Playhouse as Publicity Director in 1963, having cut her teeth on the technical aspects of summer theatre, including stage managing, at the Cape Playhouse in Dennis. She stayed at Ogunquit through 1969. In need of full-time, year-round employment, she left in 1969, returning to the Playhouse in 1985 and staying on until 1999. As Publicity Director and later Business Manager, she was part of the nucleus of people who supported John Lane and kept the dream alive.

For almost twenty-five years, Bunny also served the Barn Gallery Associates in Ogunquit as Administrator and Publicity Director. Before retiring, she ran her own business, Hart Advertising Agency, based in Ogunquit.

Front Cover Photo: Courtesy of the Historical Society of Wells and Ogunquit.